Men, Women, Passion and Power

Psychoanalytic theory has .... difficult to come to terms with issues of power with....... ....lations. Both theory and clinical practice have tende........ ....icate the cultural idealisation of men and the denigration ... women, splitting masculinity and femininity between the sexes ... a way which depletes both.

In *Men, Women, Passion and Power*, Marie Maguire argues that it is only when psychoanalytic therapists integrate the male and female in their theorising that the possibility of a more balanced and fluid psychological relation between the sexes will emerge.

Making detailed use of case material, she introduces the reader to the contemporary debates about sexuality and explores them with sensitivity from a feminist viewpoint. Looking at such topics as 'false memories' of sexual abuse, 'perverse' sexuality, homo-sexuality, pornography and bulimia, she shows how current think-ing is trammelled by sexist, homophobic and culturally biased assumptions about gender identity and sexual orientation. She concludes that only when a feminist perspective has been truly integrated into theory will the psychoanalytic project realise its full radical potential.

Marie Maguire is a psychoanalytic psychotherapist in private practice in London. She is a member of the Guild of Psychother-apists Training Committee and teaches on psychotherapy training courses. She is the co-editor of *Living with the Sphinx*.

1995

0415074339

'This book provides a most moving testimony to the often ignored session-to-session movement in patients' gendered experience of themselves and their therapists toward less defensive refusal, more accepting recognition of both female and male, maternal and paternal sexuality. Through detailed observations from her own practice, therapist Marie Maguire draws us into recognizing our persisting tendency toward sexualizing envy, emotional pain and grief, childhood deprivation and abuse, in therapy and other transactions with others. Never forgetting the social context of sexual inequality and its varied psychological construction and impact, Marie Maguire eloquently conveys the complexity involved in current therapy debates about men's sexual vulnerabilities, battered women, 'false memory syndrome', perversion, eating disorders and the normality or otherwise of gay and lesbian sex. In sum: a most readable and timely book.'
Janet Sayers, author of *Mothering Psychoanalysis*

'*Men, Women, Passion and Power* is a major contribution to the literature on gender, psychology and psychotherapy. Writing in a clear and accessible style, and using powerful and moving examples from her own clinical work, Marie Maguire brings current psychoanalytic thinking on gender to life. It is rare to encounter a book with such an accomplished integration of theory and practice in such a complex and important area.'
Stephen Frosh, Birkbeck College, London and the Tavistock Clinic

Men, Women, Passion and Power

Gender Issues in Psychotherapy

Marie Maguire

London and New York

First published 1995
by Routledge
11 New Fetter Lane, London EC4P 4EE

Simultaneously published in the USA and Canada
by Routledge
29 West 35th Street, New York, NY 10001

© 1995 Marie Maguire

Phototypeset in Times by Intype, London

Printed and bound in Great Britain by
TJ Press (Padstow) Ltd, Padstow, Cornwall

British Library Cataloguing in Publication Data
A catalogue record for this book is available from the British
Library

Library of Congress Cataloging in Publication Data
A catalogue record for this book has been requested

ISBN 0–415–07432–0 (hbk)
ISBN 0–415–07433–9 (pbk)

Contents

Acknowledgements

My greatest thanks must go to my patients who made the writing of this book possible. My colleagues and friends Eleanore Armstrong-Perlman, Nina Farhi, Iona Grant and Jean White read my manuscript, discussed ideas and supported me throughout the entire process. Julia Vellacott enabled me to get started and Russell Southwood provided practical help and encouragement in the early stages. Many other people read chapters, discussed ideas and gave me relevant literature. I'd particularly like to thank Lyn Agley, Clare Allen, Roger Bacon, Mary Barnett, Les Burton, Sue Einhorn, Sheila Ernst, Lucy Goodison, Marilyn Lawrence, Jo Ryan, Valerie Sinason, Margot Waddell and Mike Wilson. Barbara Taylor's editorial midwifery and general encouragement were absolutely invaluable. Without Myrna Paraan and Maureen Maguire's help I would never have met my deadline. Finally I'd like to thank Edwina Welham, my editor at Routledge, for all she has done.

Introduction

The inequality between the sexes is one of the most intractable features of human culture. Even today, as the relative position of women in western society improves, sex-based patterns of power and submission continue to be reproduced in our most intimate relationships. Why is this? How is it that gender inequities come to be inscribed in our very psyches, even when we believe passionately in the need for change? In this book I explore the ways in which psychoanalytic and feminist theorists have addressed these questions, as they examine the impact of early experience and unconscious fantasy on the formation of psychological gender.

Looking at theorists from Freud onwards, and utilising my own clinical material, I offer a critical perspective on psychodynamic concepts of sexual difference. In our society each sex has access to different forms of power and control which arouse intense envy in those who lack them. I consider the way in which psychoanalytic theories have shifted between an emphasis on the child's envy of paternal authority and potency and a focus on the mother as the more powerful and enviable parent. I examine the relationship between sexual orientation and identity, and between biological sex and gender characteristics.

What are 'masculinity' and 'femininity'? Every society has ways of distinguishing the sexes – socially, culturally, psychologically. Historically, however, the way this division has been drawn has varied enormously. What counts as maleness or femaleness in one period or cultural setting can look radically unlike its equivalents in other times or places. And similarly, how an individual comes to identify him or herself as belonging to a gender also varies greatly. The unconscious meaning each of us gives to our biological sex depends on a complex interaction of personal and cultural factors; it is never simply a result of anatomical difference. According to prevailing gender stereotypes in the west, women are expected to live vicariously through idealised others, including men and children, to whom they submit, denying the strength of their need and aggression. Men, in contrast, are usually encouraged to assume a stance of pseudo-independence where their own emotional need is transformed into domination of those on whom they depend. Femininity, in other words, is still associated with passivity, and masculinity with activity, as Freud argued (Freud 1905a). But, as my clinical examples show, there is as much variation within each sex as between the sexes, since women and men simultaneously conform to and resist gender stereotypes. Although individuals may present themselves as having a fixed and unified sense of what it means to be male or female, this is often a veneer, a masquerade. Sexual identity – the psychological meaning each of us gives to being a woman or a man – is always fluid, and never exactly what it seems.

The roots of gender expectations lie in our ideas about the psychological division in parenting. In our society the mother is expected to look after the baby's physical needs, and to help her or him to contain, think about and eventually verbalise feelings and thoughts. The father's role is associated with boundary-setting, and helping the child find a pathway out of the symbiotic preoccupations of infancy into the world at large. However, I assume that the capacity for both these parental functions exists in all women and men and, as my clinical examples show, some mothers prefer fathering, while their husbands may have more highly developed maternal capacities.

One of my main themes is the way each sex deals with aspects of personality seen culturally as feminine or masculine. In many societies girls and boys react against the early power of the mother by idealising paternal authority. As a result the work men do and 'masculine' qualities tend to be valued more highly than those associated with women. This devaluation of women has profound implications for each sex, since we all identify to some extent with conventionally 'masculine' and 'feminine' aspects of both parents, and with the paternal and maternal functions of each.

Theories about sexuality have always been central to psychoanalysis. Yet they have also been the focus of fundamental disagreements which have divided the analytic community. These disputes have coincided with rapid changes in the organisation of sexual and family life, in turn accompanied by shifting attitudes towards gender. Although the analytic and feminist literature in this area is vast, surprising gaps exist. Key papers are scattered and sometimes hard to find. The issues which have aroused most controversy over the years are often discussed from polarised positions with little dialogue between opposing factions.

In this book I draw together and re-evaluate psychoanalytic theories of psychosexuality, using case histories from my own psychotherapy practice to review issues which have recently become controversial within the analytic community. These include questions about 'false memories' of sexual abuse or incest. I also look at a series of psychoanalytic debates about 'perverse' sexuality. Is homosexuality perverse and/or pathological? Should certain types of psychological problems among women, for example eating disorders, be described as perversions? Can women be perverse, or is perversion exclusively male? These are now hotly contested issues, as is the question of how the gender of the patient and analyst affects the therapeutic transference and countertransference. Some of these topics raise fundamental questions about the aims of psychotherapy and the stance clin- icians should take towards social norms and political institutions.

Much of the theory I discuss in this book has been written by psychoanalysts working with patients who they see in the classic fashion, five (or in Freud's case, six) times a week, lying on the couch. Psychoanalytic psychotherapy, although it is founded on the same basic premises as psychoanalysis, involves less intensive treatment. For practical and stylistic reason I use generic terms such as analyst or therapist to refer to all who practise psycho- therapy.

Psychoanalytic psychotherapy is distinguished from other forms of therapy by an emphasis on helping the patient to understand their own unconscious processes as they are re-enacted within the transference relationship. The psychotherapist also uses her own countertransference – her emotional reactions to the patient, and especially to the transference – in a variety of different ways, to further the work of analysis.

Some of the patients I discuss came to see me for intensive psychotherapy, two to four times weekly for up to eight years, often lying on the couch. Others came for once-weekly brief psychotherapy over a period of six to nine months, in publicly funded clinic settings. In order to preserve patients' confidentiality I have altered biographical details. Whenever possible I asked for permission and used material from ex-patients to avoid disrupting an ongoing psychotherapy.

Although Freud claimed universality for psychoanalysis, it is the product of a particular culture and historical epoch, a social theory with moral and political effects, as well as an analysis of individual suffering and development. Different views on the interaction between unconscious fantasy, culture and physiology, including cross-cultural critiques, are therefore vital to my discussion.

Contemporary girls are brought up with a promise of sexual equality which, for the most part, our society fails to deliver. Although individual women attain influential positions, men as a sex retain control over institutions of authority – political, educational, juridical and medical. British women on average work longer hours than men, frequently doing the equivalent of two jobs where men do one. Not surprisingly the emotional toll on women is statistically visible. Women are far more likely than men to seek psychological help of all kinds, to be prescribed psychotropic drugs, and to spend time in psychiatric hospitals.

I argue that inequality between the sexes continues to be reflected in the theory and practice of analytic psychotherapy, despite periods of intense debate between feminists and psychoanalytic clinicians. European struggles for women's suffrage shadowed the first period of controversy about female sexuality. A half-century later a new generation of feminists – myself included – turned to psychoanalytic psychotherapy in the 1970s to understand why we could not will ourselves into being the New Women we had hoped to become. Like many of my contemporaries I thought at first that I was struggling mainly with oppressive outer realities. But gradually I realised that I was also grappling with unconscious feelings and fantasies which often contradicted my conscious political beliefs.

Like many British psychotherapists I am a theoretical hybrid, incorporating diverse influences within my clinical practice. My experience of working in two radical psychotherapy projects, Battersea Action and Counselling Centre and The Women's Therapy Centre, was formative. The founders of these organisations drew on certain British psychoanalytic theories, especially the work of W.R.D. Fairbairn, to analyse how real inequities of class, race and gender are structured into the personality and emerge within the therapeutic relationship. Despite this kind of pioneering work, which has often been inspired by the Women's Movement, we still do not yet know exactly how cultural and social changes impact on the psyche. However, I remain absolutely certain that we are primarily a product of our personal and cultural histories, and that we carve out an identity for ourselves through giving meaning both to what happens to us in childhood, and to what those around us expect and desire of us.

Theoretically I am steeped in the tradition of British psychoanalysis, with its insights gleaned from child analysis about the infant's earliest experience of mothering and the maternal body. In my clinical work I have been influenced by contemporary Kleinian theories about modes of thinking, symbolisation and early identificatory processes. But I also maintain a critical distance from some aspects of object relations theory. My own analysis was Freudian, and I consider Freud's theory of psychosexuality, including his concept of bisexuality, his emphasis on how the child deals with Oedipal rivalry and desire, and the way patriarchal power is structured into the personality, absolutely essential to the practice of psychotherapy.

Although I believe we are formed primarily through culture, I also think that the anatomical differences between women and men impact on the psyche, affecting unconscious anxieties and fantasies. Because male and female bodies are constructed differently and we have different physiological and sexual capacities, our experience of sex, reproduction and physiological life-stages such as adolescence and the menopause will inevitably be different.

I am not arguing for the existence of inborn anxieties or for certain preconceived patterns of feeling or fantasy. Nor do I think that any particular psychological characteristics can be found universally in one sex rather than the other. I do not believe that we are born with tendencies towards heterosexual 'femininity' or 'masculinity', or that there is any core of 'real' personality which transcends culture. In fact language-patterns, cultural symbols, belief-systems and values will be fundamental determinants of how physiological sensation is interpreted in any given society. If we want to abolish inequalities between the sexes, we must understand and radically alter the way we interpret and symbolise the embodied experience of women and men.

This may well be a controversial position for a feminist to take. But it is in no sense ahistorical. During the twentieth century women's relationship to their bodies has changed dramatically in our society. For the first time, women can control their fertility whilst also remaining sexually active, and living openly in partnerships with other women or men. We no longer spend much of our adult lives pregnant or breast-feeding, and therefore, most women do not need to be financially dependent on men unless they choose to be. In other words, women's bodies are becoming more like men's, and this will inevitably be reflected in our psychic lives.

In my view theories of narcissism are essential to an understanding of how gender power inequalities are woven into our most fundamental passions and desires. The narcissistic wish to avoid confronting our ultimate helplessness in the face of psychic pain, loss and death exists unconsciously in all of us. Recognising that both sexes are anatomically different, yet equal, would mean facing up to the fact that the most important aspects of existence elude our control. Those we love and on whom we depend are psychically separate from us. Unless we maintain an illusion of ecstatic fusion with others – a defence associated with stereotypes of femininity – or imagine ourselves to be so powerful and independent that we have no emotional needs – the stance culturally linked with masculinity – we have to acknowledge that our love-objects are essentially unpredictable.

I begin the book with an account of the 1919–35 controversy about female sexuality. In the first three chapters I summarise opposing analytic and feminist arguments about envy and power which had their origins during this period of controversy. Envy, described in Webster's Dictionary as 'chagrin or discontent at the excellence or good fortune of another', originates in early disappointment in relation to the mother, the original source of life. To Freudians and Lacanians the role of the father, female penis envy and male dread of paternal castration remain central. Mother-centred theories, including those of Klein and Winnicott, emphasise that ambivalence towards maternal power underlies all female envy of male privilege and authority as well as men's repudiation of femininity. I look at the relevance of these opposing theories of sexual identity to my own clinical work with male and female patients.

Since the psychoanalytic literature is so extensive I have structured the book around the writings of those analysts and feminists who see the early debate on female sexuality as a central point of reference. This 1920s/30s controversy focused on Sigmund Freud's theories and Karen Horney's counter-arguments. Significant contributions were also made by Ernest Jones, Joan Riviere and others who were influenced by Melanie Klein's new theories. Many feminists including Juliet Mitchell have been inspired by the work of Jacques Lacan, who saw the controversy as a watershed where psychoanalysis lost its subversive core. I also draw on the work of many other analysts and feminists who address this book's central themes. I am particularly interested in the work of Janine Chasseguet-Smirgel who pioneered a reassessment of the debate in the 1960s, Jessica Benjamin who analyses the way culture binds our erotic desire, and Luce Irigiray, who – like Chasseguet-Smirgel and Benjamin also – attempts to combine the insights of Freud or Lacan with a more mother-centred perspective. I argue that we need to draw on the strengths of different psychoanalytic and feminist theories since no one perspective offers a complete understanding of sexual identity.

Throughout the book I address a series of related topics which need reassessing in the light of dramatic cultural changes. For instance the early psychoanalytic interest in the erotic life of adult women has faded, to be replaced by a preoccupation with their maternal function. In many contemporary case studies the mother dominates her children in indirectly sexualised ways, but is not the subject of her own desire (Welldon 1988). Ironically, given women's increased sexual independence, there has been a long period where we have heard little about their actual sexual relationships, with men or other women. After the Second World War in Britain and the USA the father's role in the psyche received little theoretical attention. Only since the 1980s have psychoanalysts begun to acknowledge that in many post-industrial societies men's expectations of sexuality, marriage and fatherhood are very different from those of Freud's patients.

In Chapter 4 I ask, 'Are men really fragile?' Freud argued that men were not so prone to neurosis because of a less problematic sexual history. Later object relations theorists (e.g. Stoller 1968) emphasise the relative fragility and emotional impoverishment of male identity. I argue that this latter argument needs to be combined with an understanding of how cultural dominance is structured into the male psyche. Men can fully recognise their difference from the mother only when they recognise her otherness in themselves, once maternal and 'feminine' aspects of themselves are acknowledged rather than projected onto others. If women and femininity are devalued in the psyche and in culture then there really is no possibility that men can achieve equality in heterosexual or homosexual relationships, since the partner who is seen as more psychically 'feminine' is likely to be denigrated and objectified. I look at some of the reasons why men are less likely to seek change through psychotherapy, and at the particular combination of psychic 'femininity' and 'masculinity' displayed by those who do.

Although some contemporary object relations theorists imply that women are emotionally the more powerful sex, the real lack of economic and social power experienced by the female sex as a whole is rarely acknowledged. In Chapter 5, 'The power of women's sexuality', I connect this discrepancy with the psychoanalytic emphasis on the elusiveness of female desire. Cultural imagery constantly depicts women as gaining pleasure from being attractive, rather than from exercising their own desires. Women who feel that desire pulls them towards surrender and self-sacrifice may choose to deny their need for erotic pleasure altogether. Other women patients describe a disturbing clash between internalised images of female submissiveness and conscious hopes of sexual and social equality. For the girl, masculinity is not a threat, as femininity is for the boy, but an unattainable ideal (Benjamin 1988). The difficulty many women have in experiencing themselves as independent beings with their own needs and desires can be linked to the problems girls have in identifying with paternal qualities in the mother or father. I look at how far it is possible in psychotherapy to break into this cycle and help patients to develop the capacity for more equal relationships.

Writing about the analytic transference, Janet Malcolm uses the analogy of romantic love relationships, which are 'at best an uneasy truce between powerful solitary fantasy systems', where we 'must grope around for each other through a dense thicket of absent others' (Malcolm 1982: 6). Chapters 6 and 7 explore the interface between fantasy, reality and erotic desire in the transference and countertransference. In Chapter 6 I look at how gender power inequalities emerge within the therapeutic setting through the impact of the patient and therapist's sex on the transference

and countertransference. I ask whether homosexual and heterosexual erotic transferences are experienced differently by male
and female analysts and explore some of the difficulties psychotherapists may have in working with cross-gender transferences.

In Chapter 7, 'False memories of sexual abuse?', my focus is
on contemporary psychoanalytic debates about false memories of
incest. It is often suggested that the psychotherapist's emotional
influence could be used in ways which are counter-productive for
the patient, perhaps reinforcing existing inequalities of gender or
generation. I locate dramatic shifts in psychoanalytic theory about
the 'real event' of childhood incest within a context of heightened
public concern that psychotherapists might either deny the reality
of these experiences or encourage patients to fabricate false memories. Through clinical material, including an account of the
psychotherapy of a patient who thinks she may have been sexually abused but has no concrete evidence, I explore the technical
difficulties of working with those who are uncertain whether or
not they are incest survivors.

Women's masochistic avoidance of erotic pleasure has been a
constant psychoanalytic theme. Freud argued that women express
sexuality indirectly through hysterical conversion symptoms and
physical self-abuse. Perversion has until recently been seen as
predominantly male. In recent decades it has often been
attributed to the presence in men's lives of seductive, castrating
mothers (e.g. Rosen 1979a). In Chapter 8, 'Female and male
perversions?', I look again at psychoanalytic theories about
male and female perversion and hysteria. Using detailed case
material I discuss why the use of hard-core pornography as a
substitute for sexual relationships might be more commonly
found in men while eating problems such as bulimia are more
prevalent in women.

When psychoanalysts label sexual behaviours as perverse or
pathological they are also, of course, giving clear signals about
their own anxieties and prejudices. This has been particularly
obvious in relation to homosexuality, where the profession is only
now beginning to confront a deep-rooted, partially hidden bias
against homosexuals, both as patients and potential colleagues.
The final chapter, 'Is homosexuality pathological?', explores the
origins of sexual orientation, touching on fundamental questions
about the aims of psychotherapy. Contradictions in theory can be
traced back to Freud, who argued that psychoanalysis should not

encourage adaptation to prevailing norms of sexual behaviour since these were often a root cause of human misery. Yet at the same time he linked adult homosexuality with arrested development and perversion. As a result, some contemporary psychoanalysts describe an analytic 'cure' as synonymous with the attainment of heterosexual 'maturity'. (For opposing views, see Socarides (1979) and Mannoni (1968).)

Current debates over homosexuality within the psychotherapeutic world are in some respects reminiscent of the 1920s/30s dispute over female sexuality, inasmuch as both test many of the central assumptions on which psychodynamic therapy is based. And both controversies also reflect the challenge which gender politics poses to psychoanalysis, as feminists and gay theorists offer new interpretations of psychosexual development which confront older orthodoxies. It is essential that psychoanalytic psychotherapists be willing to accept these challenges and to rethink our theoretical and clinical work in the light of new perspectives. I hope this book contributes to this process.

Part I

Theories of female and male sexuality

Chapter 1

Sexual controversy

It was in the wake of the mass feminist struggles for women's suffrage that the first significant controversy over female sexuality broke out within the psychoanalytic movement. The egalitarian demands of the suffragists formed a backdrop for the entire debate. Between 1919 and 1935 at least nineteen prominent analysts wrote papers on the topic, arguing vigorously with each other and with Freud. This debate, which centred on Freud's theory of female penis envy, set the agenda for discussions of sexual identity for the rest of the century.

Freud's attitude towards women's demands for equality was highly contradictory, in common with most other early male psychoanalysts. In his writings on female psychology he revealed a deep ambivalence over the question of female inferiority, at times implying that women actually are inferior while at other moments suggesting that they are simply viewed in that way within a male-dominated society. For instance, in 1933 he suggested that a female patient's long-held wish for professional and intellectual success might turn out to be sublimated childhood penis envy (Freud 1933). But he had also insisted, against opposition from other male colleagues, and at a time when many professions barred females, that women should be able to train and take up prominent positions within the psychoanalytic movement. He was a sexual liberal, supporting the radical causes of his day, including the legalisation of homosexuality, the liberalisation of divorce laws and a woman's right to abortion.

During the 1920s one of Freud's most influential opponents, Karen Horney, a young German psychoanalyst, accused Freud of 'male bias', of creating a theory which devalued women (Horney 1924, 1926). Freud's theory revolved around the child's relationship to the father and its struggle to come to terms with the authority and privilege of the patriarch, a struggle in which the mother seems to become almost a bystander. Horney's view was that each sex has something uniquely valuable which arouses fierce envy in the sex lacking it. This argument and other aspects of her critique of Freud won influential support from colleagues who later transformed the role of the mother in psychoanalytic theory. For British object relations theorists and North American ego psychologists, women – far from being deficient – have enormous emotional power based on the ability to reproduce the species and the utter dependence of the human infant at the beginning of life. From this theoretical perspective the influence women have over the psychic lives of children is seen as far more significant than the political and economic power wielded by men. At issue here are divergent notions of power and control and arguments about which parent is viewed by the child as most potent and enviable.

Feminists have always remained divided as to whose views on sexual identity were the more radical – Freud's or Horney's. A crucial area of disagreement was over whether women and men are born heterosexual or 'made' so by culture. For Freud the girl only begins to desire men sexually and want their babies once she realises she can never be male; Horney, on the other hand, argued that women are born with tendencies towards heterosexual femininity. By emphasising innate womanliness in this way, Horney intended to defend women against the Freudian charge that we are merely men *manqué*. But present-day feminists have pointed out that in doing so she 'threw the baby out with the bath-water', abandoning one of Freud's most subversive insights, his theory that all sexual identities are formed through the influence of personal history and culture rather than being the inevitable outcome of biological sex (Mitchell 1974).

The dispute between Horney and Freud raised fundamental questions about the transformative potential of psychoanalysis. If women have inborn tendencies towards a certain kind of feminine heterosexuality, then the possibility of change in female identity, and any subsequent shift in power relations between the sexes, might be limited. Freud had argued against the idea that psychoanalysts should encourage patients to conform to prevailing social and sexual norms. But if his theory showed a bias against women, who was to judge what counted as genuine therapeutic success rather than mere conformity to current notions of authentic femaleness? Contributors to the debate probed such questions, wondering to what extent the prejudices of the psychoanalyst influenced the course of a treatment. They also speculated about whether the psychoanalyst's gender shaped the way the transference unfolded and whether opposing theories of sexual identity might in turn reflect varying experiences of the therapeutic relationship.

The debate was crucial to the future of psychoanalytic theory and the practice of psychotherapy. For the first time Freud's authority as theoretical leader was challenged in an open and sustained way by dissenters who stayed to argue their case. The psychoanalytic movement began to split, its members taking fundamentally different paths, but still seeing themselves as part of the same community. Opposing factions in the debate coalesced into theoretical tendencies which continue to dominate contemporary psychoanalytic thinking about psychosexuality and identity.

Prior to the outbreak of hostilities between himself, Horney and others, Freud had had little to say about female sexuality as such. His *Three Essays on the Theory of Sexuality* (1905a) offered the outlines of a general theory of psychosexual development which did not dwell on the differences between male and female development. In the *Essays* Freud asked a series of questions about what sexuality was and how it came to be associated with the onset of neurosis. He concluded that sexual libido was a wild, insatiable force, the 'most unruly' of all the instincts. In order to build civilisation it was necessary to repress desire and sublimate sexual libido into culturally constructive pursuits. But this resulted in psychic conflict in individuals who could not tolerate the way society restricted their sexuality. Neurosis was the inevitable result, particularly for women who were denied pleasure and knowledge through the sexual double standard.

Freud's infant is a hedonist who at first seeks 'auto-erotic' pleasure from its own body, purely for pleasure's sake. In Freud's theory sexuality is not intrinsically linked with reproduction or with the need for closeness. (Here Freud differs from later object relations theorists who argue that the infant seeks human intimacy rather than sexual pleasure from the moment of birth.) Neither, according to Freud, does infantile sexuality have any pre-determined object. Instead it is diffuse and 'polymorphously perverse', experienced in relation to everyone and everything the infant encounters. Only after a primary period of narcissistic self-preoccupation is the infant seduced into intimacy through the physical ministrations of the mother.

Freud stresses the continuity between adult and infantile sexuality and between erotic desire and other forms of love. The mother derives erotic pleasure from her child, responding to it 'with feelings that are derived from her own sexual life: she strokes him, kisses him, rocks him and quite clearly treats him as a substitute for a complete sexual object' (Freud 1905a: 145).

Central to Freud's theory of sexual identity was his argument that all children are born bisexual, psychically androgynous, possessing a complex combination of 'masculine' – active – and 'feminine' – passive – mental characteristics. Heterosexuality only begins at the Oedipal, genital phase as the infant becomes less preoccupied with the oral pleasures of feeding and the anal struggles of toilet-training and becomes more aware of genital sensations and the fantasies which accompany them.

Until female sexuality became controversial amongst his colleagues, Freud had written mainly about the boy's experience. In his early writings on sexuality he assumed that the girl's experience would be a reverse mirror-image of the boy's and that for her too the opposite-sex parent, the father, would be most significant.

Freud confirmed some of his theories of sexuality through his analysis of three-year-old Hans, a 'positive paragon of all vices' (Freud 1909: 179). As his Oedipal desire for the opposite sex parent grew, Hans wanted his mother to touch his penis because 'it's great fun' (Freud 1909: 182). His father was at these moments a hated rival. He had fantasies about marrying his mother and having a baby with her. Hans also reported eroticised daydreams about the plumber visiting him in the bath and penetrating his stomach with a great big 'borer'. These homosexual desires are an expression of the negative Oedipus complex – Hans had also taken the same sex parent as erotic love-object and felt rivalry towards his mother.

Freud says that ideally the son relinquishes his Oedipal desire for the mother because of a real or imagined threat of castration by the father, and accepts that he must wait until adulthood to possess his own woman sexually. The little boy sublimates his incestuous desire through identifying with the father's potency and cultural privilege. This identification forms the basis of the male super-ego or conscience. If the Oedipus complex is not resolved in this way the boy may grow up to feel an intense hatred and contempt for women. Freud argued that this kind of misogyny is an expression of male castration anxiety – the man is terrified that he will lose his masculinity and become like the women he hates and fears.

It was not until 1924/5 that Freud published his ideas about female sexuality – and then in some haste, with incomplete clinical data. In apologising for the schematic character of his arguments, he cited his failing health as the reason for hurrying into print, but it is also possible that he wanted to stake out territory and re-assert his theoretical leadership against challengers such as Horney. The battle-lines were being drawn, and Freud's own famous interjection – 'Here the feminist demand for equal rights for the sexes does not take us far' (Freud 1924a: 320) – indicates how heated and oppositional the theoretical atmosphere was becoming.

In spite of his provocative tone Freud was preoccupied with questions which are still relevant for contemporary women. For instance he noted that little girls seemed initially to be 'more intelligent and livelier than boys of the same age'. He asked how those assertive little girls came to lose their intellectual confidence and capacity to act directly on their desires (Freud 1933: 151). Freud observed that, whether through nature or nurture, it is at the point where the little girl becomes interested in the father and men that she appears to become more passive.

Freud's explanation for this is that the little girl goes through a phase where she is a 'little boy psychologically' and is active or 'masculine' in her love for her mother before she becomes heterosexual. It is penis envy, Freud argued in 1924, which sets the girl on the path towards psychic womanhood. As soon as she sees the boy's penis the girl recognises her inadequacy 'in a flash' and blames her mother for sending her into the world ill-equipped (Freud 1925: 336). Neither she nor the boy knows of the existence of the vagina until adolescence. Both imagine that the clitoris is a stunted penis. In bitter disappointment at her lack, the girl turns to her father in the hope of gaining a penis and becoming like him. When she realises that she can never be a man, she reluctantly accepts the second-best option of femininity. She begins to feel heterosexual desire and to hope for the father's baby – ideally a boy, a penis by proxy. According to Freud the girl has a series of psychological disadvantages. She has to make three renunciations in order to become a heterosexual woman, none of which are required of the boy. She must give up her first love-object, the mother. Secondly, she must relinquish her active sexual strivings, experienced in relation to her mother. Her aggressive urges turn inwards, as she becomes more passive, or receptive in relation to the father and men. In the process, the girl often loses much of her own sexual desire. Thirdly, at puberty the girl must give up her early interest in the clitoris for the vagina. From these painful renunciations 'difficulties and possible inhibitions result which do not apply to men' (Freud 1931, 1933). Not surprisingly, Freud thought that many girls never do become entirely heterosexual. They may remain attached to the mother, identify with the father, or lose interest completely in sex. Freud described how a woman may marry in order to have a penis-baby, and then transfer her love completely to the infant. A marriage is only consolidated, Freud later said, when the woman has also made the man into her child (Freud 1933).

Freud argued that girls are further disadvantaged in the moral sphere. They cannot identify with the father's authority, and penis envy clouds their objectivity. Women have a weaker super-ego, their judgements being more tinged with emotion. They have a stronger sense of pity, disgust and shame, due both to the repression of their sexuality and to penis envy. 'I cannot evade the notion (though I hesitate to give it expression) that for women the level of what is ethically normal is different from what it is in men', Freud said in 1925 (Freud 1925: 342).

By the early 1930s, after a decade of pressure from his female colleagues, Freud had become more able to recognise the intensity of the early mother–daughter relationship. He now saw it as a foundation, a crucial determinant of later experiences with the father. For instance Freud now argued that penis envy had its roots in the inevitable narcissistic wounds of breast-feeding, which only become organised into a sense of gender-inferiority once the girl sees the boy's penis. The 'reproach against the mother that goes back furthest is that she gave the child too little milk –

which is construed against her as lack of love ... the child's avidity for its earliest nourishment is altogether insatiable ... it never gets over the pain of losing its mother's breast' (Freud 1933: 155–6).

Female sexuality always remained mysterious and elusive to Freud, but by 1933 he was more able to detect the maternal transference than he had been with his earlier patients. For instance his patient H.D., the symbolist poet, assumed at first that he represented a father-figure, but Freud insisted that she had transferred her early feelings about her mother onto him. He told H.D. that mistakes had been made in the early days because psychoanalysts did not realise that some girls never do transfer their affections from the mother to the father. He went on to tell her, 'I do *not* like to be the mother in the transference, it always surprises and shocks me a little. I feel so very masculine.' She asked him if others had mother transferences to him. He said 'ironically ... and a little wistfully "O, *very* many" ' (H.D. 1956: 147). From a reading of some of his earlier case histories including his work with Dora, it seems clear that Freud had always been able to elicit strong maternal transferences from his patients, but had not been able to recognise that this was happening (Freud 1905b). This may have been because of his own unresolved conflicts about his sexual identity – his difficulties in acknowledging aspects of himself which he might have seen as feminine or maternal.

In 1931 Freud suggested that female psychoanalysts could go further than him in researching the mysteries of female sexuality. As 'more suitable mother-substitutes' they had a greater capacity to elicit the early maternal transference. Some prominent women analysts, including Helene Deutsch, Jeanne Lampl-de-Groot and Ruth Mack Brunswick, declared their agreement with Freud's theory of female sexuality. Each of them remained deferential to Freud, although each gave far more importance to the mother–daughter relationship than he had done, while also insisting that the mother was central to female psychology. Some of them fully endorsed Freud's belief that women analysts would have access within the transference to aspects of the female psyche that their male colleagues would never encounter. In a postscript to the debate Mack Brunswick argued in 1940 that a certain kind of woman would never enter psychoanalysis with a male clinician. 'The undeveloped, primitive woman with scant heterosexuality and a childish, unquestioning attachment to the mother, presents herself almost regularly to the woman analyst. This type of individual does not consult the male analyst because of a total lack of contact with the man' (Brunswick 1940: 62).

HELENE DEUTSCH

Helene Deutsch was typical of Freud's contemporary female supporters in that she always stressed her loyalty to his views on penis envy without acknowledging that she disagreed with him fundamentally about female sexuality in general. Most significantly Deutsch was certain that the psychological differences between the sexes were rooted in biology. She also abandoned Freud's central emphasis on the father, focusing instead on a mother–daughter identification based on the shared child-bearing function over the course of the life-cycle. Her mother-centred perspective, like many contemporary theories, focuses on what women possess – the capacity to bear children – rather than on what they lack.

Deutsch argued that women tend to focus inwards, seeking gratification through children and family life, because their psychic life revolves around the reproductive cycle and sexual organs located inside their bodies. In contrast, men, she argued, are driven to possess women and sublimate their sexuality in the external world. She attributed this partly to the penetrative urges of the penis, whose location directs men's attention outside themselves (Deutsch 1924).

Freud didn't know whether women were naturally more passive or became so through cultural repression of their sexuality. But Deutsch became notorious with later generations of feminists for insisting that three traits – narcissism, passivity and masochism – were integral to female psychology (Deutsch 1930).

Deutsch asks, as many contemporary feminists have, why women have accepted throughout history the 'social ordinances' that prevent them from gaining sexual gratification while simultaneously denying them the possibility of sublimating their sexual urges through artistic or cultural achievement (Deutsch 1930). She argues that it must be the 'magnificent gratification' women gain from their reproductive capacities. Yet her writings are concerned with a painful paradox in female experience. According to Deutsch many women gain little pleasure from the passivity and self-sacrifice required of them in vaginal intercourse and motherhood. This is because they are born with a component of active 'masculine' sexuality – the clitoris, a stunted penis, the remnants of which do not allow them to submit without conflict. Therefore many women find little gratification in heterosexual intercourse, to which they feel they must resign themselves. They may also be highly ambivalent about pregnancy, childbirth and mothering, especially if their identifications with their mothers are ambivalent (Deutsch 1924, 1930).

This biological re-interpretation of Freud became profoundly influential and was widely perceived as the Freudian orthodoxy, particularly in the United States after the Second World War. It was hardly surprising, then, that feminists coming to psychoanalytic theory in this period perceived it as deeply conservative, particularly when influential analysts actually used the theory as a stick with which to beat the feminist movement. Freud, as we have seen, did this. So, too, did Karl Abraham, who in 1920, in the first shot fired in the debate, argued that feminist demands for equality were not just a response to social inequities but also a sign of penis envy, the desire to be a man (Abraham 1920).

KAREN HORNEY

Karen Horney, in a 1922 paper delivered to a packed conference hall, fiercely rebutted the idea that 'half the human race were unhappy with their sex' as insulting to women and unscientific. Like all the other contributors to the debate Horney agreed that penis envy existed. She differed from Freud in that she thought it to be transient and relatively unimportant. In this paper, published in 1924, Horney argued that the little girl initially envies the boy's highly visible penis which is so satisfying for him to masturbate with and to show off. But she went on to say that this envy usually diminishes rapidly as the girl becomes aware of the wonders of her own female body (Horney 1924).

Horney disagreed with Freud's theory that the little girl does not know about her vagina and goes through a phallic 'masculine' phase before becoming heterosexual. She argued that girls have their own separate line of sexual development based on their different physiology. In her view girls are born 'feminine' with heterosexual tendencies and an early awareness of their vaginas (Horney 1924, 1926). The wish to be a man should not, Horney says, be taken at face value, since it is usually a defence against a deeper and more dangerous desire – the little girl's Oedipal love for the father. Horney described how some girls, unable to tolerate the intensity of their own desire, become terrified that the father will actually penetrate and damage their small vaginas. Unable to face their guilt these girls may retreat from wanting to possess the father into the wish to be like him. So, rather than being impelled towards heterosexuality by penis envy, as in Freud's theory, Horney's little girl regresses into envy of men because she cannot tolerate her own female desire (Horney 1924).

One of the many ironies of this debate is that Horney was replacing Freud's theory of penis envy with another father-focused argument, at the time when Freud himself was being encouraged by his female supporters to explore the influence of early mothering on female development. Horney's focus on the girl's 'natural' Oedipal desire for the father also prevented her from considering the nature of the father's desire and the possibility that there might be real external reasons why some girls' dread of paternal rape becomes so overwhelming.

Freud often responded to followers who deviated from his theories with scathing attacks. His 1924 paper certainly could be read as a direct rebuttal of Horney's earlier paper – a fact she may have found wounding or offensive (Odes Fliegel 1986). At any rate, from that point on Horney's own writings became more and more polemical, concentrating on the 'male bias' within psychoanalysis which reflected a general cultural devaluation of women. Why, she asked, did male analysts focus on the relative size and visibility of the male genital, ignoring the more fundamental physiological difference between the sexes – that women can reproduce the race, while men cannot? Surely this reflected the sexual fantasies of the little boy rather than any objective truth about human nature?

> At this point, I as a woman ask in amazement, and what about motherhood? And the blissful consciousness of bearing a new life within oneself? . . . And the deep pleasurable feeling of satisfaction in suckling it and the happiness of the whole period when the infant needs her care?
>
> (Horney 1926:10)

Horney came to believe that male womb envy is far more virulent than female penis envy. Both male cultural achievement and men's urge to dominate and exclude women are, in her view, an unconscious attempt to compensate for men's tangential role in procreation (1926). 'Men are evidently under greater necessity to depreciate women than vice-versa', Horney remarked tartly in 'The flight from womanhood' (Horney 1926: 12). She described how a 'dread of the vagina', a defence against early envy and fear of sexual rejection by the mother emerged rapidly in the maternal transference between male patients and female analysts.

> When one begins, as I did, to analyse men only after a long experience of analysing women, one receives a most surprising impression of the intensity of this envy of pregnancy, childbirth and motherhood, as well as of the breasts and the art of suckling.
>
> (Horney 1926: 10)

Horney's theories won influential support, notably from Ernest Jones, founder and first President of the British Psychoanalytic Association, and Melanie Klein, who settled in London in 1926. 'There is a healthy suspicion growing that men analysts have been led to adopt an unduly phallo-centric view of the problems in question, the importance of the female organs being correspondingly underestimated', Jones wrote, entering the fray on Horney's side (Jones 1927b: 438). The central question for him was whether girls are 'born' feminine or 'made' so through culture. Jones strongly supported Horney's argument that girls have inborn tendencies towards heterosexual femininity, do not feel themselves to be castrated and have an early awareness of the vagina (Jones 1927b, 1935).

MELANIE KLEIN

In Jones' own papers on female sexuality, however, the figure on whom he relied was Melanie Klein. Klein did not directly join in the debate, but nevertheless issued a strong indirect challenge to Freud's theory of sexual identity in a paper written during the years of controversy (Klein 1928). She disagreed with Freud that Oedipal feelings arose first around the age of 3 or 4, in relation to the father. Instead she argued that the first signs of the Oedipus complex arise in early infancy in relation to the mother's body. The infant does have a relationship with the father from early on, but he is at first experienced only as part of the mother.

Klein agreed with the main arguments of all Freud's challengers, including Horney's theory that penis envy is superficial
and secondary, a defence against a deeper dread. For Klein the
girl's fundamental terror is that the mother will destroy her
capacity to bear children as retaliation for the daughter's own
envious fantasies of destroying the inside of the maternal body.
In 1928 Klein also completely contradicted Freud's theory that the
girl goes through a 'masculine' phallic phase before she becomes
heterosexual. Children of both sexes, Klein argued, go through a
primary 'femininity phase' where they form a very early identification with the mother. Both sexes are feminine insofar as they
want babies, resulting in envious attempts to steal the siblings
imagined to exist inside the mother's womb. Whereas the girl
dreads retaliatory attacks to the inside of her body the boy fears
that the mother will retaliate by attacking his genitals.

Through the influence of Klein, who was a pioneer of the
post-war school of object relations theory, Horney's theories –
particularly her emphasis on womb envy and her argument that
each sex had their own separate line of sexual development –
became subsumed into the mainstream of British psychoanalysis.
In this way, Horney had a profound influence on the development
of mother-dominated psychoanalysis.

Jones' 1935 paper, 'Early female sexuality', was intended as
the first in a series of exchange lectures to discuss the theoretical
differences between London psychoanalysts influenced by Klein,
and Freud's circle in Vienna. Instead this paper marked the end
of the period of debate on female sexuality, which ended in
deadlock rather than resolution (Jones 1935).

Present-day psychotherapists and feminists continue to discuss
the issues left unresolved by this debate, particularly the vexed
notion of penis envy. To my mind, Horney was right in arguing
that male womb envy is far more intense than penis envy and
may be an underlying motivation for excluding women from
political and economic power. As Horney pointed out, Freud's
denial that there is anything enviable or valuable about women
may well be a male defence against envy, an attempt to denigrate
what is most coveted so that it does not evoke such painful
feelings of inferiority and lack. What is most striking is that Freud
so rarely mentioned women's capacity to reproduce the species,

leaving his female colleagues to explore this central aspect of female experience.

I also agree with those who argue that the girl's most fundamental anxieties are about damage to the inside of her body, to her female organs, rather than her lack of a penis. This also seems to be the consensus amongst clinicians in Britain and North America. For instance, American analyst E. Lloyd Mayer argues that today it is possible to see that Horney was clearly right, now that we know more about the physiology of female sexuality, and the taboo on discussing it has lessened. Lloyd Mayer describes 3-year-old Emily, who, like Freud's little Hans, assumes that everyone's body must be just like hers. Hans told his mother, 'I thought you were so big you'd have a widdler as big as a horse' (Freud 1909: 173). Emily muses thoughtfully, 'and Mummy has a vulva . . . and Emily has a vulva . . . but Mummy, Daddy has something funny in his vulva!' Emily, like many contemporary girls, not only knows about her vagina, but has been given a word to denote her external genitalia. Emily's fantasy is the precursor, Lloyd Mayer argues, of the conviction she finds in many female patients that men are 'so closed' that intimacy with them is impossible. These women are projecting onto men a fundamental female anxiety, the dread of losing their genital openness (Lloyd Mayer 1985).

But why did Freud win so much support from his female colleagues? Perhaps in his day women actually were more pre-occupied with envy of men. The American feminist Elizabeth Janeway, born in 1913, wrote that in her youth all hopes existed only in the male mode. Then women copied men in their dreams because there was no one else to copy (Janeway 1982: 13). It is now possible, theoretically at least, for some women to operate as men's equals in professional life. In 1972 Helene Deutsch said, 'Yes there is penis envy, but in a society open to women, with accepting parents, the impact will be very different than it used to be' (Strouse 1985: 165–6).

Does the pattern of our anxieties vary from culture to culture? Some of Freud's contemporaries argued that this was the case. In 1929 Girindrasekar Bose, founder and first President of the Indian Psychoanalytic Association, wrote to Freud saying that the Indian boys' Oedipal anxieties were different from those of their European counterparts. In a culture where bodies were less hidden the difference between the sexes was no surprise and

Indian men felt less dread of castration (becoming feminine). Their cross-sexual and generational identifications were more fluid and Indian men were far more able to accept conscious fantasies of being female, Bose wrote (Bose 1929 quoted in Kakar 1989).

In his reply to Bose, Freud was polite and equivocal, observing that more information was needed on these issues. But he told the poet H.D. during her analysis in 1933, 'On the whole, I think my Indian students have reacted in the least satisfactory way to my teaching' (H.D. 1956: 68).

Some feminists argue that Freud was not devaluing women but simply describing their unenviable position in a society where they were seen as second-class. 'No phallus, no power, except those winning ways of gaining one', Juliet Mitchell wrote in 1974 (Mitchell 1974: 96). I certainly agree that men do not usually want to give up the privileges of belonging to the more socially valued sex, however much they might want to wield power over, or even appropriate, women's procreative power. But is this really what Freud meant? As so often, it is very difficult to tell. But he frequently seems to suggest that he is describing a symbolic system that prevails in the unconscious regardless of cultural variation.

This is the assumption made by many of his feminist critics who argue that, according to anthropological and archaeological evidence, no universal symbolism can be attributed to the penis (or phallus). For instance Lucy Goodison points out that women's different, more highly valued status in prehistoric Crete is reflected in religious symbolism that revolves around powerful images of the female body and womb, rather than the male penis (Goodison 1990).

Freud and Horney argued as much about cultural as clinical issues. In this area it is hard to prove either point of view. Freud said that it was predictable that women analysts and 'men analysts with feminist views' would see the concept of female penis envy as unconsciously designed to justify men's 'innate inclination to disparage and suppress women'. And obviously those who oppose feminism would 'think it quite natural that the female sex should refuse to accept a view which appears to contradict their eagerly coveted equality with men'. He concludes: 'The use of analysis as a weapon of controversy can clearly lead to no decision' (Freud 1931: 46).

The theories that we feel are right will probably be those that resonate with our own personal experience of family and cultural life. For instance Horney may well have been able to stress the positive, enviable aspects of motherhood, and challenge Freud so forcefully, because of her identification with an idealised dominating mother and her intense hostility towards a denigrated father. Deutsch's more negative identification with a harsh mother who seems to have wanted her to be a son might have predisposed her towards Freud's theory of female penis envy. Because of her early experiences Deutsch could not celebrate womanhood, childbirth or mothering as Horney did. Deutsch idealised her father and this may also have prevented her from being able to state her quite considerable theoretical differences with Freud (Sayers 1991).

Freud offers some subtly varied explanations of the way we simultaneously seek and resist change in the area of sexuality and identity. I find the ambiguities in his theory refreshing, because there is much that we still do not understand about the relationship between culture, physiology and psychic life. For instance, there is still great controversy about how far physiology might determine sexual orientation.

Freud was always contradictory about the role culture and physiology play in determining sexual identity and orientation. His opponents in the debate and many of his followers claim far more certainty about the origins of sexual identity than he did. Freud seems never to have fully made up his mind on this issue, and has therefore been seen by some as a committed biologist and by others as a pioneer of environmental theories of sexual identity.

On the one hand he was vehement in his opposition to the biologism of his opponents.

> I object to all of you [Horney, Jones, Rado, etc.], to the extent that you do not distinguish more clearly ... between what is psychic and what is biological ... I would only like to emphasise that we must keep psychoanalysis separate from biology just as we have kept it separate from anatomy and physiology.
> (Freud 1935a: 328–9)

Yet he himself was obviously profoundly ambiguous about whether women's inferior status is biologically fixed. 'Anatomy is

Destiny', he said, while discussing female penis envy in 1924. Freud eventually acknowledged that the discrepancies in his theory had led to confusion. 'The sight of the penis and its function of urination cannot be the motive, only the trigger of the child's envy. However, no one has stated this' (Freud 1935a: 329).

I prefer to believe, as Freud sometimes seemed to, that we piece together our own sense of what it means to be psychologically male or female and our sexual orientation through the influence of family and culture. The radicalism of Freud's theory is flawed, though, by his phallocentrism. For Freud, women exist only as envious or lacking in relation to men, not as individuals with their own assets and dilemmas. Horney has earned a place in psychoanalytic and feminist history through her spirited denunciation of his 'male bias' and her insistence that he was using the infantile theories of the little boy to analyse her sex. Her account of women's devaluation within culture remains as inspiring and relevant as if it had been written yesterday.

Yet Horney's theory of inborn femininity was an equally problematic alternative. For instance, how are we to view the many female contributors to this debate who either did not become wives and mothers, or did so only with great ambivalence? Theories which describe a true psychic femininity, based around heterosexual desire and the wish for children, pathologise women who may choose other paths towards happiness. Freud, in contrast, argued that there was no point in encouraging people to conform to what society demanded of them, particularly in the sphere of sexuality and gender, since they could never fully do so and repressed desire might well lead to neurosis.

But Freud's theory also linked heterosexuality with the relinquishment of the girl's active 'masculine' strivings. This raises questions about whether heterosexual women, or those interested in mothering, can also remain forceful and competitive enough to survive in the 'masculine' world of work outside the home.

JOAN RIVIERE

In one of the most interesting papers of this period, 'Womanliness as a masquerade', the British psychoanalyst Joan Riviere struggles to understand some of these questions which were so important to her generation of female psychoanalysts (Riviere 1929). Riviere's concern is with the growing number of women like herself who divide their time between traditionally 'feminine' and 'masculine' spheres of activity. Until recently a woman who engaged in conventionally male pursuits would, Riviere observes, have made no secret of her wish to be like – or even to be – a man. Riviere is puzzled about how to classify these new women who do not want to close the door on femininity or motherliness in order to succeed professionally.

Riviere draws on the opposing theories of Freud and Jones – both her ex-analysts – to ask what psychic womanhood is. Like Horney, Jones and Klein she assumes that women are born with tendencies towards heterosexual 'femininity'. But Riviere also stresses the difficulties of the girl's transition from an oral attachment to the mother to a genital desire for the father, arguing that the girl may be left feeling intense envy and hostility towards both parents. Riviere is concerned with a particular category of women whose early ambivalence towards both parents is so strong that they remain emotionally and sexually suspended between mother and father in the internal world. Even if they engage only in sexual relationships with men, these women are, Riviere argues, neither fully lesbian nor heterosexual.

Riviere describes a female patient who gains satisfaction from a conventionally 'feminine' lifestyle, including marriage and family life, whilst also being successful as a professional. She has identified with her father and feels that through her 'masculine' achievements she has symbolically stolen the paternal penis. She tries to appease her father and ward off retaliation from men through ostentatious flirting with 'father-figures' after every successful public-speaking engagement. In this way she cancels out and disowns her 'masculine' success (Riviere 1929: 93).

This is an example, argues Riviere, of how womanliness can 'be assumed and worn as a mask' for defensive reasons (Riviere 1929: 94). She points out that the patient hides her masculine identifications with a masquerade of femininity just as some men hide their homosexual desire through exaggerated displays of heterosexuality. Riviere lists many everyday situations where women conceal their 'masculine' skills, sabotaging their own efforts through mockery and self-deprecation. These women feel such guilt and anxiety about male retaliation, Riviere argues, that they take up an attitude of extreme passivity with men, as if to say, 'I must not take. I must not even ask. It must be given me' (Riviere 1929: 101).

For the patient Riviere describes, both parents are hated rivals. But, according to Riviere, like all girls she feels most dread and hatred of her mother, since she imagines she has also robbed her of the paternal penis, perhaps by identifying with the father. The patient obsessively engages in fruitless attempts to restore to her mother the stolen penis, through daughterly displays of 'masculine' skill and prowess. Although the patient has a fulfilling sexual life with her husband, Riviere argues that she is psychically a lesbian. Homosexuality differs from heterosexuality only in the degree of early hostility, and the way the girl manages to deal with it, she says.

Having established that much apparent feminine heterosexuality is not what it appears, Riviere then asks how true 'womanliness' differs from the 'masquerade'. Is there some core of 'genuine' femininity which can be clearly delineated from the pseudo-womanly mask? Riviere answers, quite unequivocally, as far as I can see, that there is no essential difference between the two. Whether 'radical or superficial' womanliness and the masquerade 'are the same thing' (Riviere 1929: 94). This statement, which has endeared Riviere to many late twentieth-century feminists and Lacanians, is one with which I agree. I do not think it is possible to say that some aspects of the psyche are more genuinely feminine or masculine and more resistant to the pressures of cultural expectations or familial wishes than others. But Riviere, like Freud, sometimes writes in an ambiguous way, which may reflect her actual position, poised between two ex-analysts who were in theoretical conflict. This has enabled others to argue that she believed strongly in inborn tendencies towards 'true' heterosexual femininity, as Jones and Klein did. (See Hughes 1991.)

Riviere's question about how women can draw on their psychic 'masculinity' while also preserving more traditionally feminine strengths and activities is central to this book. I ask how women can take possession of their lives, and retain their fighting spirit, without losing the possibility of intimacy and sexual passion. The question is just as fundamental when reversed: how can men integrate qualities associated culturally with femininity? Can they be strong without depending on women as a receptacle for disowned aspects of psychic life? The difficulty both sexes have in this area is compounded (or perhaps created) by the fact that women and 'femininity' are still valued so much less than men and 'masculinity', and by the power differentials between the sexes. Men and women are very differently located in the cultural hierarchy, and this difference also affects the analytic encounter, a topic raised by Horney. She described how rapidly envy, fear and contempt arise in the maternal transference with male patients. Likewise, Freud acknowledged the discomfort he felt when his female patients perceived him as feminine or maternal.

This brings me to the second major theme of this book – the clinical and political implications of power and envy. Freud and Horney's opposing views about penis and womb envy have found expression in theories which privilege the power of one parent rather than the other in the mind of the child. This, of course, raises fundamental questions about what mothering and fathering are, and whether we are discussing actual biological parents or the functions associated with them. Can the theory and practice of psychotherapy help us understand and change cultural power-differentials or does it merely replicate them?

Interest in some themes of the debate appears to have died out. Such is the case with the question of whether women are more masochistic than men. This highly controversial question is rarely asked openly today, although perhaps it is now being raised in more covert ways. Contemporary analysts and feminists still ask why women tolerate cultural restrictions and painful or frustrating personal relationships. Object relations theorists also look at the different ways women and men might mobilise aggression or defend against pain, focusing on symptoms which prevail in one sex rather than the other, such as serious eating problems and certain male sexual perversions. Examining such phenomena invariably raises all the questions so central to the earlier debate. What are 'masculinity' and 'femininity'? How do they arise, and are they more the property of one sex than the other? And given the way inequitable divisions of power and prestige have permeated the erotic life of women and men, is it ever possible to eliminate such deeply entrenched inequalities or have they become necessary to our sexuality? Uncomfortable questions, with still no easy answers.

Chapter 2

From the penis to the womb: male sexuality

Debate over the issues surrounding female sexuality abated after the 1920s/30s controversy, and did not revive until the 1960s, when feminism generated a new wave of interest in the psychology of gender. In the intervening years there had been some significant theoretical shifts in British psychoanalysis and North American ego psychology. This chapter focuses on changing theories about envy, the Oedipus complex, and the role of the father in the male psyche, which I discuss in the light of my own clinical work.

> After the 1930s hardly any British analyst was likely to be an uncritical supporter of Freud's theory of female psychosexual development in its phallocentric aspects, and by the 1980s it is regarded as more dated than most of Freud's theories.
>
> (Rayner 1991: 104)

This description by Eric Rayner certainly fits in with my experience of training as a psychoanalytic psychotherapist. Most of my colleagues and teachers seemed to regard this aspect of Freud's theory as too anachronistic and irrelevant to merit serious discussion. In Britain during the early 1980s only Lacanians criticised the prevailing view of the mother as the most powerful and enviable parent. Juliet Mitchell, who drew on Lacan in her early writing, said: 'The debates of the 1930s bequeathed, instead of an interest in the psychology of femininity, a heritage of a mother–child obsession' (Mitchell 1974: 229). In North America and France the psychoanalytic climate was different. Freud's theory was re-formulated in new ways and his writings on female sexuality have continued to be taken far more seriously as a subject of debate.

Freud had prophesied that his theory of a subversive sexuality which could never be fully tamed by culture would alienate many of his psychoanalytic followers, and this was indeed the case with British object relations theorists who argued that Freud focused too much on the relief of physical tension, rather than seeing erotic desire as inextricably linked with the capacity for loving intimacy or defences against it (Meltzer 1978, Symington 1986). Gradually most British psychoanalysts moved away from Freud's emphasis on the child's need to relinquish incestuous desire, concentrating rather on the need to renounce the illusion of fusion with the mother. Until recently relations with the father were virtually ignored.

This tendency to regard the father as an increasingly peripheral figure both reflected and reinforced social trends during the era when object relations theories were developing. Freud's perspective was formed through the experience of Victorian upper-class European families, where mothers were often squeezed out by authoritarian fathers and a parade of nannies. The theories of Winnicott and Bowlby, by contrast, were forged in post-Second World War Britain. There, panic during 1945–7 about the falling birth-rate ensured that the target of post-war social policy was the mother, who was spoken about as if she constituted all there was of the family. Increasingly the mother was seen by policy-makers as a synonym for all women, the needs of other female groups being ignored (Riley 1983). Today theories which stress male fragility and womb envy may be seen to reflect men's current anxieties about the erosion of patriarchal power as traditional family structures disappear. The lives of women may seem more desirable and enviable to both sexes now that the female sex has access, in theory at least, to traditionally male as well as female spheres of activity.

As the 1980s went on, however, there was also a noticeable revival of analytic interest in the role of the father. Andrew Samuels, a Jungian analyst, in 1985 described how men he knew expected to be far more actively engaged with their children than their own fathers had been, a social shift reflected in childcare manuals of that decade (Samuels 1985). This may be so, yet it may also be true that the increasing economic dispensability of the father (given the growth in female employment) has induced anxiety in some male analysts. In 1991, for example, the British psychoanalyst Adam Limentani lambasted a feminist clinician who had suggested that children often benefit from being brought up solely by the mother (Limentani 1991). At the same time, feminists have also become concerned that in psychoanalytic theory mothers are being held solely responsible for the problems of their children (e.g. Chodorow 1989). Clearly this is a critical moment in the changing patterns of male/female relations: can psychoanalysis take on board these shifts in family life, and the way they reverberate in the individual unconscious? If the actual power of men is under threat, what meaning does this have for psychological gender?

THE BRITISH SCHOOL OF PSYCHOANALYSIS

Writing as a turn-of-the-century patriarch, Freud was well aware of the benefits men gained from identification with the father's authority and cultural privilege. He also idealised the mother–son relationship, saying, 'A mother is only brought unlimited satisfaction by her relation to a son; this is altogether the most free from ambivalence of all human relationships' (Freud 1933: 168). According to Freud men's greatest rivalry is with other men, rather than with women's unenviable lot in life. Once the boy sees that the girl lacks a penis, is 'castrated', he will 'tremble for his masculinity henceforth'. Freud explained male misogyny by arguing that the woman-hater dreads being in the 'castrated' submissive position in relation to another man and therefore abhors the female sex and qualities he sees as 'feminine' in himself and other men.

For Freud, then, the ultimate obstacle to analytic progress in both sexes was the dread of femininity. He argued that women might be unable to resolve neurotic conflicts because they could not face the fact that they would never be men. According to Freud men resist the analytic process because they see the acceptance of help as synonymous with humiliating submission to (or castration by) the analyst within the paternal transference (Freud 1937).

In contrast British psychoanalysts such as Klein and Winnicott argue that it is envy of the mother rather than rivalry with the father which impedes psychic change. Klein, who believed that the boy's early rivalry with his mother was particularly intense and asocial, created a new psychoanalytic reading of envy. She described how all infants are born with varying tendencies towards envious hatred, a wild, unbearably destructive state of mind experienced most strongly towards the mother in infancy rather than the Oedipal father in toddlerhood (Klein 1957). Contemporary Kleinians make a fundamental distinction between the thirst for knowledge, including the desire for emotional insight, and the converse – envious and intrusive curiosity – the impulse to gain power and triumph over or control others in the interests of denying feelings of infantile vulnerability, humiliation or need. In Kleinian theory, both envious curiosity and the desire for knowledge arise in the context of the infant's urge to explore the inside of the mother's body.

Klein radically redefined the Oedipus complex, focusing as much on emotional and intellectual development as on erotic desire. In her theory the child's most crucial task is to re-own its own hatred and fear and to tolerate the guilt and depression that follow the recognition of destructive feelings towards love-objects. The attainment of psychic health, including the capacity for self-reflection and symbolic thought, is dependent on becoming able to tolerate the fact that the mother is a separate being with a life of her own, including a sexual relationship with the father (Britton 1989).

Klein's views on the origins of envy touch on psychoanalytic controversies about how far aggression is inborn and the extent to which the very young baby experiences itself as separate from other people.

D.W. WINNICOTT

Winnicott's view that envy can only arise as a reaction to experiences of severe pain or frustration contrasts sharply with Klein's theory. Winnicott sees the baby as so incapable of surviving on its own that it is meaningless to discuss it as a separate unit outside its natural context, which he assumes to be the mother–baby couple. The baby who feels secure, satisfied and contented will, by and large, exist in a state of pleasurable unity with the mother. For 'this child the breast is the self and the self is the breast. Envy is a term that might become applicable in the experience of a tantalising failure of the breast as something that is' (Winnicott 1971: 96). I agree with Winnicott that envy is not inborn but arises because of experiences of pain, loss or lack. The envious child may well have been the object of deeply destructive parental envy.

Winnicott followed Horney in arguing that male womb envy and fear of domination by the female is far deeper than women's envy of men. He describes a male patient who has been unable fully to accept the fact that he is male. A dissociated female part of this man's personality, which Winnicott called 'the girl', could not allow analysis to end until her existence was fully acknowledged even though the patient had already received twenty-five years of treatment with different psychoanalysts. There was a breakthrough when Winnicott recognised this entirely split-off 'pure female' aspect of his patient's personality, and understood that it was a response to the mother's failure to acknowledge that her infant son was male. Once the strength of 'the girl' had been acknowledged the patient could begin to accept his psychic bisexuality, rather than needing to split off his femininity entirely from awareness (Winnicott 1971).

Despite his emphasis on environmental factors in personality development, Winnicott, like most British object relations psychoanalysts, believes that there is a congenital disposition to be psychologically, as well as anatomically, masculine or feminine, maternal or paternal. Of the father of one of his patients he wrote, 'one could say that he is so maternal that one wonders how he will manage when he becomes used as a male and as a true father' (Winnicott quoted in Davis and Wallbridge 1981: 133). Ultimately, though, Winnicott believed that upbringing is crucial, and this is why some men are more maternal than their female partners. Women, like men, are psychically bisexual and also possess the 'male' capacity for 'doing'. But ideally the environment reinforces innate tendencies, Winnicott says. Therefore, most 'males become men and most females become women' (Winnicott 1964: 184).

Winnicott recognised that cruel and discriminatory customs were in operation against women in most cultures. He argued that human beings would have less need to wreak revenge on 'Woman' through cruel cultural customs and exclusion from political leadership if they could face up to the absoluteness of their early dependence on the mother. He traces men's tendency to seek out danger, in fighting wars for instance, to envy of the risks women take in childbirth. These insights are, in my view, absolutely crucial to a feminist understanding of gender power differentials. Yet, Winnicott who, like Freud, remained profoundly ambivalent about women's struggles for equality, argued in the same essay that feminism is an identity disorder – the result of the girl's inability to accept that she could not be male (Winnicott 1964).

There is a tendency for psychoanalysts who emphasise women's power in psychic life to ignore men's financial and social power. Thus they disregard the fact that motherhood is circumscribed by medicine and the state, often in ways which increase women's sense of helplessness and isolation. Refusal to recognise such realities can lead to the assumption that women, as the stronger sex, simply give away the emotional power they gain from their procreative role (e.g. Temperley 1984). The reality is that in our culture qualities seen as 'masculine' are more socially valued and linked with mental health (Frosh 1989).

Maleness, in our society, is a sign of power and privilege. Yet, given this, why do some men wish to abandon it? Indeed, far more men than women seek actually to change their gender, penis envy notwithstanding. Why is this? Robert Stoller, an American psychoanalyst who has researched gender disorders, argues that because men have to 'dis-identify' with the mother after an initial period of female identification, their gender identities are more rigid and fragile than women's (Stoller 1975). According to this theory it is early anxieties about differentiation from the mother rather than fear of castration by the father which cause men to dread becoming female or homosexual. Stoller goes on to argue that the male mind is often dominated by a three-way conflict – between the desire to regress to an illusion of symbiosis with the mother, a dread of the ensuing loss of male identity, and a longing for revenge on the mother for her part in this dilemma. This conflict results in the cruelty, misogyny and emotional detachment that characterise men in our culture, and can also give rise to states of serious gender confusion which are less often found in women.

Stoller argues that an immutable sense of being male or female – a 'core gender identity' – is fixed mainly through cultural rather than biological forces by the age of 3 – earlier than in Freud's theory. He offers powerful evidence that if a child's biological sex is incorrectly assigned at birth (for instance in the case of genital or reproductive abnormalities) the child will believe itself to be the sex it has been told it is, rather than the one it was born with. If the boy is not encouraged to 'dis-identify' and instead has a 'timeless, excessively close physical and emotional intimacy' with the mother he may in extreme cases become transsexual, convinced that he is a psychological female trapped in a male body (Stoller 1979).

It is striking that Stoller barely mentions the role of the father except to say briefly that in these cases he is either absent or oppressive and threatening. Sometimes Stoller even appears to be blaming the mothers of his patients for choosing husbands who will collude with their sexualised possessiveness, as if all responsibility for marital choice lay with women! (See Limentani 1991: 575.) The British psychoanalyst Adam Limentani has slightly more to say about the father's role in creating serious confusions of sexual identity. He argues that male transsexualism develops from a background of early disturbance in symbol formation exacerbated by intrusive or absent fathering (Limentani 1979, 1991). Similarly, Limentani says, female transsexuals who feel psychically fused with the mother are unable to think symbolically and so can conceive only of the most extreme and concrete way of differentiating themselves – through gaining a male body surgically.

For 'most men the problem is women', we are told in a contemporary American anthology on male psychology. 'Masculinity is often defined in relation to and in contrast to women; as boys and men we are dependent upon, threatened by, vulnerable to, and envious of women' (Fogel 1986: 9). The contributors to this anthology argue that the father is no longer seen by his sons as a threatening patriarchal presence but as absent or ineffectual, leaving his son at the mercy of the parent who really is imagined to be powerful – the mother. This results in a 'martial masculinity', a brittle, artificial and aggressive version of manhood formed as protection against identification with the powerful mother, argues Munder Ross in the same volume. In a classic British object relations anthology on sexual perversion, almost all the patients described are male, and maternal seductiveness or over-stimulation is given as a reason for the son's difficulties in almost every case. The mothers of these male patients are typically seen as castrating, smothering or emotionally neglectful (Rosen 1979a).

Some of these contemporary theories focus on the supposedly 'real' characteristics of each parent, as described by the patient at the beginning of psychotherapy. But unconscious communications between family members and the child's own fantasies can be as significant as actual events, and as the patient becomes more aware of these unspoken undercurrents during psychotherapy, his perception of each parent may change dramatically. For instance if a child is brought up mainly by one parent, perhaps the mother, what is important is her own relationship to her internal male aspects, including her identifications with her own father and the 'masculine' or paternal qualities of both parents. A single mother may be more able to help a son achieve a sense of psychic separation than a heterosexual couple who have profound difficulties in that area themselves. And an absent father can dominate the child's mind at least as much as one who is present throughout childhood.

THE RETURN TO THE FATHER

Since the 1980s there has been renewed interest in the father and in male psychology amongst British and North American psychoanalysts. In general, however, the role assigned by these analysts to the father in psychic life is much diminished compared to the part Freud assigned to him. In most cases, the father is seen primarily as an adjunct to the mother whose unique nurturant functions can only be performed by the female parent. His role in the structuring of mental life tends to be played down. Adam Limentani, for example, has argued that the father should not intrude in the early, delicate mother–child relationship (Limentani 1991). Winnicott barely mentioned fathers, and when he did it was to assign them the auxiliary role of providing a 'protective covering' for the mother–infant couple against external impingement (Winnicott 1957). Later the father might also balance the mother, providing a more objective attention that would help the child to cope with emotional ambivalence.

Other psychoanalysts, including some contemporary Kleinians, have adopted a more radical stance on the mobility of parenting functions, arguing that fathers may provide 'maternal' containment, and that mothers too may help children gain a sense of psychic autonomy and assist their move into the wider world. Kleinians in general have tended to place greater emphasis on the father's importance both as a real figure and as an object of early fantasy: an emphasis which has been developed much further since the 1980s, as Kleinian theorists demonstrate the crucial role played by a child's feelings and fantasies about the father in the formation of its early relationship with the mother. At the same time, however, the mother's role in helping the child negotiate its relationship with the external world is also stressed.

According to Kleinians, a child's capacity to manage its perceptions of relations between its parents is crucial. The child who has not internalised a secure early relationship with the mother will experience evidence of its relationships with others as catastrophic to its inner security and cling to the illusion of symbiosis in order to ward off feelings of psychic disaster. This may lead to distortions in thinking. The capacity to think about and learn from one's own emotional life only arises once links can be recognised, including those between the parents. Once the child can acknowledge parental intimacy and the separate relationship it has with each of them, a triangular space develops in the mind which enables the child to distinguish internal and external reality and to reflect on itself and others. The child will then become able to think symbolically, initially about how to repair attacks made in fantasy on the mother's body (Britton 1989).

However, despite this new emphasis on the paternal role the father's function is still secondary to that of the mother in post-Kleinian theory. He does not intervene as a powerful sexual presence, a representative of authority and culture, as in Freud's theory.

In an interesting re-appraisal of the object relations neglect of the father, Adam Limentani admits that in his own past work he sometimes colluded with the family's desire to exclude the father from consultation about the psychological problems of their children. He himself overlooked the way in which he became a positive paternal figure in the analysis of patients, including transsexuals. Limentani argues that if the psychotherapist focuses only on the mother this may fulfil the patient's unconscious desire to preserve the illusion of being central to the mother's life. The theoretical neglect of the father may mean that little is expected of him or that important facts about his position in the family are ignored in clinical work. Limentani says that, especially in the latter part of the analysis, the 'acquisition of the second object is our fundamental therapeutic task, a fact that is so obvious that it gets overlooked' (Limentani 1991: 577).

Limentani's paper fits in with a contemporary tendency to

emphasise the positive aspects of the father–child relationship – to find a clear role for the 'Cinderella-figure of developmental theory' (Samuels 1993). For instance Melvin Glasser, a contemporary Freudian, argues that initially the boy internalises the father as an ally, the 'wall of a fortress' against fears of merger or annihilation by the mother. The father will then gain significance as an alternative love-object with whose body and gender the boy can identify (Glasser 1984).

Despite these efforts at rehabilitation the father remains a shadowy figure in much contemporary theory. British psychoanalyst Gregorio Kohon draws on Lacan to argue that object relations analysts 'have managed to castrate the father, and desexualise the theory; the penis of the father has become another breast, an organ of warmth and reparation, the giver of babies but not of sexual pleasure'. He quotes a senior British woman analyst, 'What is the function of the father,' she exclaimed, 'but, of course, to fuck the mother?' (Kohon 1987: 225).

The recourse to Lacan in Kohon's essay is significant, since it points to one of the most fully elaborated – and controversial – attempts to reinstate the father at the heart of psychoanalytic theory. Lacan was deeply critical of the contemporary psychoanalytic preoccupation with the mother–infant relationship on a number of counts. In particular he identified the Oedipal moment – rather than the pre-Oedipal relationship with the mother – as the crucial point of psychic structuration. The preverbal child, dwelling in its dyadic union with the mother, is living inside an imaginary world which must be ruptured by the entry of a 'third term', the symbolic father, if the child is not to become psychotic.

Lacan argues that the boy suffers in a particular way from being 'idol-ised' by the mother, who does not envy or idealise the girl in the same way. The boy needs the father to break into the intense 'luring' relationship the mother has with the infant, a relationship structured around the mother's lack of a penis and the son's wish to become the 'phallus', the sole object of maternal desire (Lacan 1964).

Lacan is describing the role of the symbolic, rather than the actual father. His focus is on the way patriarchal laws are reproduced in the unconscious. It is the father who helps the child to face reality, originally of the differences between the sexes and the generations, while the mother is associated with helpless dependence and the dangerous lure of psychotic illusion.

Inevitably, then, his theory reflects the devaluation of the mother and idealisation of the father which prevails in our society. There is a paradox inherent in it too, since the 'liberation' offered by the father places the girl and boy in different positions in male-dominated culture. Through identification with paternal power the boy can triumph over the mother and deny the strength of his early physical and emotional dependence on her. It is also worth noting that in most actual families the mother does much of the work of preparing the child for independence, while the father may well provide some maternal containment for the infant.

Different theoretical views about the importance of the father will obviously influence the way psychotherapists work. For instance some object relations psychotherapists expect to be seen mainly as a maternal transference figure during the early stages of treatment (Limentani 1991). This may reflect a belief that the patient must internalise a secure enough maternal object before he or she can face the existence of the father. From a Kleinian perspective, it is stressed that the psychotherapist must maintain a secure 'holding environment', a therapeutic setting and bound-aries which remain as consistent as possible. Interestingly, while object relations theorists often associate this consistent frame-work with the mother–infant relationship, one contemporary Freudian sees the therapeutic boundaries as paternal, providing evidence for the patient that if they regress to an illusion of fusion with the mother in the session, they can and must after-wards return to external reality. Chasseguet-Smirgel (1986b) argues that the 'analytic boat has sides which can be grasped in order to get out, and the analytic cot has bars one can hang on to so as not to become lost in a timeless sleep' (Chasseguet-Smirgel 1986b: 41).

In contrast with this approach, Lacan follows Freud in empha-sising the need for the analyst, 'like the forbidding father to represent, and point out to the analysand, the Other' (Benvenuto and Kennedy 1986: 208). The analyst must speak from the posi-tion of the symbolic father, one of whose functions is to point out the inescapability of sexual difference, castration and lack, and locate the child's desire to move out of the narcissistic posi-tion associated with the early mother. Too great an emphasis on 'internalising' a maternal good object is described as collusion with the patient's illusion that he exists in an exclusive therapeutic dyad. The patient has to come to terms with lack – the object of our desire is always outside us, and we can never fully possess the presence or qualities of another.

In the next section I explore a fragment of my work with two male patients, looking at the relevance of two different perspectives on maternal and paternal power to clinical practice.

THE SPIDER DREAM

A male patient, Mr C, had been coming to see me once a week for two months before the Christmas break. Returning from the break, he told me a dream he had had over the holidays which had disturbed him greatly. As soon as the sessions had stopped, he said, he had felt overwhelmed by unfamiliar feelings of terror, rage and isolation. Then he had a dream in which he woke up and noticed a small multi-coloured spider on his bedroom door. He went to pick it up gently but saw that it was growing larger and moving nearer to him. It was made of shiny foil with a lot of red in it, like Christmas decorations. Bits of it kept sticking in him 'like fibre-glass, which gets under your skin and becomes infected if you don't protect yourself'. It then changed, becoming a matchstick animal, standing on the table near him. It was mainly female but also a bit male.

Eventually as the spider/animal continued growing he told it, 'I'm bigger than you and can walk away.'

My patient woke up immediately the dream was over, feeling overwhelmed by powerful, confused feelings. Although it was still the middle of the night he started to write about his feelings about psychotherapy. Recounting this in the session after the break, he said that he associated the shiny red spider with me, since I often wore red. He went on to say: 'These sessions have become very important to me, but I realised that I did feel very angry about you being away. I started to write down things you'd said to me before the break. At the time, they made sense, but later I felt criticised by you.' When he finished writing his mood changed. He had acknowledged his own ambivalence towards me so his depression lifted.

The primal spider creature might have combined elements of fantasy and real experience. Mr C's feelings of insecurity in relation to his mother seemed to have been compounded by an intolerable feeling of exclusion from parental sex. He often talked about how the entire family, who had been very poor, had slept in the same room until he was 4. Mr C told me that several times in his teens in the swimming-pool, adult men had rubbed themselves against his genitals. He had found this both exciting and profoundly disturbing, and wondered whether he had suffered any sexual abuse earlier in his childhood. When he was 14 he had also made several attempts to force himself on his elder sister sexually and she had only managed to fight him off with great difficulty.

Discussing the dream in the session, he told me that there was something sexual about the spider/animal. He went on to say that just before Christmas he had become aware of feeling attracted to me. During the break he felt so abandoned that I, like the little spider, altered in his mind, becoming an increasingly overwhelming, predatory and threatening figure. Whereas he had previously found my interpretations helpful, now he experienced my words as having pierced his skin. Left to fester they had become as painful and hard to remove as bits of fibre-glass. My break, enforced evidence that I had a life apart from him, had provoked an overwhelming dread of annihilation or engulfment.

In his associations to the dream Mr C said that there had been a 'lack of empathy' in his 'baby-relationship' with his mother, for which his rather distant, uninvolved father could not compensate. Mr C had therefore not had a maternal figure of either sex who could help him digest and think about his earliest feelings and fantasies. So he had never developed the capacity to tolerate and understand his own emotional life, and could only deal with his raw, unprocessed feelings of pain and destructiveness by projecting them outside himself. Once imbued with feelings Mr C could not bear to acknowledge as his own, other people, including myself, could turn into nightmare creatures, looming dangerously over him like the spider in the dream. It was easier for him to see me as a wicked retaliatory maternal figure than, for instance, to face his fear that I might be at risk from the part of him that had nearly succeeded in overpowering and sexually assaulting his elder sister.

Contemporary Kleinians argue that if parental intercourse is felt to intrude into the child's mind before she or he has internalised a secure maternal object, as may well have happened in Mr C's childhood, the Oedipus complex does not appear in its classical form. The predominantly female multi-legged spider, who is also a bit male, would, from this perspective, be a very primitive early infantile image of the combined parents in intercourse. The threatening four-legged matchstick animal might represent the omnipotent maternal body which is imagined by the infant to contain everything in it, including the father's penis. Contemporary Kleinians argue that it is only as the infant develops the capacity to perceive others, initially the mother, as whole persons, that an image of the original parents and their respective qualities can occur. Mr C would have needed to bring together within the maternal transference his different experiences of me – as cruel and abandoning, yet also helpful and containing – so that he could gradually see himself and others as more benign and stable, less terrifyingly unpredictable. Then his image of the combined parents might divide out into the more easily recognisable Oedipal three-person scenario (Britton 1989).

The dream indicates that as yet Mr C has little capacity to envisage triangular relationships, or to think about the emotional links between himself and others. He is hardly able at an emotional level to recognise his father's existence in relation to his mother or himself. According to contemporary Kleinian theory, this is because his father is still experienced as a hostile force whose presence would annihilate the emotional link with the mother. The full recognition of parental sexuality is then dreaded as a mental catastrophe, or even experienced as a threat to life (Britton 1989).

From a more Freudian perspective the spider could represent the phallic mother, an image which is defensive against castration anxiety or a denial of the small boy's inability to satisfy the mother (Chasseguet-Smirgel 1984). Or the spider might represent a primal image of increasingly threatening parental intercourse where the mother is imagined to have incorporated the father, and might be about to do the same to him. From this perspective Mr C's dream might represent an attempt to incorporate a paternal element into a potentially suffocating therapeutic dyad. He is in the grip of a universal male conflict between the desire to re-enter the maternal womb, and the dread of being swallowed up in an incestuous symbiosis where he would lose any sense of being male. Freudian or Lacanian clinicians would argue that Mr C needs to confront the existence of the Other, a paternal force who can help him to face Oedipal issues, rather than to internalise a more secure maternal presence. Chasseguet-Smirgel argues that the father's penis represents a stop, which protects from symbiosis, from the melting of the boundaries between the ego and the non-ego, and from death (Chasseguet-Smirgel 1986b).

Mr C admitted in the session that he would like to tell me, as he told the spider, that he is bigger than me and can walk away. At the point where the boy is beginning to separate psychically from the mother and identify with the father he can become fixated and may then activate his anal sadism and contempt in an attempt to protect himself from incestuous merger with the mother and Oedipal anxieties about sexual rivalry with the father. At this juncture the boy may repudiate the mother and his own identification with her through an assertion of his more privileged position within patriarchy. Many boys unconsciously decide then that the mother is not worth the pain of so much desire and that they will never again allow a woman to have so much power over them (Jukes 1993).

Male-dominated social structures provide opportunities for men to deny their own envy and dependency needs, while forcing women into confrontation with infantile aspects of their own experience. Chasseguet-Smirgel argues that men encourage penis envy in women and make it part of their social institutions in order to avoid experiencing their own envy and feelings of sexual inadequacy in relation to women. The woman becomes the man's unacknowledged 'feminine part', whom he can master and control (Chasseguet-Smirgel 1964b). Indeed in our society it is still more socially acceptable for a man to put his female partner into the position of childlike helplessness or humiliation which he once occupied in relation to the mother, although women's increasing economic independence is giving them more possibility of resisting the emotional subservience that can accompany financial dependence. Another way in which men can deny their emotional need for others is by treating objects as a substitute for people, and relating to them with a fervour once reserved for the mother. Some men form their richest relationships with systems of ideas or pieces of machinery and relate to people as if they are things.

Is it possible to integrate the insights of Freud and Lacan with more mother-centred theories? Certainly the psychotherapist must be aware of Oedipal issues from the beginning of therapy, but some patients will be able to face these issues more rapidly than others. In contrast to Mr C who had very little capacity to recognise triangular relationships, because they represented such a threat to his psychic equilibrium, the next patient I describe had as a child begun to recognise his parents' sexual closeness. But his pain at exclusion was so intense that he simultaneously evaded the full significance of this knowledge, turning a blind eye to it (Steiner 1985). In psychotherapy he was so determined to avoid facing his Oedipal rivalry and humiliation that he barely mentioned his father for the first two years of twice-weekly psychotherapy.

THE FATHER ECLIPSED

This patient told me in his first session that his problems had begun in his fourth year. A first child, he was greatly cosseted and indulged by both parents, but was expected to grow up suddenly when a sister was born that year. He felt that he'd been ejected with traumatic abruptness from a womb-like atmosphere. In that fourth year his family had also moved house and he had been sent to a nursery school some distance from home. He also described how at 14 he had hit his sister on the chest and his father had responded by hitting his son – something he had never done before. His own aggression towards women emerged strongly towards me as a mother or sister from the beginning but it was a long time before we were both able to recognise in the transference the strong paternal figure who had been able to lay down the law to his teenage son.

Psychically he had wiped his father out because he had not wanted to acknowledge that he himself was not the sexual and emotional centre of his mother's life. In order to cling to the belief that he was the sole focus of maternal desire he had created an illusional system 'free from the demands of the exigencies of life, like a kind of reservation' (Freud 1924 quoted in Britton 1989: 183–7). This system was designed to prevent him having to face what he already knew about. He felt curiosity about parental sexuality to be potentially disastrous because the arrival of a third – the new baby – had destroyed his fantasy of existing in an exclusive couple with his mother. He defended himself against feelings of humiliation and inferiority in relation to his father by illusions of triumph. In one dream he climbed out of bed with his mother while his father glowered impotently from the other side of the room. Everyone has these illusions to a certain extent, but in his case they had been strong enough to prevent the working through of Oedipal rivalry and relinquishment of incestuous desire. Ronald Britton, a Kleinian psychoanalyst, describes expectations of an endless humiliating exposure to parental triumphalism or a horrific, sado-masochistic or murderous intercourse that he has found in patients who cannot face their knowledge of parental sex. This patient certainly did dread unbearable humiliation, and he was also preoccupied with murderous fantasies towards parental figures. These are issues I discuss in more detail in Chapters 4 and 6.

As he began to work through some of his overwhelming grief about abandonment by his mother after his sister's birth, my patient began to acknowledge that in fact his father had given him considerable attention during that traumatic period. The relatively strong relationship he had had with his father had been covered up and buried by his pain at the loss of his mother.

Meanwhile, as he became less preoccupied with anxieties about separation from his mother and myself he began to make dramatic progress in his career. Then for the first time he began to recall, through dream-images, the hours his father had spent with him playing patiently with maps, trains and models. He now related this to his intellectual confidence and the organisational abilities he was beginning to utilise in his work.

If the psychotherapist focuses entirely on early conflicts about the mother a sense of stagnation may begin to prevail within the therapeutic relationship. The father has been obliterated and there is a sense that something is missing from the therapeutic discourse which may suddenly come to life again once the father's presence within the transference is acknowledged.

The first time I became aware that I represented this patient's father in the transference was during a session when he complained bitterly that he couldn't listen to me, although he agreed rationally with what I was saying. The problem, he kept reiterating, was that the room, which usually felt warm and soft, today did not provide the womb-like, softly-upholstered environment he needed. Eventually I began to feel useless, impotent, invisible. The atmosphere changed when I said this, and then went on to link this feeling with the way his father had been wiped out, never mentioned in the sessions. I went on to suggest that he was unable to make use of what I was saying to him today, even though he agreed with it, just as he had been unable to assimilate the hours of patient attention his father had given him after the birth of the new baby. Now, as then, he felt too preoccupied with the loss of soft maternal comfort to partake in a different kind of relationship. He felt that I was speaking to him in a paternal way whereas he wanted everyone to be the same and to treat him in an identical way.

It soon became obvious to both of us that he still felt unprepared to face the Oedipal reality of the difference between the sexes and the generations. He began for the first time to acknowledge the strength of his early identification with, and envy of, his mother. Perhaps now that he had recognised the power of his internal father he felt more able to explore aspects of himself which he thought of as feminine. As his confusion of identity became evident, he described himself as having been 'twenty-four when his mother was born'. He'd always had fantasies about heterosexual intercourse with me. Now he described bisexual fantasies about having my body inside his, keeping him warm. 'It feels as if I've got a baby inside me, and that the baby is you', he told me. This reminded him of how he had told his teacher 'I'm having a baby' before the birth of 'my baby', as he had called the second sister, born when he was 8. Later in psychotherapy he came to understand that the reason he had always wanted many children was so he could out-do his mother. For him the minimum number was one more than she had had.

Having begun to work through his envy of his mother as well as his desire for her, his identification with his father grew stronger. He could now begin tentatively to confront the intimacy between his parents. He dreamt about them as a united couple but still resisted the implications of this. When I discussed the dream in the next session he said, 'I don't like you putting both of my parents together and talking about them in one sentence'. But gradually he became able to notice and even enjoy the fact that in reality his parents still seemed to gain great pleasure from physical and emotional closeness with each other. He also began to express the hope that I had a sexual partner, because he did not want me to be lonely. Once he had mourned the illusion of a lost exclusive relationship and recognised the link between his parents, he became increasingly able to reflect on his own experience and to observe relationships between others.

As psychotherapy progressed it became clear that his father had been exceptionally involved in his son's early childcare, even though his mother had remained the primary parent. He became convinced that his father had contributed to the early feeling of womb-like security he had experienced in infancy.

Another way of working with this man would have been to confront him much earlier with the fact that he was obliterating his father from the therapeutic discourse. Would earlier, more forceful interpretations about the absence of a third have had a positive effect? The father had a far stronger presence in this man's mind than in that of Mr C, whose dream I described earlier. Nevertheless I am not sure that he would have been able to make emotional sense of interpretations about Oedipal pain and rivalry until he became less overwhelmingly preoccupied with the loss of an early maternal intimacy to which his father also contributed. In childhood he had been expected to grow up too suddenly. If I had confronted him earlier with his pain about having to share his mother with a sexual rival he might have experienced me as repeating his parents' mistake. I think that one of his reasons for choosing a female psychotherapist was an unconscious wish to avoid facing the existence of his father too soon. However, as I show in Chapter 6, it is questionable how far the therapist's sex does impede the emergence of such transferences. Although it took this patient a couple of years to begin facing the implications of his parents' sexual love, he had already begun this task in childhood and so once his father emerged as a tangible presence in the transference he quickly became able to put his parents together in his mind, and recognise the links between himself and each of them.

Male patients come into psychotherapy with different kinds of psychic disturbance, including varying capacities to deal with triangular issues. In some patients like Mr C there is little sign of the Oedipus complex in its classical form. Others may either have denied their knowledge of these issues, or come into psychotherapy ready and able to begin work in this area.

The boy needs simultaneously to identify with the father and men, and to face that he is not central to the mother's life, and will never possess her sexual or reproductive capacities. At the same time he can resolve his womb envy by identifying with the mother's nurturing capacities, as well as her psychic 'masculinity'.

As his identification with the father grows stronger the boy need no longer be so terrified of fusion with the mother, and may then feel less nostalgic for it, and hence more free to seek other love-objects. If he attempts a false differentiation, through entirely repudiating his own psychic 'femininity' and his early helplessness in relation to the mother, women will be idealised, while simultaneously becoming the object of intense destructive envy.

Men in psychotherapy may express envy of women's capacity to reproduce the race, but there is little evidence that they want to relinquish their position as the more powerful and highly valued sex. In a society where men retain more political and economic power, boys can deal with infantile humiliations by triumphing over the mother who they once experienced as all-powerful. Through identification with the father and men they can further consolidate a sense of possessing a cultural status and value the mother lacks.

CONCLUSION

At different periods psychoanalytic theory has tended to emphasise the centrality and power of one parent rather than another in the mind of the child. Since the 1980s there has been a new attempt to bring both parents together in the theoretical mind and to highlight Oedipal issues. But theory in this area has always been riven with political bias and ethical value-judgements, and this is all the more obvious now that family life is changing and male power is under threat.

Each of the theories I have discussed tends to reproduce aspects of the gender power-imbalance which prevails in our society. For instance those analysts who have recently reacted against theoretical neglect of the father by stressing his positive attributes often fail to acknowledge how the mother is denigrated in different psychoanalytic theories. Freud argued that the child sees her as castrated and unenviable, while contemporary mother-centred theories tend to focus on her enormous potentially destructive power over human life.

In psychoanalytic theorising about Oedipal issues there is often great confusion about the psychic significance of the anatomical sex of parental figures, and it is often unclear whether it is the actual behaviour of the parents, or their symbolic function which is under discussion. Many unanswered questions emerge. For instance, is it desirable to have two parents who fulfil different functions? Or is it possible for the biological mother to fulfil the paternal role of facilitating psychic separation? Can a grand-mother, aunt or lesbian lover play the part of father, or should we then assume that the child has two mothers? Such queries are fundamental to my exploration of how the realities of male social power and female personal influence interact within the psyche and are played out within the therapeutic transference relationship.

In the following chapter I discuss different theories about the interaction between sex-based discrimination and women's own psychic prohibitions against the realisation of their independent needs and desires. In particular, women's eroticism, like men's, often seems bound up with prevailing patterns of power and submission. Femininity, like masculinity, is a psychosexual product of the most intimate inequalities, although how the psychically female person is created continues, as we shall see, to be a source of intense controversy.

Chapter 3

What do women want?

Women 'frequently do not feel whole, we feel undeserving and fraudulent in significant ways', the feminist psychotherapists Susie Orbach and Luise Eichenbaum claimed in 1987, while fifty years earlier Freud had described how all women develop a sense of inferiority 'like a scar' (Eichenbaum and Orbach 1987: 56, Freud 1925: 337). That women somehow become bruised and scarred by the process of becoming female has been an ongoing theme within psychoanalytic theorising, although the ways the process has been understood have often been very different.

What Does Woman Want? Freud demanded in 1933, and four decades later a new generation of British and American feminists returned to this question. Initially the answers they gave to it were, for the most part, fiercely anti-psychoanalytic. In North America a strongly biological version of Freudianism had become assimilated into the medical establishment, where it was often used to bolster conservative ideals of 'women's place'. British psychoanalysis likewise aroused feminist suspicions, since the mother-centred theories of Bowlby and Winnicott had been used after the Second World War to justify the withdrawal of nurseries for working women who were encouraged to return to the home, vacating their jobs for returning soldiers (Riley 1983, Ernst 1987).

But gradually during the 1970s some feminists began to look towards psychoanalysis for a better understanding of why it was so difficult to alter feelings or fantasies through will-power or collective action alone. As this turn 'back to Freud' (or versions of Freudianism) occurred, so the issues raised in the 1920s/30s controversy re-appeared, with theories polarising around problems left unresolved by that earlier debate. In this chapter I contrast the mother-centred perspective of North American and

British feminists who continue Horney's tradition of opposition to Freud, with French Lacanian theory which revolves around an analysis of the father's role in the reproduction of patriarchal power. In the final section I draw on these different arguments to discuss clinical examples of female penis envy. Through exploring the intricate interplay between what my women patients wish to possess and what they want to be, I raise questions about the interaction between envy and desire and psychic 'masculinity' and 'femininity' in both sexes.

WOMEN'S LACK: A FEMINIST PERSPECTIVE ON MOTHERS AND DAUGHTERS

'It is an ironic and cruel phenomenon of patriarchy that the already oppressed shall prepare the succeeding generation for a similar fate' (Eichenbaum and Orbach 1987: 59). British feminist psychotherapy aims to restructure the female personality through a new experience of nurturing within the maternal transference. In its focus on the strengths women gain through maternal identification this theory has many similarities with the pioneering work of North American psychoanalytic feminists, particularly Nancy Chodorow (Chodorow 1978).

In 1933 Freud located the origins of women's narcissistic wounds in an ambivalent early relationship with a mother who could not adore her daughter as she did her son since the girl could not provide her with masculinity by proxy (1933). He argued that this failure to arouse idealised desire in the mother later becomes organised into penis envy, a narcissistic wound which leads women to become highly dependent on the love and esteem of others. Women love in order to be loved, to compensate for their own feelings of inferiority, according to Freud, in contrast to men who love in order to satisfy their instinctual needs (Freud 1914a).

A half-century later Orbach and Eichenbaum strongly refuted this theory, arguing instead that a girl's sense of inadequacy originated in the mother and daughter's shared identification as second-class citizens in a male-dominated world. This maternal ambivalence would disappear, they argue, if there were true equality between the sexes. Under current conditions of inequality, however, women are in fact the stronger sex, on whom men rely for their emotional support. Striving from infancy to nurture her emotionally deprived mother (with whom she identifies) and thus to gain loving attention vicariously, the little girl becomes a compulsive carer. But these skills of feminine caring are devalued in a society which prizes 'male' characteristics, such as emotional detachment and rationality, more than 'feminine' attributes such as empathy and intuition (Eichenbaum and Orbach 1982).

In Britain the writings of Eichenbaum and Orbach have had considerable popular, as well as professional, success, probably because they manage to articulate the very deep feelings of vulnerability and inadequacy many women have, without pathologising individual mothers or stereotypical 'feminine' attributes. The writers transmit their own passionate conviction that women can transform themselves through psychotherapy, while simultaneously fighting to improve the social status of their sex. The validation of culturally denigrated characteristics and the presentation of positive role-models seems to be a vital part of the process by which oppressed groups gain confidence in their capacity for personal and political change.

Eichenbaum and Orbach's theory originated in a period of optimism after the cultural flux of the 1960s, when it was believed that female and male identity might change over several generations if family and sexual life were re-organised. They stress the necessity for fathers to share childcare equally, so breaking the cycle of emotional deprivation between mother and daughter. (See also Chodorow 1978, Dinnerstein 1978.) This theoretical approach assumes a quite fluid interchange between the psyche and the external world, a certainty that as culture changed, so would internal reality.

I was initially impressed by this theory and incorporated it into my own work on the virulence of mother–daughter envy (Maguire 1987). But I was also uneasy, recognising immediately that the schema did not fit exactly with my own childhood experience, nor that of many of my female patients. Orbach and Eichenbaum describe how personality is formed very directly through 'real' experiences of parenting but their early work reflects an initial feminist tendency to emphasise the similarities between women, without acknowledging how very diverse their experience actually is. However, they did address a significant and often neglected difference between women – that of sexual orientation. Unlike many psychoanalytic feminists in the 1980s they did write about the experience of lesbians.

In *Understanding Women* (1982) Eichenbaum and Orbach describe how core gender is fixed within the first year or two of life through external forces imprinting themselves on the personality. Then, according to their theory, mothers and fathers fulfil their conventional roles, which results in boys becoming 'masculine' and girls 'feminine'. The problem seems to be that they conflate the formation of core gender identity with socialisation into gender stereotypes. While it is possible to argue that core gender identity – the knowledge of being biologically male or female – is fixed and inexorable, there is no reason why stereotyped masculine and feminine personalities should follow from this. And, even if girls do know that they are female, this conscious awareness is often fraught with unconscious conflict and uncertainty, as I illustrate through clinical examples later in the chapter.

As the 1980s progressed, however, psychoanalytic feminist writing placed far more stress on how stereotypes of femininity vary within as well as between cultures and historical epochs. The sexuality of black women, for example, is usually represented in western society as primitive, powerful and 'free' from cultural constraints, as opposed to the 'delicate, repressed hysteria' associated with white middle-class women for much of this century (Flax 1990).

In reality gender identification is complex, chaotic and often only partially successful. A daughter may simultaneously resist and absorb the awareness that she is female, knowing she is a woman yet feeling that she is in some way male or masculine psychologically. Mothers may identify strongly with a son rather than a daughter and fathers are sometimes more conventionally 'maternal' than their wives. The mother may be the parent who is more absorbed in her career, or may distance herself from the conventional maternal role. Some families unconsciously value daughters more than sons. In certain classically patriarchal cultures girls are still taught that they should submit to and serve their fathers, brothers and husbands, and that the penis is the most valued sexual organ. In contrast, as Nancy Chodorow points out, daughters from other cultural groups, including Afro-Americans, are taught that women are far stronger and more dependable than men (Chodorow 1994).

Although these variations will affect a girl's sense of identity and self-worth, in a society where women are second class an unconscious knowledge of her inferior social status will inevitably be imprinted on her psyche. There is no escaping the fact that she is female, and, whatever her personal characteristics or experience, she always belongs to the inferior sex. Nevertheless there is plentiful evidence that girls do not slip easily into the restricted roles that society continues to offer them.

I also find unconvincing the notion that the infant remains passive while outside forces stamp themselves on its personality. Identification – through which the subject assimilates aspects or attributes of another and is transformed partially or entirely after the model the other provides – is a process in which the child engages actively, although unconsciously. She (or he) takes inside herself – introjects – bits and pieces of experience which have been infused with fantasy. The child's view of the world around her is also structured through what she projects onto it from inside herself. Identifications are formed through a subtle and intricate process of layering and fusion of memory, fantasy and desire. Fragments of language and image are constantly worked over, influenced always by fantasy.

It has become clear during the past twenty years that many psychic and social obstacles stand in the way of sexual equality. For instance, statistics show that mothers are still primarily responsible for childcare, and that where fathers have tried to take a leading role the impact on gender stereotypes has not been as dramatic as was originally predicted (Segal 1990). We all know consciously that the world around us is altering, but psychoanalysts have always had very different views about whether cultural change impinges on the depths of the psyche immediately, after a time-lag, or not at all. Feminists have also become increasingly interested in an issue central to the early debate on female sexuality, the question of why women continue to accept their second-class social status.

Parents may consciously believe in equality between the sexes while actually transmitting unconsciously a belief that women would be happier in their traditional roles. The internalised value system may be constructed not through what children are actually permitted or prohibited from doing, but through what they absorb unconsciously of their parents' own super-egos, the conscience or values of a generation before. In periods of rapid cultural alteration new prohibitions develop and others lose their old authority but something in the psyche may resist easy change. Reserves of primitive moral feeling may remain beneath a façade of liberal personal change. So for example in the decades following the permissive 'swinging sixties', there has been a resurgence of self-proclaimed 'traditional' values (Richards 1989).

Women, so the feminist arguments I've been discussing generally run, are trammelled socially and psychically by cultures in which femininity is a subordinate state. Women themselves do not bear responsibility for this situation, it is implied: they are its unhappy victims. But some psychoanalytic feminists disagree, believing that women have a more active part to play in our life destinies. These feminists have tended to look towards Klein and Freud, both of whom emphasised the ways that individuals participate in the intrapsychic processes which shape their lives.

Margot Waddell, a British psychotherapist, uses post-Kleinian theories to explore how, from the beginning of life, the infant engages actively in the processes of identification which are so crucial to the formation of gender identity. She describes gender identity as a series of concentric circles, with a fragile and brittle outer ring of pseudo-masculine or feminine identifications and an inner core capable of bearing the pain of fundamental psychic change and creative development. The baby who does not have enough opportunity to identify with the maternal 'function' – who is not helped by parental figures to tolerate, process and understand her own earliest feelings and fantasies – will have to construct an identity through her own devices – narcissistically (Waddell 1989, 1993).

Lacking the inner strength to face the possibility of psychic pain or loss, such an infant will have to find ways of denying or evacuating her own emotional experience. She may live vicariously through others with whom she identifies, having endowed them in fantasy with idealised or denigrated aspects of herself which she cannot bear to acknowledge. Or she might construct an identity by imitating stereotypical gender character-traits and conventional sexual mores, rather than creating her own original version of psychic bisexuality through an inspired examination of what psychological masculinity and femininity mean to her. An example of this kind of stereotypical pseudo-maturity is the woman who compulsively nurtures others in an unconscious attempt to restore a barren internal world full of dead and damaged objects. The infant who does not feel securely 'held' in a maternal psychic skin may be unconsciously preoccupied with relationships where tyranny and destructiveness prevail. In adulthood such states of mind can be reflected in an incapacity to combine sexual passion with loving concern for others.

This subtle and intricate analysis of the interaction between an unthinking adherence to conventional gender-codes and the inability to confront and learn from emotional experience is extremely useful in clinical practice. Particularly valuable in Waddell's argument is her stress on how 'maternal' functions can be found in men, while paternal functions also exist in women. But Waddell describes a process of identity formation which seems identical for the boy and girl, offering no explanation of how the position of the sexes within patriarchy turns out to be so profoundly asymmetrical. As a Kleinian, Waddell also emphasises inborn disposition as well as environmental factors, and her use of words such as 'true', 'genuine' and 'real' suggests that she thinks some aspects of psychic experience might be relatively impervious to social change and influence. I agree with Klein's observations about the significance of pre-birth experiences. However, I believe that identity is constructed through culture and language and that each individual's notions of emotional 'truth' and 'reality' are also formed within a particular social and historical context.

In her ground-breaking 1964 anthology *Female Sexuality* Janine Chasseguet-Smirgel argued for the need to draw together the insights of all the leading protagonists in the early debate on female sexuality, thereby integrating the role of the mother and father theoretically. She draws on Freud, Jones and Klein to describe the plight of many girls who, when faced with early difficulties in separating psychically from the mother, resort to the culturally favoured solution of denigrating their own sex and enviously idealising the father. In contrast the boy can assert his physiological difference and his more privileged place within culture, thus triumphing in fantasy over a mother once experienced as omnipotent.

'Basically penis envy is the symbolic expression of another desire. Women do not wish to become men but to detach themselves psychically from the mother and become complete autonomous women' (Chasseguet-Smirgel 1964b: 118). Chasseguet-Smirgel argues that the daughter's idealisation of men is a defence against envious hatred of the father. Guilt about this repressed desire to castrate him may result in intellectual and creative inhibition.

Because of this repressed envious guilt towards her father, a woman may relinquish her own needs and beliefs and see herself as the man's 'thing', the object of male desire. This particular kind of 'feminine guilt' can create sexual frigidity and masochism, Chasseguet-Smirgel argues, since the woman both fears dangerous penetration and also experiences the inside of her own body as destructive to the male penis (Chasseguet-Smirgel 1964b: 97). Repressed envy and hatred of men may also lead to creative and intellectual inhibitions, since women unconsciously dread trespassing on spheres of life which they still see as a male preserve. In these ways women collude in maintaining their second-class position within culture and sexual relationships.

American feminist Dorothy Dinnerstein also drew on Freud and Klein in her influential *The Rocking of the Cradle and the Ruling of the World*. Dinnerstein described how both sexes tacitly collude in a gender-based division of power and labour, once a social necessity, but now a threat to the race, since biotechnology has become dangerously out of control. Both sexes cling to these out-dated arrangements because of an unconscious wish to deny that the most important features of existence elude our control. At the basis of this collusion is an unwillingness to face the original loss of the illusion of blissful unity with the mother, which would also mean confronting the inevitability of human frailty, psychic pain and death. Because of their particular difficulties in separating from the all-powerful early mother, daughters welcome the apparently more limited authority of the father. Later they attempt to recapture their original feeling of fusion with the maternal body by retreating into motherhood and family life, so avoiding responsibility for the challenges of history-making. Men develop a capacity for mastering the universe and a compulsive preoccupation with what can be predicted, possessed, piled up and counted in order to deny the strength of their early physical and emotional link with the mother. In the short term, men benefit more from gender inequities and therefore are less inclined to expose them (Dinnerstein 1978).

It is vital, then, to understand how the girl internalises a sense of cultural devaluation both through an early identification with her mother's knowledge of being socially second class, and at the point where she begins to be aware of psychic difference. As she begins to recognise her own psychological separateness the girl's distorted sense of gender-difference becomes entrenched, and the pattern of idealising men and masculinity and devaluing her own sex grows stronger. To the toddler of both sexes the father may well represent exuberance, excitement and agency (Benjamin 1988). Above all he is different to and autonomous from the mother, and his patriarchal authority may appear less all-encompassing than maternal power. The daughter may also feel intense fear of losing her mother's love through arousing her envy and retaliation if she achieves more than her mother has done. If the girl defends against envy by devaluing the mother this will merely reinforce her envy of paternal power and privilege. The resulting envious guilt towards the father may combine with real external discrimination to create serious inhibitions about competing professionally with men and self-assertion in personal relationships. And, in a society where each generation of women has more opportunities than the last, the mother – and indeed the father – may in reality envy the daughter.

In these ways culture and the psyche intersect to reproduce women's cultural subordination through the generations. In order to break into this cycle the girl needs to identify with the father and the psychic masculinity of both sexes without devaluing womanhood. But how can she separate psychically from the mother without entering into another relationship where she relinquishes her will and desire? First of all we need to recognise that the girl gains positive strength from her early identification with the mother, who can encourage her to move out into the world. The girl's desire for autonomy need not simply represent a contemptuous rejection of the mother or hatred of dependency. Then we need to explore how the daughter can form an identificatory relationship with the father without idealising his sex. But how is this to be achieved within a social system where both she and her mother are valued less than the father? Some feminists have turned to Lacan's theories, arguing that the Women's Movement needs to look again at Freud's father-centred theory in order to understand the resilience of patriarchy – the way it continues to reproduce itself in the unconscious mind however family life is structured (Mitchell 1974).

LACAN – THE RETURN TO FREUD

If feminism is to change a phallocentric world, phallocentrism needs to be dealt with and not denied.

(Gallop 1982: 18)

Lacan believed that the 1919–35 debate on female sexuality marked the beginning of the deterioration of psychoanalysis, the point where the subversive and radical core of Freud's theory – his stress on sexuality and the unconscious – was abandoned. In his theory Lacan focused on these two basic concepts of Freud's, adding a new concern with linguistics. Lacan argued against Klein's theory that the baby arrives in the world with tendencies towards a male or female sexual identity, which is confirmed (or not) through real interactions with others and fantasies about them. Lacan saw biology as having no place at all in psychoanalytic theory and stressed instead that the unconscious is constructed through the words of others – the language of the family, culture and epoch into which we are born.

Lacan kept a sceptical distance from all prevailing notions about self, truth, knowledge and power. In some object relations feminist writings there is an implication that we should and can feel 'whole' psychically, entirely sure and confident in our sense of sexual identity. This is impossible, Lacanians argue, since human beings are fundamentally alienated both from themselves and each other. What appears to be an identity is in fact a mirage arising through identification with others' perceptions of, desires and expectations for the subject. Although the analysand may consciously believe that she is certain of her identity, her unconscious will reveal a fragmented subjectivity, which is shifting and precarious (Mitchell 1984).

Lacan criticised those object relations theorists and ego psychologists who chart an ideal line of development from infantile satisfaction at the breast through to adult heterosexual fulfilment, describing some relationships or states of mind as 'mature', 'healthy' or 'fulfilled'. Such notions, he argued, romanticise conventional ways of structuring sexual and family life (Lacan on Dora, 1985). Instead Lacan stressed that adult sexual and love relations are inevitably unsatisfying because the loved one is always a displacement of, and a substitute for, the primal maternal lost object. Desire comes into existence through experiences of absence or lack (of the breast or the mother initially), not as the result of satisfaction. There is then something intrinsically painful and insatiable about desire itself. Any later experience of satisfaction always contains that first loss within it. As Freud said, 'We must reckon with the possibility that something in the nature of the sexual instinct itself is unfavourable to the realisation of complete desire' (Freud quoted in Mitchell 1984: 255).

Lacan returned to Freud's theory that it is the possession or absence of the penis (phallus), which distinguishes one sex from the other, rather than the existence of different sexual and reproductive capacities, as argued by Horney and Jones. But Lacan rewrote Freud's theory in linguistic and symbolic rather than biological terms, differentiating the penis from the phallus more than Freud had done. In Lacan's theory the paternal figure separates the child from the dangerous engulfing mother, as representative of the Law and an embodiment of the power of the phallus. The child must accept the Father's authority and phallic status in order to have a place in the socio-symbolic order, a name and a position from which to speak. There can be no symbolisation without the phallus, the 'signifier of signifiers', the mark which positions the subject as male or female, and locates him or her in terms of power, authority and speaking position. The phallus signifies what men think they have and what women are believed to lack. Under patriarchy women represent for men a lack which men have disavowed (Lacan 1977).

However, Lacan's theory is, like Freud's, deeply ambiguous. Lacan argues that neither sex possesses the phallus, but each sex longs either to possess it (in the case of the boy) or to be it (if a girl). Yet at the same time the male enjoys a special relationship to this privileged, albeit symbolic, term. Although Lacan rejects the idea of the 'natural' or pre-given, he says that the name of the father has been identified with the impersonal law which structures the personality at the Oedipal phase since 'the dawn of history' (Lacan 1977: 67). At times Lacan seems to echo Freud's uncertainty about whether women really are in some way inferior, as for instance when he says:

> the fact that the penis is dominant in the shaping of body-image is evidence of [an autonomous, non-biological imaginary anatomy]. Though this may shock the champions of the autonomy of female sexuality, such dominance is a fact and one moreover which cannot be put down to cultural influence alone.
>
> (Lacan 1953: 13 quoted in Grosz 1990)

Certain feminists argue that neither Lacan nor Freud were supporting patriarchy. They were simply describing what they saw around them: a world where women were second class and their social position entirely unenviable (Mitchell 1984). But in order to arrive at this conclusion Freud and Lacan must be read in a very selective way. Lacan's phallic signifier is not a neutral term against which both sexes are positioned symmetrically. I agree with Grosz who says, 'Unless the symbolic order is conceived of as a system where the father and the penis are not the only signifiers of social power and linguistic norms, feminism is no better off with Lacan than without him' (Grosz 1990: 145). It is quite clear that Lacan's theory has the same weaknesses as Freud's. Both are fundamentally profoundly phallocentric, and focus primarily on male subjectivity.

Lacan's lack of attention to female subjectivity resulted in a backlash from some French feminists. Under pressure from these critics he acknowledged the strength of female sexual pleasure and tried to side-step the controversy aroused by his theory that women were the complementary sex. He now described women as having a 'supplementary jouissance' that men know nothing of. Like Freud, Lacan stressed the mysterious inaccessibility of women's desire, and sought from female colleagues the enlightenment which he was unable to gain in the usual analytic way – from his patients. At the same time Lacan made a sardonic dig at the feminist predilection for theories of female sexuality which revolve around mothering: 'We have implored our women psychoanalysts, on our bended knees, to tell us about it (the enjoyment of the women) but mum's the word' (Lacan 1972–3 in Benvenuto and Kennedy 1986: 69).

POST-LACANIAN FEMINISM: BACK TO THE MOTHER

Perhaps Lacan is so ignorant of women's 'incalculable pleasure, which grows indefinitely from its passage in/through the other' because he does not know how, or where to listen (Irigiray 1977: 350). This is the argument of Luce Irigiray, a French feminist psychoanalyst, who claims that Freudian and Lacanian psychoanalysis recognise only masculine desire and see all desire as masculine. Psychoanalysis reproduces one of the 'sexual theories of children', Irigiray argues, the fantasy that there is only one sex, that that sex is male, and that women are castrated, defective versions of men. Her project is to seek other ways in which women can speak of and for themselves.

While most feminists minimise sexual difference, Irigiray seeks to maximise it. She argues that the only way forward for women is to assert their difference through the creation of a powerful female symbolic to represent them against the omnipresent effects of the male imaginary, which negates their existence as subjects. Many psychoanalysts and feminists argue that the only way to break into the cycle of suffocating merger between mother and daughter is for the father to intervene or become involved in early childcare. In contrast Irigiray believes that it is women themselves who must alter their position in society by creating new ways of speaking about and for their sex. This may mean existing separately from men for a period of time.

Irigiray argues that the problem for women is that the relationship to the mother and the mother's body is not symbolised often or adequately enough in our culture. At the moment women exist in a state of 'dereliction', outside society and the symbolic order, as if abandoned by God. Deprived of their own symbols, gestures, imaginary, denied access to their own auto-erotism, the mother–daughter relationship is the 'dark continent of the dark continent, the most obscure area of our social order'. And, without that 'interval of exchange, or of words, or gestures, passions between women manifest themselves in a rather cruel way' (Irigiray 1984: 103 quoted in Whitford 1989). Both mothers and daughters must create a new language in which their identities as women can be articulated. At the moment the daughter has no woman with whom to identify.

Since, in her view, psychoanalytic theory is not sexually neutral, but specific to men, Irigiray argues that the model could be inadequate for women, and imposing it on them could further reinforce their inferior position within patriarchy. For instance, classical psychoanalytic interpretations might block rather than free the expression of women's desire. Through research into senile dementia and with analysands diagnosed as hysterical or obsessional, Irigiray claims to have discovered that there are significant differences in the impairments of women's and men's speech. She has also explored the parameters of the psychoanalytic session, looking at factors such as the gender of the analyst and analysand, and the effect of gesture and other non-verbal factors on patients of both sexes. For instance she discusses the different meaning for the woman and the man of lying down in the presence of another, who sits behind them. She also implies that women should create forms of psychoanalysis appropriate for them, as various groups of women have tried to do (Whitford 1989).

Irigiray points out that Freud and Lacan constructed their theories around the boy's experience of his body while denouncing as biologist anyone who attempts to do the same for the girl. She explores the female body as it is made meaningful in language, articulating the ways in which it is used as a site both for patriarchal power relations and for symbolic representational resistance. When she describes some typical female erotic pleasures, such as 'Caressing the breasts, touching the vulva, opening the lips, gently stroking the posterior wall of the vagina, lightly massaging the cervix', it is immediately obvious that such experiences are rarely if ever referred to in psychoanalytic literature (Irigiray 1977: 348). Instead we hear much about the power of the penetrating penis, and the smothering potential of the womb. Women do not need, Irigiray argues, to find something external to touch themselves with – a hand, women's genitals, language – as men do: 'A woman "touches herself" constantly without anyone being able to forbid her to do so, for her sex is composed of two lips which embrace continually' (Irigiray 1977: 345). Woman 'has sex organs just about everywhere. She experiences pleasure almost everywhere . . . one can say that the geography of her pleasure is much more diversified, more multiple in its differences, more complex, more subtle than is imagined – in an imaginary centered a bit too much on one and the same' (Irigiray 1977: 348).

Obviously Irigiray is right in arguing that our culture represents all agency and power in phallic terms and that there is no equivalent symbol to suggest female desire or potency. Does the hidden nature of women's sexual and reproductive organs reinforce this cultural inequality? Psychoanalysts have often suggested that men may find it easier to mobilise aggression and desire because they can symbolise these powerful emotions through the more visible penis which they can imbue in fantasy with magical powers for destruction or reparation (Freud 1924a, Klein 1928). It may be easier to control anxiety through a symbolic and physical focus of sensation. Women often experience intense sexual excitement as dangerous, frightening and destructive, perhaps because they cannot so easily link it to any external organ that would localise it in space and allow them to visualise control of its duration. This lack of anatomical anchoring could have a correlative effect at the symbolic level (Noel Montgrain quoted in Benjamin 1988). The difficulty for women, Benjamin argues, is in recognising our desire as truly inner. Spatial images can be used to convey images of female desire, as opposed to phallic activity. We need metaphors for describing inner space, which emphasise holding and self-exploration as the active side of receptivity. And Benjamin, like Irigiray, points out that women need to recognise the sensual capacities of their whole bodies, the totality of space between, outside and within our bodies as the site of pleasure.

Each of the theories I have described has strengths, but some of them neglect important aspects of female psychic life. Lacanian feminism provides a powerful challenge to conventional ideas about identity, power and language, and a counter-balance to the idealism and romanticism of object relations theory. Study of the role of the (symbolic) father is also vital for understanding how patriarchal structures reproduce themselves even when parents make a conscious effort to avoid reinforcing them. But, like Freud's theory, it is constructed from the perspective of the male, and women tend to be ignored or denigrated. As in Freud's theory it is the mother who is associated with boundless narcissism and regression to archaic early experiences. The possibility of early paternal receptivity, or the father 'holding' the infant emotionally, is ignored in these theories. Neither is it considered that the mother – or the child itself – may have urges towards moving out into the world, although many mothers are heavily committed to employment outside the home as well as to childcare.

In contrast, object relations and post-Lacanian feminists struggle to articulate women's previously hidden experience as mothers, daughters and autonomous sexual subjects. It is obviously true that the girl has particular difficulty in separating herself psychically from the much-envied early mother, who is initially experienced as omnipotent, because the daughter, unlike the son, possesses no mark of difference or privilege. Psychic and cultural difficulties with this process of psychic differentiation are exacerbated by the problems many girls have in identifying with the father and qualities seen culturally as 'masculine' in both sexes.

Both sexes need to develop and build on their early identifications with the paternal and maternal functions of both sexes
and with a version of the psychological characteristics associated
with each sex. The girl needs to be recognised as being like both
parents psychologically. She also needs to have access to images
of women as active sexual beings and agents of their own destinies. But how is this to happen? And how far must women rely
on a change in male attitudes towards emotional life and family
responsibilities? It is vital that men become more involved with
early childcare, and fulfil conventionally maternal functions, as
well as helping the daughter separate psychically from the mother
and find a pathway to the outer world. However, this traditional
paternal function can also be performed by women.

And it is women themselves who must continue the fundamental task of creating new forms of symbolism and imagery to
represent all aspects of female experience. The expectations and
wishes which are transmitted from generation to generation
cohere around bodily experience. We need to understand more
about how physiological sensation is mediated through culture
and becomes inscribed on the psyche, so that we can read and
interpret it in new ways. Only then will girls and boys come to
see women as full subjects with their own needs and desires.

It is necessary, then, to combine the object relations emphasis
on how women's second-class status is structured into the personality through early maternal identifications, with a feminist Freudian analysis of how, in toddlerhood, as the girl struggles to gain
psychic autonomy, her perception of sexual difference becomes
distorted. At these two points of interaction between culture and
the psyche fundamental questions arise about the girl's capacity to
symbolise and act on her own desires. Difficulties in externalising
aggression and articulating desire are exacerbated by the fact that
in our society agency and potency are routinely associated with
men and masculinity.

PENIS ENVY

Although many women express dissatisfaction with their position
within culture they do not necessarily struggle to change it. In
this section I use clinical examples of female penis envy to explore
how women's fighting spirit becomes twisted into envy, self-
devaluation and contempt for their own sex.

Freud argued that penis envy was central to female sexuality, and, when extreme, resulted in interminable analyses (Freud 1937). His present-day critics imply that it may have been Freud himself who created the chronic envy, guilt and despair he detected in his female patients, by interpreting their penis envy in a dangerously literal way as the desire for something unattainable – to be a man, or to possess a penis (Grossman and Stewart 1976). In Britain, the USA and even to some extent in France, a clinical consensus seems to have been reached since the late 1960s that penis envy is defensive against early conflicts about the mother. Indeed Freud himself traced the origins of penis envy back to early disappointment at the mother's breast. Nowadays the girl who wishes for a penis, or imagines herself as a proxy male, may be seen as expressing a need to separate psychologically from, or avoid, Oedipal rivalry with the early mother on whom she so utterly depends. Or, alternatively she may want a penis in order to become the object of maternal desire (Chasseguet-Smirgel 1964b).

In Britain clinical discussion of penis envy is rare. In the papers that do exist, object-relations theorists can be extreme in their refusal to recognise that penis envy might represent a desire for the privileges of men. For instance Enid Balint argues in 'What does a woman want?' that a female patient who dreams of going to the chemist to buy a penis unconsciously wishes to use the penis to 'warm up' a depressed internal mother with whom she is overwhelmingly preoccupied. The woman is not seeking masculinity and is not lesbian, Balint says. What she lacks is an internal sense of 'mutual concern' which she failed to experience within the mother–daughter relationship (Balint 1973). I find Balint's argument unconvincing, leaving too many questions unanswered. Why, for instance, should her patient want to warm up her mother with a penis, unless she feels some lesbian desire, or believes that she would be more attractive and lovable if she were male?

No doubt psychotherapists find ways of confirming their own beliefs. Freud and his colleagues assumed the centrality of female penis envy and therefore found it where many contemporary clinicians would find unresolved early conflicts about the mother. Freud's father-centred theory and his own gender may have elicited envy of men in his female patients. Or perhaps women then did feel more envious of men?

It is also true, though, that patients sometimes seek out

psychotherapists whose theories make sense of their own experience. For instance I found that women who came to see me while
I was working at The Women's Therapy Centre, which was well
known for its focus on early mothering, were likely to be preoccupied with mother–daughter envy, while those referred to my private practice from more orthodox psychotherapy organisations
were as likely to have psychic conflicts about the father.

In general though I find that female patients are more likely
to express envy of other women, or to describe their fear of
losing the love of significant women (including the therapist in
the maternal transference), if they succeed at work or in personal
life. This may be both a defence against their own envy of their
mothers and a reflection of the reality that many women do envy
their daughters. Perhaps women are more conscious of their
envy of their own sex now that, theoretically at least, they have
access to many traditionally male as well as female spheres of
activity.

Where extreme penis envy does exist it often seems to be
associated with an early life where the general cultural devaluation of women has been reinforced through intense sexual denigration or discrimination in favour of boys within the family.
Through two clinical examples I show how, in order to understand
the complex and multi-faceted nature of penis envy, we need to
draw on theories which locate it in early envy of the privileges
and functions of both parents.

The gender of my soul is male

A woman patient told me: 'The gender of my soul is male. I can
hear Freud saying, "I told you so." He'd say I suffer from penis
envy. . . . Deep down I am a man.' This woman was the youngest
child of a large working-class family and had four elder brothers
and two sisters. She described how in her family 'men were always
right' and female sexuality was the constant butt of denigratory
jokes. 'Women in my family had no status . . . the girls in my
school talked about two CSEs then marriage. The boys expected
jobs, and I wanted that too', she said. A bawdy highly sexualised
atmosphere prevailed in the family. Everyday physical and
emotional contact was eroticised and her teenage brothers left
pornography lying in places where a child might find it. This
atmosphere had a profound effect on her erotic imagination, and

she developed an overwhelming feeling that sex would always involve an intense objectification of the female body.

She had initially felt painfully abandoned by a mother who she described as distant, emotionally uncontaining, but also rigidly controlling of her bodily functions. As a young child she had consoled herself with being close to and feeling herself similar to her father and brothers. She went fishing with him, rather than shopping with her mother, telling herself that she was glad to avoid female talk of 'diets and hairdos'. However, in her teens she became preoccupied with her weight and appearance and felt that no amount of make up and feminine clothes could make her feel attractive and womanly. In her adult life she still wanted to be recognised as a man when with men, and described how, when she was with a lover and his male friends, her greatest pleasure was in imagining that she was 'one of the lads'. In her family there were, she told me, no images of how a woman could get on in professional life, which she consequently still regarded as a male sphere of activity. Remarkably in the light of this, she was the only member of the family who had been academically successful. However, she did not now know how to use her numerous talents.

Paradoxically her unconscious attempt to deny pain and envy through fantasies of belonging by proxy to the more highly valued male sex resulted in a gender confusion which further increased her envy of other women, including myself, who she perceived as more comfortable with their femininity. She had not wanted to be like her mother, yet did not know how to identify with her father while valuing her own womanhood. She told me how uneasy and out of place she had felt on one occasion when working with a group of women who all seemed to dress in a stereotypically feminine way. She had rushed from the room, feeling overwhelmed. In the session she asked, 'What makes me a woman – is it my body? Is it because I dress in female clothes? Or do I have a woman's mind?'

Although she could identify with Freud's theory of penis envy, this patient's history would also fit Horney's counter-argument that girls retreat into masculinity as a defence against unbearably intense Oedipal anxieties about penetration by the father (Horney 1924). But whereas Horney seems to assume that fantasies of paternal rape are simply the result of the girl's own over-heated imagination it was clear from my patient's description that her father exposed her to his own debased sexual fantasy-life. This then created in her a combination of excitement and fear lest the incest boundaries actually be breached. My patient described her companionship with her father as alarmingly sexualised even though there were no sexually abusive acts. 'You notice little girls having heterosexual love-affairs with their fathers,' she said, 'but at a certain point he says, "Enough!" My father didn't set any boundaries so I had to, by dressing like a boy.' As time went on a picture emerged of a father who made inappropriately sexualised comments to his daughters, yet was actually far more preoccupied with his wife than his children. As a result my patient seems to have felt simultaneously over-exposed to and painfully excluded from the parental sexual relationship.

Her feelings of envy and inferiority emerged very quickly towards me as a maternal transference figure. She was very disparaging about her mother's appearance and intellect, and at first she was similarly dismissive of my personal qualities. For instance she insisted that she had been told I was an inexperienced psychotherapist by the person who had referred her, although this had not been said. This belief that I was a beginner was belied when, after a few months of psychotherapy, she discovered a book I had co-edited which had been required reading for a professional course she had attended. She told me, 'I suddenly realised your name was on the cover. . . . I've had the book a while but I never look at names on covers.' The book was a collection of essays with one chapter by myself on mother–daughter envy. She went on to make dismissive remarks about non-fiction which she said was less creative than novels or poetry. But she also admitted that she had enjoyed my chapter but could not remember what the theme was. When she eventually did remember, we were able to begin looking at the different ways she defended against envy of myself as a maternal figure, by denigrating what she admired in me, or denying that I possessed any valuable qualities, so that I no longer aroused feelings of inferiority and envy in her.

Early in psychotherapy she had been critical both of her mother's appearance and of mine, stressing her belief that men would always prefer a younger woman. But as time went on, it became clear that she had felt great sexual rivalry towards her mother, which was emerging towards me in the maternal transference. Her dreams and fantasies also revealed feelings of attraction towards other women. She told me that she had never acted upon these desires because she felt that lesbian sex would be a 'pornographic act, driven by a desire to humiliate and gain power'. She was afraid of objectifying another woman, since she felt that this was the inevitable outcome of any sexual act. And also, she imagined that lesbian sex would make her feel very envious of men since her body was not designed for intercourse with women.

She told me,

> It was my father who decided whether or not I looked attractive and what should be done about it. . . . It's all about needing to have my sexuality controlled and directed by men because it's so rampant. My father thought there were women who did – dirty bitches – and women who didn't. My mother's attitude was that it is dangerous to give in to appetite.

She could only imagine herself in control of her own sexuality by putting herself in the position of the male. 'What I need is something to express my aggression with sexually, and what else could that be but a penis?' she asked. However, her image of a voyeuristic, dominating male figure may have gained some of its strength from her early experience of her mother as rigidly controlling and physically intrusive.

In this woman's childhood there had been no escaping an awareness of women's subordinate sexual status, or the fact that in our society female desire is represented through phallic imagery. Her wish to be male was a logical response to a family atmosphere devoid of positive representations of womanhood. Yet this devaluation of women was a defence against rejection by a mother experienced as omnipotent, possessing everything, monstrous yet alluring. There had been no obvious way for her to differentiate herself from her mother, just a series of false trails. Initially her alliance with her father and brothers gave her a vicarious sense of power and value. But in denigrating her mother she denied all the strengths that she might have identified with in her. She could never fully belong in the world of men but, having rejected the idea of being like her mother, she then had no protection against her father's contempt for women and female sexuality.

If the girl cannot come to terms with her early envious

ambivalence towards her mother she may idealise male power, as this patient did. But penis envy can have other origins. Some women may, for instance, maintain an envious idealisation of the mother, albeit one which is tinged with an unconscious knowledge that they share an inferior status under patriarchy. The father may be denigrated, or become a very weak presence in the internal world. But, whatever the family constellation, the girl still has the same dilemma: how to value herself as her own woman, whilst identifying with a range of 'feminine' and 'masculine' emotional attributes in each parent. The next patient I discuss did not suffer from any strong wish to be a man and felt little confusion about her gender-identity. Instead she felt all-too feminine, too like her mother and myself.

The experimental penis

Ms L was in her fifth year of three times weekly psychotherapy and was beginning to think about the possibility of leaving. She told me,

> I dreamed a wonderful dream. You'll love it. I was fascinated by an ENORMOUS erect penis. I was in a kitchen. Actually, the penis was on a man. The man was the brother of my teenage friend. She was someone I really loved. I started to play with the penis, and then I took it right off (effectively castrating him, but painlessly). I carried on playing with it. Later, I was putting it in my mouth, trying it on for size, when I heard someone coming into the kitchen. I think it was a man but he was too shadowy to see. I quickly hid the penis in the drawer. Later, when it was all clear, I pulled it out, only to find it had shrunk. Now this was a letdown in some ways, but a blessing in others – I could slip it into my pocket to play with it later. When the time came I did my best to make it 'come alive' again and cause an erection, but it didn't work, so I tried to eat it. It tasted foul, perhaps dead, like chloroform and very rubbery.

My patient associated her attempt to devour the penis with the lack of her father's influence in her childhood. He had died when she was 2. Now she wanted to strengthen her identification with him, partly in order to differentiate herself from her mother psychically. When she thought of leaving psychotherapy she realised that she lacked a paternal figure who would intervene between us, within the maternal transference. It was traditional in her culture for male relatives to step into the role of a dead father, yet her mother had resisted family pressure to share her parental duties.

> If my father had lived there might have been a balance in the family. My mother was very rigid, but she didn't help me develop any boundaries or limits of my own. I can't get away from her. I have her body.

This woman thought of herself as having some sexual inhibitions, although far less than when she first came for psychotherapy. Although psychotherapy had enabled her to become professionally successful, she still described herself as a 'people-pleaser', who dared not fight aggressively for what she wanted. She wanted to see what men had that enabled them to assert their desires with more apparent ease. She also responded to the male penis whenever she saw it with a complex combination of fascination and repulsion. This combination of feelings – 'penis-awe' – results, Phyllis Greenacre has argued, from abusive or frightening exposure to the male penis in childhood. My patient did in fact remember at least one man 'flashing' his penis at her in an alarming way (Greenacre 1979).

Discussing the dream I referred to her 'wanting a penis'. She responded indignantly, making it clear that her desire for a penis was not predominantly to do with any wish to be a man.

> What gave you that idea? Do you think ALL women want a penis? ... I wanted it to try on, to experiment and play with, to see what it's like. I didn't actually want to have a penis permanently attached to me. Though I suppose there is what having a penis represents. ... In my experience, men are always more confident sexually, more assertive and able to get what they want.

What she coveted was the ruthless determination to put her needs first in professional and sexual life, a quality she associated more with men than women. But some women had it too, she pointed out. She thinks her father may have been more 'soft' and conventionally maternal than her tough dominating mother, who she saw as quite psychically 'masculine'. She also saw this ruthlessness in my adherence to my own holiday times, and the endings of sessions. 'You do what suits you and don't alter your plans because of my needs', she complained enviously. When she had first come for psychotherapy she had felt obsessed with looking at herself and with being watched. No longer content to be the object of others' desire she wanted to experiment with having the 'masculine' potency and privilege she associated with the penis.

When the girl becomes heterosexual, Freud argued, her desire to have a penis attached to her body, or to ingest it, becomes a desire to enjoy it sexually. Freud told Jones in 1928 that one of his most deeply held beliefs about female sexuality was that the 'first conception of sexual intercourse is an oral one – sucking on the penis as earlier on the mother's breast (Freud to Jones, 22 February 1928, quoted in Gay 1988: 501). My patient had not made up her mind whether she wanted a male or female sexual partner more – unconsciously she felt torn between her mother and father. Her image of a combined nipple–penis provided a temporary solution to this bisexual conflict. She told me that in the dream she had put the penis into her mouth as a baby does when it explores the world around it, sucking on it as she once sucked on the nipple. 'The penis was like a tough, springy plastic toy,' she said, 'a kind of eroticised nipple.'

The dream reflected her current 'part-object' relationships with men. In the past she had had sexual relationships with both sexes. Now she was going through a phase where she loved women and desired them a bit, while having heterosexual affairs where she often made it clear that she was only interested in having a bit of the man – temporary use of the penis during sex. She also wanted to see whether a penis would make her more desirable to women. She was curious, she told me, about what men had that made her women-friends attracted to them, rather than to the 'other half of the human race, nice people like me'.

Hélène Cixous, a French feminist, wrote:

> I do not want a penis to decorate my body with. But I do desire the other for the other, whole and entire, male or female; because living means wanting everything that is, every-thing that lives, and wanting it alive. Castration? Let others toy with it. What's a desire originating from a lack? A pretty meagre desire.
>
> (Cixous 1976: 262)

My patient, who identified with this quote, wished to experiment with the attributes and privileges of both sexes. She wanted to see whether a penis would make her more desirable to women. And she wanted to be the agent of her own destiny, to be in command of her own needs and passions. Identification with the paternal penis also represented the possibility of greater autonomy from her mother. But once she felt more separate from her mother, then she might also be able to draw on her identification with maternal 'masculinity'.

It is interesting that both of the patients I describe were either actively bisexual or desired both sexes. We know little about this aspect of female sexuality. Freud said, 'Some part of what we call "the enigma of women" may perhaps stem from this experience of bisexuality in women's lives' (Freud 1931: 385). But he was able only to make brief references to mother–daughter sensuality, since his main focus was on the father–daughter relationship. Within orthodox psychoanalysis female sexuality has either been ignored in favour of maternal nurturing, or viewed from the perspective of the male. In this as in other areas of female psychology we need to combine an understanding of eroticism between mother and daughter with feminist theories of father–daughter Oedipal sexuality.

Theory is still polarised along the lines of the early debate. As a result certain features of female experience are neglected, or discussed in a limited way. Penis envy has a different meaning for each woman, and, in order to understand it fully, it is necessary to draw on theories which emphasise the way patriarchy reproduces itself in the unconscious as well as focusing on the girl's early feelings of envy and inadequacy in relation to the mother's emotional power.

It is clear from the clinical material I have discussed that sexual identity is convoluted, tenuous and fragmented. We need theories which show how women simultaneously resist and embrace gender stereotypes and which acknowledge that the qualities and functions we identify with in each parent may have little to do with conventional notions of what women or men are like. An image of feminine or masculine certainty presented to the world may be a masquerade, unconsciously designed to hide, or compensate for, chaos, damage or gender confusion in the internal world.

We need to understand more about the nature and origins of

female sexuality, recognising that although it is shaped within culture it is mediated through the body. Desire cannot exist outside prevailing social structures, but neither can psyche and soma ever be seen as distinct from each other. It is important to explore how women could re-own characteristics projected into men, such as anger and forcefulness, which could then be acted upon constructively to improve women's lives. Furthermore, women's sexual lives would be enriched if they could tolerate their aggression enough to acknowledge the strength and power of their sexual desire.

The clinical material I have described raises issues I continue to explore in the following chapters. The great difficulty many women have in articulating and fighting for what they want emotionally, sexually and professionally has led some to argue that women unconsciously collude in their own oppression. In Chapter 5 I look at how the gender power imbalance has become eroticised, so that women's powerful desire sometimes emerges through images of powerlessness and subjugation. Chapter 8 focuses on the tendency some women have to express unresolved psychic pain through physically located, indirectly eroticised symptoms, such as eating problems, in contrast to men whose unconscious conflicts are often more floridly sexualised.

In the next chapter I return to the theme of male sexuality, exploring the rigid fragility which characterises an identity built on a repudiation of early identifications with the mother and the 'feminine' world of pre-Oedipal intimacy.

Part II

Contemporary debates in clinical practice

Chapter 4

Are men really fragile?

Cultural conceptions of masculinity and femininity vary between cultures and alter over historical time. But during the twentieth century the speed of technological and political change in the western world has been dazzling. Men's position in the family has been irreversibly transformed since the 1950s. Questions about men's role as father, their attitude to housework and domestic violence were rarely mentioned in childcare manuals, sociological surveys or contemporary literature during that period (Segal 1990). Those issues were simply not on the agenda for discussion by individuals or social commentators. In contrast most men today have a much closer relationship with their children than their fathers did and it is no longer automatically assumed that women will service men in the home.

For women who know what life was like for their sex when Freud began writing the changes appear astounding. 'We are part of a reversal of history, an absolute shift in the quality of reality', wrote Elizabeth Janeway, the American novelist and critic, describing in 1982 the revolutionary changes she had seen in the organisation of sexuality and gender since her birth in 1913 (Janeway 1982: 17).

Men often express more ambivalent feelings in the psychotherapist's consulting-room. Usually they absolutely support the idea of women's equality and often describe their mothers as having been exploited within the home. Yet sometimes male patients enter psychotherapy because of an emotional crisis caused by the changes in women's position that they themselves believe should happen. 'Something is happening to men of my age', a 30-year-old patient told me. He and many of his friends had been thrown into depression and self-doubt because their girlfriends, having complained that they were emotionally ungiving and uncommitted, had eventually left them. He linked this new female assertiveness to the fact that women's lives no longer revolved around the family. They had careers and other interests and were 'no longer prepared to spend their lives cooking and knitting for men and children'. This man had been shocked into acknowledging insecurities about his masculinity including feelings of weakness and vulnerability, which he had previously projected onto the female sex. His experience typifies a cultural tendency for men to exhibit more outward signs of emotional distress as their traditional roles are eroded. For instance male unemployment has risen faster than women's since the mid-1980s in Britain and so have suicide, illness, psychological stress and earlier death amongst men (Miles 1991).

These trends would lend weight to the contemporary psychoanalytic theories that describe men as psychologically the weaker sex. But it seems very contradictory to stress the vulnerability of the culturally dominant sex. Despite images of a softer, more 'feminine' masculinity, men as a sex still retain control over institutions of authority – political, educational, juridical and medical. Work outside the home is still mainly organised according to traditional gender roles with the work women do being less well-paid and socially valued. Bearing this in mind, it can be argued that contemporary fathers 'have the best of both worlds: they retain power in the public sphere while having greater access to the satisfactions (often without the frustrations) of family life' (Segal 1990: xi).

Now that men cannot maintain such absolute control over women within the family and in society it is clear that most psychoanalytic theories are constructed around an acceptance, even a justification, of gender power differentials. Most theory reflects a cultural inability to view women as individuals with an identity separate from men and children. 'Men's loss of absolute power over women and children has exposed the vulnerable core of male individuality, the failure of recognition which previously wore the cloak of power, responsibility and family honour', writes Jessica Benjamin (Benjamin 1988: 191). She argues that the breakdown of paternal authority and the resulting search for a different route towards the formation of identity has revealed a contradiction: the inability to confront the independent reality of the other. Men's apparent individuality and capacity for paternal authority belies a failure to recognise women as separate and equal beings with their own will and desire.

It is widely acknowledged in psychoanalytic literature that men's repudiation of aspects of themselves which they see as 'feminine' results in male fear, contempt and cruelty towards women and also towards men who do not appear stereotypically 'masculine'. Freud's male case histories focus on unresolved conflicts about passive and active homosexual attachments, originally to the father. He observed that treatment often foundered on men's inability to understand that a passive attitude does 'not always signify castration and that it is indispensable in many relationships in life' (Freud 1937). The same preoccupation with dread, longing and envy for the mother's 'femininity' is reflected in contemporary studies of gender disorders.

It is surprising then that there is still a widespread acceptance within mainstream psychoanalytic literature that, although men may initially identify with the mother, ideally they should go on to become psychologically akin to the father, who is assumed to be stereotypically 'masculine'. Children will have difficulties in later life if they cannot accept that anatomically they belong to one sex rather than the other, but it does not follow from this that they must either develop the psychological characteristics associated with 'masculinity' in their culture, or become heterosexual. The unconscious meaning each child gives to their biological sex will vary.

If there is a father in the family, he may be seen by the child as the more 'feminine' and maternal parent. The mother may have a strong component of psychological 'masculinity' with which the boy can identify. Nowadays she is sometimes the parent who is more orientated towards the external world, working longer hours or investing more of herself in life outside the home. However, this does not alter the fact that father and son share the same physiology, which denotes membership of the culturally dominant sex. Nor does it affect the strong unconscious fantasies of symbiosis which may exist between mother and infant even if parents attempt to share childcare equally.

The boy has the advantage of being able to use his different physiology and more privileged social status to differentiate himself psychically from a mother who he once saw as all-powerful, possessing everything. And he does not have to change his primary love-object in order to fulfil the cultural requirement of becoming heterosexual. But in western cultures he is expected to relinquish his mother both as an object of identification and Oedipal desire with traumatic suddenness. This is why the lost maternal object so often returns in male fantasy as a denigrated female body which can be controlled and abused, rendered powerless and humiliated as the boy once felt himself to be. Through fantasies and real external relationships of domination over women on whom they depend, men can disown their own psychic 'femininity' – their infantile helplessness and vulnerability, and their wish to return again to an early illusion of symbiosis with the maternal body. This psychic defence against early fear and anxiety is consolidated in male-dominated societies through institutions which exclude women, reinforcing in them the feelings of inadequacy, fear and envy which men deny in themselves.

But with increasing financial independence women can no longer be relied on to 'carry' emotional helplessness and vulnerability for both sexes. Male patients who recognise that they are unable to use their cultural power in a sustained way to exert emotional control over female partners, often describe how changes in sexual and family life have forced them to confront aspects of their emotional experience which their fathers could more easily avoid. In this chapter I discuss the complex interplay between the psychological patterns of male social dominance and female emotional power as they are acted out between myself and male patients. My clinical material illustrates how major shifts in class or culture can exacerbate contemporary men's confusion about rapidly altering images of masculinity. I argue that, in order to cope with the rigours of more equal emotional relationships between the sexes, men need to integrate a range of identifications with the 'masculinity' and 'femininity' of both parents within the therapeutic transference relationship.

CHANGING VIEWS OF MASCULINITY: THEORY AND CLINICAL PRACTICE

Mr A sought psychotherapy because of serious panic attacks and phobias. At work he also found it difficult to use his own personal authority and initiative and was under-achieving. Despite a brilliant academic record, professional promotion eluded him. Mr A described a disturbing gap between his competent, sophisticated man-about-town exterior, and the distraught toddler he felt himself to be. This disjunction was reflected in the clothes he wore to sessions which ranged from pinstripe city suits through jeans and leather jackets to a torn and grubby blue running suit that became known as his 'baby-gro'.

When he moved to London from a small town in Scotland Mr A lost the traditional structures of lower-middle-class life. He compared himself to his father who in contrast had not needed to make a great number of individual decisions. His father had been able to rely on the bureaucracy of work and solace from the Church when in personal difficulties, whereas his son had needed to pay for my professional help.

Mr A described how his father had been 'propped' up in his role by the networks of Scottish small town life – female relatives, the local Church and community. His father had, he said, been 'another dependant, nesting under my mother, the Queen Bee. My father had three maternal figures, including his own mother and his mother-in-law, within the space of half a mile, to support him as a father and authority figure.' Within the family his father could rely on lifelong maternal support and also on clear, even rigid, expectations of male and female behaviour. In contrast Mr A was not able to hide unresolved infantile conflicts beneath a veneer of patriarchal authority.

At the age of 4, after his sister's birth, Mr A had felt 'pushed out of a love-nest' with his mother. He described how, up to that point, he had felt 'swaddled . . . emotionally protected in a close and attentive way'. At 4 he was suddenly sent off to school dressed up in a formal uniform. He blamed himself for the way life had suddenly changed so dramatically for the worse. He told me about the very high expectations his parents had for him, as the only son, and his envy of his sisters who seemed to be loved just for who they were.

After graduating from a southern university Mr A married and the couple had a child. He and his wife wanted to operate as personal and financial equals. But equality proved difficult, even with the support of his men's group. At times Mr A found himself taking over the household completely, as he played out his identification with his mother, a conventional 1950s housewife. Or he would go to the other extreme and collapse into the role of the helpless, cosseted son who must be totally cared for by an all-protective maternal figure. When his wife left him after three years Mr A's mother-in-law told him that he 'hadn't let his wife be a woman'. This increased his confusion since his wife had been adamant that she didn't want to play a traditional housewife role.

After the separation Mr A, who felt absolutely bereft, became a part-time single parent. He expected himself to play a far more active role in mothering his daughter than his own father had done. Although he appreciated his daughter's affection and company Mr A lacked practical support in his single-parent role and felt extremely isolated and self-critical. Lacking the internal capacity to process and think about his own emotional life, he could not mother his daughter in this way. But nevertheless she was a companion and a consolation to him. The phobias and panic attacks which had begun during a prior separation from his wife intensified, until he felt forced to seek professional help.

Mr A's psychotherapy was to last seven years, twice-weekly. During the first few months he could not bear to have the consulting-room door shut. He felt trapped in psychotherapy as in the nursery class-room and wanted to curl up like a foetus in a corner of the room or crawl under the table as if into a womb. He felt himself to be an utterly uncontained 'skinless' creature, bursting with anguished and violent feelings.

Mr A defended against these experiences of infantile helplessness through fantasies of absolutely controlling or annihilating me, as the much-needed maternal object. Halfway through his last session before my first long summer break Mr A mentioned an old lady he'd read about who'd been murdered. I suddenly sensed an alarmingly strong murderous feeling in the room. 'I noticed that, as usual, the flat is empty apart from us. I never hear any neighbours around', he said. Feeling utterly chilled by this, I then said that I thought he was having murderous feelings about me. Through letting me know about these feelings he was trying to make me feel as frightened and vulnerable as he did about my impending holiday. 'I don't know. Perhaps I am trying to frighten you', he replied, before going on to talk more lucidly than he had before about his fears of loneliness during the break. He had agreed surprisingly compliantly with my interpretations. But, whereas I had felt quite shaken by the strength of his violence, I was not sure he had fully recognised the intensity of his own emotions. Later, he was to say about these persistent murderous fantasies which had their origins in the period after his sister's birth, 'It's not a man attacking a woman. It's a child attacking a mother and a child.'

Whenever I said something that put Mr A in touch with early vulnerability and humiliation, he would retreat into grandiose fantasies of winning my admiration with heroic feats, or over-powering me with his sexual passion. He fantasised that he was Albert Einstein, and I was an adoring student or a secretary, hanging on his every word. He imagined himself piloting Concorde outside my window rather than having to listen to me.

At other times when he felt trapped and humiliated he with-drew into florid sexual fantasies. Sexuality had become powerfully implicated in his unconscious attempts to maintain an illusion of fusion with maternal figures. His fantasies ranged in atmosphere from childhood innocence to adult conquest. Sometimes his fan-tasies revealed a cold violence which seriously frightened me. He began with talk of 'tearing my body to bits' – criticising me – and went on to describe his thoughts of raping me. In his dreams he'd seduce me powerfully, and I'd submit passionately, or we'd sit on the floor and play with toys together.

In psychotherapy Mr A's fantasy of existing in a symbiotic 'love-nest' with me was shattered by another separation – my unexpected absence after a sudden bereavement. Initially he retreated into murderous fantasies and threats of rape as a defence against his anxieties about abandonment. I worried that I might be in real physical danger. I explored my own fears of male violence while thinking about the precautions I might take in case he really did act on his violent or murderous feelings. Gradually both my own anxiety and the intolerable fear of his own aggression projected into me by Mr A subsided as he became able to articulate the feelings of loss beneath his murderous rage.

I used to exist in a bubble here. My mother didn't make me feel secure ... she needed me to grow up suddenly when she had my sister. . . . I'm not so important in your life, just any old therapy client. I used to feel special. You could stop therapy with me.

The catastrophic shock of my absence was ultimately a grow-ing-point for Mr A. He dreamed of a baby wearing his blue baby-gro who played with himself and his daughter. 'I realised the baby could look after itself ... change nappies, put itself on the pot. . . . I'm less helpless.' Through the experience of having me listen, contain and think about what he was telling me, Mr A was becoming more able to process and understand his own anxieties. But the dream also revealed that there was still a pseudo-grown up baby part of him which clung narcissistically to the illusion of self-sufficiency. He still felt like an infant who could change its own nappies.

In another dream Mr A illustrated the interchangeability of the female figures in his life, all experienced alternately as mothers, sisters and erotic love-objects. In the dream he was dipped in a swimming pool filled with chemical water that had magical properties, by two young girls wearing print dresses identical to each other and also to one he was wearing. He stayed in the pool long enough to be changed, but not to burn his skin off. 'Probably', he said, 'your caustic comments.' The two young girls represented myself and a new girlfriend. He associated the printed dress he was wearing with his 'pretty looks' and likeable manner. Psychotherapy, like the caustic pool, was dangerously powerful in its transformative potential. He was responding passively 'with his dress on' because it was difficult for him to listen to what I was saying and then examine it for himself.

Narcissism is present in all of us to the extent that we all yearn for the illusion of fusion with an idealised other – originally the mother – as happens, for instance, when we fall in love. Narcissistic relationships are superficial, with friends and lovers being seen as interchangeable. Other people are experienced as part of the self rather than as separate beings with their own distinct identities. In fantasy Mr A glued himself onto me, forming a kind of 'adhesive identification' (Bick 1968), which enabled him to avoid the recognition of the differences between us. So strong was his illusion of being identical to, a part of me, that he had convinced himself that we were exactly the same age. In a similar way he often felt like his daughter's peer, one of her playmates.

Mr A needed to be able to face his own feelings of loss and guilt before he could become able to love someone while recognising their imperfections, rather than relating to others as imagos – split-off idealised or denigrated reflections of a fragmented inner world. In his third year of psychotherapy he began for the first time to express remorse about his sadistic feelings towards me and his attempts to sabotage the psychotherapy process. He was worried that he might actually damage or destroy me.

This became noticeable after a session two weeks before my summer break when he withdrew into a fantasy about me as a 'disembodied cunt', perhaps the lower half of a Greek statue which he would keep for himself in a lonely moorland grotto, making visits whenever he felt like it. I connected his desire to mutilate and control me with his feelings of rage and loss about my break. He agreed rationally with this, but went on elaborating the fantasy. Apparently he was trying to avoid the emotional impact of what I was saying. He also told me that work commitments would prevent him attending his last two sessions before I left, so that he could only come twice more before my holiday.

In the following session he described how he was making his current girlfriend feel insecure because he was afraid she would finish their stormy relationship. I linked his treatment of her with the fantasy he had had about mutilating and controlling me, saying that he wanted her and myself to be the ones to feel humiliated and abandoned. 'I feel really worried', Mr A said. 'There isn't much time left in the session . . . and you're going on holiday soon. . . . I feel remorse towards P . . . and towards you. . . . I feel I've destroyed the relationship.' He returned the next week telling me that he had managed to re-arrange his office timetable so that he could come to his two last sessions 'because I realised you were concerned about my welfare'. He went on to tell me how he had tried to repair the damage he had done to his relationship with his girlfriend.

As he was preparing to leave psychotherapy Mr A described a watershed point where he had begun to realise that the most important thing was to find a partner who would love him. 'I realised that people were not interchangeable', he said. 'Only a few people are really valuable.' He was saying that he had begun to relinquish his quest for the unattainable incestuous object – myself within the maternal transference – and was willing for the first time to accept a woman who was emotionally available. At the same time, he now felt able to let one person become deeply important to him. He went on to start a passionate sexual love relationship with his closest woman friend, who he then married.

Two changes in his internal world made this transformation possible. The first crucial change was that he began to recognise that the cruel psychotherapist who abandoned him during breaks was also the person he needed and felt gratitude towards. When he began psychotherapy he had alternately idealised and denigrated me, and was unable to bring his different experiences of me together in his mind. This marked a new capacity to differentiate himself from me within the maternal transference. Secondly, Mr A's identification with his father became stronger. He began to face the strength of his early relationship with his father. During this period he began to try out and experiment with a range of identifications with both parents. Within the transference he became more able to use me as a figure who possessed the characteristics of both sexes. He then began to explore his passive homosexual desires for his father, as well as his Oedipal rivalry and humiliation. Once he began to feel more secure in his own male identity he became less frightened of fusion with me within the maternal transference.

Gradually, as Mr A began to work through some of his overwhelming grief about abandonment by his mother, he began to acknowledge that his father had given him considerable care and attention around the time of his sister's birth. They had played 'atlas games . . . trainsets on Friday evenings . . . he made me feel important'. After standing in for his boss at an academic conference and winning strong praise for his work there, he dreamt that he was starting off on a new and exciting journey with his father. During this voyage towards manhood, Mr A and his father were travelling 'in a small wooden boat that I'd built, that had been covered up or neglected for years'.

After acknowledging that he saw me as a paternal as well as a maternal figure, Mr A became more able to delve into 'the very dangerous territory . . . the fundamentals of who I am'. He embarked on an exploration of his own repudiated identification with his mother and his passive homosexual desires towards his father. He remembered giving his father 'lingering kisses' and speculated that his parents had noticed the extent of his sexual interest in adult males. He thought now that this might have been why they had forbidden him to go on a train-spotting expedition with older boys and men.

Mr A now began to face his intense envy of my reproductive capacities. He complained of a persistent hollowness in his stomach, associated with an inability to conceive ideas. He mourned the fact that he couldn't validate his existence in a fundamental way by bearing children. But he hoped that he could identify with what he saw as my feminine creative ability to weave coherent ideas out of half-articulated fragments. My capacity to link together a series of ideas about him was, he felt, tantamount to conception – a creativity of thought. He was in rivalry with my capacity to make both a real baby and a thought baby.

Now that he had acknowledged the strength of his internal relationship with his father Mr A began to discuss his feelings about me as an object with the attributes of both parents. He dreamed of me as a woman doctor, a TV presenter who possessed a professional authority he saw as male. He envied her prominent position and the style in which she conducted the 'Seven O'Clock Therapeutic Show'. At work he felt dominated by what he saw as a feminine desire to be needed. He could not set the kinds of limits he associated with a benign internal father. He compared his masculinity to a Meccano construction, rigid yet fragile. But he went on to say that he hoped within the boundaried structure of the sessions that he could build a more solid and durable sense of what it meant to him to be a man.

In one of his last sessions Mr A said, 'I don't feel I'm waiting to grow up any more. I've become a man.' He now felt equal with the heads of the organisations in which he worked, he said. Recently he'd been 'head-hunted' for a prestigious and lucrative new job, having during his years of therapy developed his own area of professional expertise.

In describing his new workplace Mr A let me know about the structural changes in his internal world. This new building had wide, very light corridors, filled with paintings and sculptures by young artists. There was even a very innovative sculpture of a water-mill in perpetual motion. He was now more accessible to himself. There were fewer dark secrets and hidden passages inside him now that his aggressive urges had become more integrated. He could accept that his parents were still sexually happy with each other and now felt more able to welcome and look after any younger siblings (young artists) they might produce. Through psychotherapy, Mr A had developed a far greater capacity to think symbolically about his own emotional experience and to be innovative in his working life. Margot Waddell compares the symbolising functions of the artist with those of the psychother-apist and the mother, each of whom nourishes and develops the internal creativity of those who engage with them (Waddell and Williams 1991).

This new organisation had (like himself now) less of a liberal image, but was if anything more genuinely humanitarian. For instance there were people with severe physical disabilities in the top jobs. The firm was also putting considerable resources into training women for leadership roles. Mr A told me that, despite a progressive veneer, his previous firm would not have placed people with physical disabilities in prominent positions because of a fear that they'd have put off important clients. Mr A compared this to his own tendency to project his own vulnerability outside himself onto less privileged social groups.

I might go out of my way not to be prejudiced. But underneath, I might not want to look at people with physical disabilities. But really, it's the frail part of me, the disabled part. . . . 16 years ago, a weakness came to light – an emotional stroke. You have therapy for strokes. Therapy is still going on inside me, healing me.

Mr A had integrated his frail and disabled parts much more and was surprised to find that he could display them without frightening himself or others. He was also working towards a greater acceptance of his own 'feminine' aspects. In this context it is significant that Mr A's anxieties came to the surface when he became a part-time single parent. Apart from coping with his wife's abandonment he was also forced to confront the infantile states of mind which men have traditionally disowned and projected onto women.

INTEGRATING MALE 'FEMININITY'

Men who objectify women and set up relationships where they control and dehumanise their female (or male) partner deprive themselves of the possibility of intimacy, since the other cannot be recognised as equal but different. The process of projecting out rather than processing emotional experience undermines the capacity to acknowledge and repair real or fantasised destructive acts. Instead a vicious circle is set up, whereby the person who is attacked or abused in reality or fantasy becomes threatening and dangerous, so that more violence is deployed against them, or a greater amount of emotional distance arranged. But gaining a sense of personal power through destroying the unsettling difference represented by the feminine other impoverishes the male personality, creating a structure which is rigid yet precarious.

Mr A had been forced to repudiate his own early experience

with his mother and his early 'feminine' identification with her in a very dramatic way. He was expected to change from a cosseted toddler to a high-achieving schoolboy without having the opportunity to play out and integrate a range of identifications with each sex. He therefore resorted to a false autonomy based on a denial of dependency. Once Mr A had lost his sense of being similar to his mother he also felt that he no longer had her goodness and nourishment inside him. He felt utterly excluded from the world of intimacy they had shared and cut off from his own emotional life, which now seemed alien, external to him. In typically male fashion he alternated between idealising his mother and women as representatives of a lost paradise, and feeling contempt for the helplessness and dependency he now projected onto them.

His 'feminine' identification with his mother was not integrated with his organised gender identity. Yet it remained as a powerful unexplored part of himself. He struggled continually to regain contact with his early relationship with her, whilst simultaneously repudiating her femininity. He now experienced women as completely Other from him, destructive yet powerfully alluring. Accordingly, within the maternal transference Mr A resorted to fantasies of impressing me with his heroism or genius, or conquering me by passion or force. Since he remained unconsciously preoccupied with his early feelings of maternal abandonment, Mr A's identification with his father was tenuous, since he could not face and resolve Oedipal feelings of inadequacy and rivalry.

The repudiated body of the mother remains as an object to be violated, devalued and controlled, as representative of the repressed 'feminine part' of the self. In psychotherapy Mr A unconsciously dehumanised me, making me in fantasy into an object he could control and abuse. This gradually lessened only once he began to fear that he might absolutely destroy me and the therapeutic relationship on which he depended. Then he began to confront the reality of my emotional power – that I was essential to his process of psychic transformation. He had previously denied that I had anything he envied or needed, through displays of pseudo-independence and struggles for dominance.

Through a prolonged period in psychotherapy of experimenting with cross-gender identifications and expressing desire for both parents, Mr A managed to strengthen his own identity as a heterosexual male. Since he no longer had to work so hard at excluding his own 'feminine' aspects he was able to see myself and other women in a more balanced light. I was no longer so dangerous and alien. He could recognise some of his own qualities in me while also acknowledging the fundamental differences between us.

Those men who enter, and stay in ongoing analytic psychotherapy, often seem to possess conventionally creative or professional 'masculine' capacities as well as an uncomfortable awareness of their own 'feminine' vulnerabilities. This combination of cross-gender strength and fragility may make it easier for men to face aspects of themselves previously disowned as 'feminine'. Men (or women) who project all their 'feminine' need and vulnerability onto others do not usually commit themselves to long-term psychotherapy. They can usually use stereotyped modes of behaviour to protect them from their own pain. It is more likely to be their sexual partners who seek psychological help. Or they may stay in psychotherapy only until their most obvious and pressing problems are resolved.

In the following section I look at different psychoanalytic theories about the male propensity towards acts of violence and the sexualisation of psychic pain, which was so obvious in the therapeutic transference with Mr A.

MALE VIOLENCE AND SEXUALISATION OF PAIN

The preoccupation with fantasies of committing violent and murderous acts, including sexual assaults, is sometimes found in women patients, but I have found it far more often amongst men in psychotherapy. This reflects a more general prevalence of violent and murderous acts among the male population. Mr A is also typical of his sex in his tendency to sexualise his aggression, for instance in fantasies of raping me, as well as defending against his feelings of infantile vulnerability through thoughts of his own sexual prowess. Is the tendency to externalise and sexualise aggression related to the vicissitudes of male identification with the father, or to cultural or physiological factors? Or does it reflect male psychic fragility, men's overpowering feelings of inadequacy, fear and rage in relation to the early mother? Psychoanalytic explanations tend to oscillate between these two opposing viewpoints, focusing either on male womb envy, or on the problematic aspects of their identification with paternal power and authority.

Since boys are expected to relinquish their early intimacy and identification with the mother suddenly and absolutely, their unresolved infantile conflicts may re-emerge as exaggerated sexual needs and narcissistic over-valuation of the male penis. Other ways of expressing vulnerability do not fit in with stereotypes of masculinity. An example of this eroticisation of early vulnerability is the common male fantasy of a powerful woman who is always present and sexually available. The American psychoanalyst Ethel Spector Person argues that in order to satisfy such a woman, many men imagine that they possess a penis 'two feet long, hard as steel' which 'can go all night'. Through this fantasy the man assuages oral needs, as well as Oedipal anxieties about male potency and sexual rejection by the mother (Spector Person 1986: 84, quoting Zilbergeld).

Men like Mr A who are insecure about their male identity may use forceful displays of heterosexuality (or even active homosexuality) as a way of underlining their difference from the mother. In men gender identity appears to be more associated with sexuality than it does in women. Lack of desire or satisfaction in women is much less visible than in men and may therefore be less significant to female self-esteem. Ethel Spector Person argues that an impotent man always feels that his masculinity and not just his sexuality are threatened (Spector Person 1986).

Since sexual potency and prowess are often closely bound up with male identity, contemporary men's anxieties may be heightened by the recent dramatic change in popular and professional perceptions about which sex is to blame for heterosexual dysfunction. Since the 1980s there has been a huge rise in journalistic articles about male impotence, with far less mention of female 'frigidity', a central focus of early psychoanalytic study (Segal 1990).

Chasseguet-Smirgel is one psychoanalyst who attempts to understand male defences against the early power of the mother, while also acknowledging some of the privileges that the boy gains from identification with the male sex. She attributes men's greater propensity to commit murder and acts of violence to their inability to identify with the mother's procreative power. Men can, she argues, attempt only in fantasy to re-enter the mother's womb by force, destroying all obstacles in their way. She argues that women who can enter again into the maternal womb symbolically through identification with the mother, have more respect for the continuity of human life (Chasseguet-Smirgel 1986a).

So far my emphasis has been on men's psychic fragility and the difficulty they have in differentiating themselves from the mother, which results in a 'fault line' in the male psyche. In fact though, because of their privileged place within culture, men are easily able to project their feelings of vulnerability and inadequacy onto women and less privileged men as Mr A did.

Identification with the more highly valued sex offers the boy a series of psychic and cultural advantages, since he can enhance his narcissism and compensate for early infantile pain and loss either through positive achievements in the external world, or more defensively, through triumphing over the mother. But psychological difficulties may arise if he gets fixated during the identificatory process, as happened with Mr A. The failure to identify fully with male strengths and assets may lead to the idealisation of a caricature of manhood, 'false emblems of masculinity, faceless bureaucracy, violence, torture, the jackboot and the whip'. Chasseguet-Smirgel goes on to attribute these 'pseudo-manly values' to a 'society which possesses only an illusory show of paternal authority' (Chasseguet-Smirgel 1986a: 73).

According to Klein the boy has a different, potentially advantageous, means of externalising aggression, through the belief that he posseses a penis with magically destructive and reparative powers, unlike the girl whose psychic life continues to revolve around the inside of her body. But this too is a double-edged privilege. The boy's conviction that he has a deadly weapon at his disposal will also increase the likelihood of direct aggression if he cannot resolve internal conflicts in any other way (Klein 1928).

Some men's preoccupation with accumulating ostentatious wealth or with displaying their power or prestige may also originate in the little boy's inability to face the reality of being unable to satisfy his mother sexually with his small penis. Having glorified the functions and productions of his own toddler body the boy (or girl) moves on to idealise anything he can hoard that can be piled up and counted. 'Thus shining pieces of money are nothing other than odourless, dehydrated filth that has been made to shine' (Ferenczi 1914 quoted in Chasseguet-Smirgel 1985: 131).

Some psychoanalysts openly mourn the loss of traditional patriarchal authority within the family. They attribute to this many of
the contemporary social ills of this age, including increased male
violence. The French analyst Grunberger argues that the unstable
contemporary family does not foster the Oedipus complex as
Freud described it (Grunberger 1989). While Freud argued that
human beings suffer from too much guilt Grunberger says that
people today have too little guilt. The emotional absence of the
father who can provide a model of self-restraint results in a super-
ego or conscience which remains fixated at a pre-Oedipal stage
of narcissistic self-absorbtion. Cruelty and destructiveness
towards the self and others may result from a super-ego which is
harsh and punitive but without moral values.

Narcissism is sometimes seen as an individual pathology which
reveals a social malaise. Christopher Lasch, a cultural theorist,
argues that narcissistic ways of functioning, where people are
interchangeable and relationships superficial, are used as a widespread defence against the terrifying fluidity and fragmentation
of the modern world where violence always threatens to break
through the brittle glamour. In contemporary western societies
people do not build their own destinies through work and responsibility towards others, but instead seek immediate experiences
of power, glamour and excitement, or at least identification with
those who appear to have access to these qualities (Lasch 1979).

According to Grunberger the narcissistic solution is regressive,
pre-Oedipal, unlike that of the Oedipal person who engages with
the conflict and difficulty intrinsic to relationships with others
(Grunberger 1989). Narcissism impels the little boy who doesn't
try again when he feels defeated by his Oedipal rival but attempts
instead to 'abolish the paternal principle'. Like Mr A he unconsciously denies the existence of the actual father and all structures
of authority. As a result of this refusal to engage with otherness,
the possibilities of psychic change are restricted, Grunberger
argues. But is he demanding that we simply adapt ourselves to
the current status quo rather than questioning it?

Discussion of narcissism is often riven with cultural assumptions and value judgements. Most importantly these theories
idealise the Oedipal values associated with the father, while
devaluing the early infantile mother–infant dyad, which is seen
as regressive, the locus of illusion. It is also unclear whether the
subject of discussion is the actual parents or what they symbolise

in our culture. It is true that women are usually the primary parents, while the child often sees the father as representative of the wider world. But the father may also play a strong role in early maternal care, as Mr A's father did, while the mother may encourage the child to give up the illusion of being a part of her.

It is obvious that the man who has not separated psychically from his mother or resolved his Oedipal rivalry with his father will feel disadvantaged with both sexes, as Mr A did at the beginning of psychotherapy. He may, like Mr A, resort to pseudo-masculine displays of prowess and dominance. But the solution to this is not necessarily a re-assertion of paternal authority. Mr A had failed to identify fully with his father, but this was not the result of paternal negligence. Many boys do not identify with the father because they experience him as harsh or cruel. Or they may, like Mr A, be unable to face Oedipal rivalry with the father because of feelings of abandonment by the mother. For men like Mr A a fundamental problem is their inability to tolerate their own helpless dependency associated culturally with femininity, which compounds any difficulties they may have in identifying with their own sex.

Theories which stress the barren fragmentation of modern relationships also disregard the tendencies that enrich contemporary family life, such as fewer children, shorter working hours, increased paternal involvement in early stages of childrearing, family leisure and the tendency to understand rather than to discipline children (Benjamin 1988). Although many contemporary men are in crisis, there is much in today's society that benefits women. For instance women's workload in the home has been dramatically reduced and they now have greater access to equality in the workplace. With increased economic independence and the possibility of controlling their fertility, women can choose to live outside conventional nuclear family units if they wish.

It is very difficult to know quite what – if any – effect physiology has in shaping the psychological differences between the sexes as they exist in our culture. I do not believe it to be a first cause. But it may have an impact on our mental representations, for instance the way in which we symbolise and conceptualise sexual experience. But what is significant is the way in which we read or interpret such symbolism and how it is represented within culture. I do not know whether men's more visible genitalia aid them in externalising their aggression, but it is quite clear that they gain positive advantages from the favoured position of phallic imagery in a society where men are dominant. Clearly there is potential for change in representations of female and male sexuality, as can be seen in societies which have different values and mythological systems.

CULTURAL DISLOCATION

Cultural critiques of narcissism have been used to explain the impact of the 'great structuring dominations' of race, class and gender on the psyche (Frosh 1989). It is argued that contemporary cultural fragmentation militates against the creation of an atmosphere of reverie or containment in early life. The confirmed existence of the self can then be buttressed only through denigration of the other. So each racial, class and gender group projects its own sense of weakness onto those who have less power and destroys the conscious knowledge of this projection. This destructiveness may be wrought for instance in sexist or racist fantasy or acted out in real acts of violence (White 1989).

However, these projections are not necessarily received passively by different ethnic and cultural groups who may absolutely reject the values of the dominant culture and bring their children up with different ideals of male and female identity and family relations. So far I have described men who have moved from one class to another, but men who move between different cultures are often presented with even more drastically different conceptions of manhood.

Mr D

A 23-year-old man, Mr D, whose family were high-caste Hindus, expressed his conflicts about sexual identity through intense confusion about the different versions of masculinity to which he had been exposed. When he had arrived in Britain with his mother and siblings at the age of 6, to join the father he had last seen five years before, he was moving to his third different continent and culture.

Mr D came to psychotherapy because of a painful, conflict-ridden love-affair. He urgently needed to resolve questions about the way of life he wanted to follow. In his first session with me he described himself as passionately involved with the only woman he had ever loved. But revealing the ambivalence he could not tolerate in himself and habitually projected onto her, he made a slip of the tongue, telling me that he had come to psychotherapy to break up with her. It gradually became clear that he had unconsciously made a series of decisions, and had come into psychotherapy because he knew these would cause him psychic pain.

His lover was regarded by his family (and perhaps by a part of himself) as an unsuitable marriage partner because her cultural and religious background were different from his. Mr D remained obsessed with the idea that she would return to one of her previous lovers, who had been Afro-Caribbean or white. His unresolved Oedipal rivalry was projected onto these men who he imagined to be bigger, more 'macho' and more potent than himself. He felt painfully inferior to all the ideals of manhood to which he had been exposed. The greatest pressure seemed to be coming from his family, who disapproved of his lifestyle and advised him to build a future through hard work, responsibility towards others, and immersion in the family's religious and cultural heritage, instead of seeking to aggrandize himself through superficial glamour and rapid ways of making money.

Mr D knew that he was much sought after as a husband in his own community. He described how he was mobbed by young girls and their mothers at religious festivals because of his family background, his personal qualities, including his gentle demeanour and his delicate, almost pretty looks. His family were extremely concerned that their offspring should do well, and had therefore set up a business to be shared by Mr D and his siblings. But at the moment the wages were low for long hours' work, and Mr D said that he did not trust the family. He feared that his older relatives would always retain control of the organisation, since nothing was written down.

Psychotherapy represented an individual solution to problems, and in this way it too represented a part of the conflict Mr D had come to solve. In fact psychoanalytic notions of autonomy or individualism are a Eurocentric or at least a 'modern' phenomenon, and have little relevance to some cultures (Littlewood 1992). Mr D did not know whether to throw in his lot with European individualism or to identify himself as part of his family unit, which would include helping to develop the family business.

Mr D felt ambivalent about what he saw as a strong component of 'femininity' in his personality. One of his strongest identifications seemed to be with a depressed, self-sacrificial maternal figure. For several years during puberty he remembered having dreams in which he was a girl. He associated these with a terrible humiliation of which he had hardly spoken before coming to see me – the experience of having been sexually abused by a previously idealised slightly older relative, when he was 9. He had been in search of fatherly affection, he told me, and bitterly resented the fact that his parents had not protected him, or realised what was happening. Mr D often spoke of how much easier it seemed to be for his brothers to feel proud and sure of their masculinity and their place in the world. He attributed this to their having had more stable parental relationships in early life and being old enough to find alternative paternal figures amongst the extended family during the separation from their biological father. When his father was reunited with the family Mr D had felt unable to identify with what he perceived as cruel, dictatorial paternal authority. His parental imagos seem to reflect both real parental characteristics and persecutory fantasies resulting from early separations and losses, compounded by sexual abuse.

But there may also have been strong cultural reasons for Mr D's frequent fantasies about being a woman. Since the 1920s, Indian psychoanalysts have argued that men of their race are more able to integrate and remain conscious of their own feminine identifications, and their womb envy than their European counterparts (Kakar 1989). Kakar, a contemporary Indian psychoanalyst, argues that psychoanalysis operates from within the heart of European mythology, from the myths of Ancient Greece to the 'illusions' of the Enlightenment, and there has been little attempt to observe from within the way in which other mythological systems influence personality development. He points out that the dominant narrative of Hindu culture is neither that of Freud's Oedipus, nor Christianity's Adam. In fact one of the dominant mythological figures is Devi, a personification of the Great Goddess. The powerful mother Goddess, as depicted in folk beliefs, proverbs, symbols and religious ritual, is always omnipotently fierce and terrible, and possesses an inexhaustible sexual energy, which inspires intense awe and dread in the Hindu male.

Her significance is reinforced by certain aspects of Indian

family life, including the fact that within the extended family the boy will have not one but many maternal figures, who will all assume responsibility for his physical care. In contrast the father in Indian mythology is often presented as unassuming and remote, yet powerful. Kakar argues that in the face of such an overpoweringly sexual, omnipresent maternal figure, the boy deals with his anxieties about differentation in certain culturally favoured ways. The fantasies of being a woman which are often close to conscious awareness in the male psyche, and the image of the goddess as a man–woman are, according to Kakar, expressions of the Indian male's wish to become a man without having to separate psychically from the mother (Kakar 1989).

There were indeed many maternal figures in Mr D's family. For instance at one point he wondered whether to go to a religious ceremony where he would receive maternal attention from his many sisters, or to come to his session where there might be only one mother-substitute. But in spite of this Mr D had not internalised the maternal capacity to process and think about his own emotional experience. He felt that he had lacked consistent mothering, as well as fathering. There seemed to be many reasons for this, including his mother's depression, the birth of a new sibling when Mr D was 1, just before his father left the family, and the many moves and separations. As a result of this lack of maternal containment he had developed a cruel superego with which he attacked himself and those he was close to, including myself. Unlike Mr A, described earlier in this chapter, Mr D disowned his own destructiveness and ruthlessness, seeing himself as his lover's rejected victim. Whenever I referred to his once stated desire to break up with her, he would smile wryly, acknowledging that he had said it, but never exploring it as part of himself.

During six months' psychotherapy, focused around his conflicts about his love-relationship, Mr D bombarded me with intensely emotional barrages of words, leaving me little space to speak. He generated intense anxiety in me about his destructiveness towards all his enterprises, including psychotherapy, his attendance at which was constantly in doubt. Despite the fact that he rapidly became dependent on me, he found breaks and gaps between the sessions extremely difficult and frequently missed sessions. He continually attacked all the ties that bound him to other people, whether relatives, lovers, business associates, or myself.

After attempting to repair the broken links between himself and others, he would then make further attacks, always conveying a sense of anguish and helplessness about his own destructiveness. Although Mr D saw himself as genuine and caring, this was not the experience of those on whom he depended, including myself. Such states of inner persecution are another form of narcissistic self-absorption. In fact, he had not developed any deep concern for others, seeing them only as extensions of himself. It is this lack of concern for others for which the super-ego reproves the patient who, without realising it, subjects other people to ruthless emotional control, projecting onto them the same sadistic states of mind he experienced in childhood. In psychotherapy these cruel aspects of the self may become integrated with more loving feelings, eventually becoming the source of a fantasy life that generates emotional contact between people. Mr D did make the first tentative steps towards this process in his psychotherapy, beginning to acknowledge and make up for his attacks on me and others, and making some significant decisions about his life. Eventually he decided that his future lay in integrating his own western upbringing with the advantages of immersion in a very resourceful, traditional family structure where he had considerable status as a high-caste member of the dominant sex. His relationship with his lover also ended, ostensibly through her volition.

The tendency to disown aggression and to experience the self as a caring, loving victim of others' destructiveness as Mr D did, is associated in psychoanalytic and feminist literature more with stereotypical female than male behaviour. Nevertheless everyone has the capacity to bully, as well as to be victimised. Gender and culture will influence but not absolutely determine which aspect of personality any individual can more easily act out. Mr D may, for instance, have drawn more on his identification with his long-suffering mother in an unconscious attempt to avoid acting out an identification with his father's cruel authoritarianism. As I have indicated, ideals of manliness vary both within and between cultures. Yet the power differences between the sexes may still remain.

CONCLUSION

Now that rigid sex-roles and patriarchal family structures are breaking down, male psychic fragility is more obvious. Men can no longer rely on women or less culturally dominant groups to 'carry' the emotional vulnerability for both sexes. In societies where 'masculine' characteristics are associated with mental health and success in all spheres the dilemma for men is what to do with those aspects of themselves, such as envy, humiliation and need, which have traditionally been seen as 'feminine' characteristics.

I argue against the theory that the boy must give up his early identifications with the mother in order to build a sturdy, autonomous male identity, based primarily on similarities with other men. More emphasis needs to be placed theoretically and clinically on boys' early bisexual identifications with both parents. In my discussion of case-material I have shown how male identity can be strengthened through a prolonged period of experimenting with and integrating identifications with 'feminine' functions and desires.

Cultural ideals of masculinity obviously vary between cultures and over historical time. But if the society around us dehumanises and denigrates women and 'femininity' and idealises men, then our psyches will continue to reflect this. Men who for cultural or personal reasons are more 'feminine' than the cultural ideal may find themselves being treated with a fear and contempt usually reserved for women.

Although men can use the cultural objectification of women to defend themselves against psychic pain and vulnerability, they have little possibility of equal intimacy with women who are deprived of the possibility of autonomous selfhood. The cultural repudiation of femininity may well have a profound impact on gay relationships. It certainly fuels homophobia. Patriarchy does not benefit men psychologically; in profound ways it impoverishes the male personality. If men project the 'feminine' aspects of themselves onto others, their capacity for reparation and loving concern will be diminished. Their psyches will be rigid, yet fragile. Only when men begin to mourn early losses and acknowledge the anxiety and envy underlying the devaluation of femininity, will they be able to feel more equal to women and other men. For instance, when Mr A began to feel more secure in his identity as a man who also enjoyed fulfilling conventionally 'feminine' functions, his image of me as a maternal figure became less dangerous and threatening. I was no longer absolutely alien and other. He could recognise some womanly qualities in himself while also acknowledging that I would always possess attributes he could never have.

Change at the personal level will be limited if it is not accompanied by a transformation of attitudes, cultural imagery and social institutions. Each sex needs to recognise the other as anatomically different, yet equal, and to acknowledge the existence of the other in themselves. It is crucial for us to understand more about how our experience of physicality is mediated through language and cultural imagery. For instance, is a representation of the dangerous omnipotent mother who must be controlled and manipulated consolidated in the male mind through the lack of cultural images of women as separate beings with their own will and desire?

Although patriarchal relations profoundly cripple the male psyche, men also benefit from them. It is inevitable, then, that it is the female sex which has struggled for equality throughout this century. Women also express unhappiness with their lot through seeking all kinds of psychological help far more often than men do. In the next chapter I explore how far women can break the cycle of personal domination, claim their own autonomous subjectivity, and operate more as equals in their sexual relationships.

Chapter 5

The power of women's sexuality

Contemporary psychoanalysts do not usually draw links between masochism and femininity as their forebears did. Indeed the concept of female masochism, so controversial with feminists, is rarely discussed openly. Nevertheless, the questions Freud and his contemporaries raised about the nature of women's desire and our capacity to combine motherhood, professional creativity and sexual fulfilment remain highly relevant today. It is widely acknowledged that men are more likely to be sexual masochists, who can obtain gratification only through physical pain or humiliation. But Freud asked why female sexual desire so often emerges in fantasies of being punished or overpowered. He also noted a tendency in his female patients towards self-sacrifice, and questioned whether it was nature or nurture that drove women towards 'moral masochism' where they martyred themselves to the needs of others and relinquished all life's pleasures, including sexuality (Freud 1919). Contemporary women patients often struggle to break free from other patterns of self-imposed suffering, including relationships where they feel trapped and unable to extricate themselves from sexual partners who are cruel, tantalising or unsatisfying.

In this chapter I explore the difficulties many women have in recognising their own desire and asserting their needs directly. Instead they often invest their personal potency in others who they identify with or submit to, or their fighting spirit may emerge only in alienated forms, for instance through envy or self-abasement. I begin by discussing female patients who describe a disturbing clash between their conscious hopes for equality with men and an erotic life structured around images of female submission. Sexually these women seek the desire they cannot recognise in themselves through a powerful other who releases them into abandon but remains in control. This often reflects a more general difficulty in seeing themselves as the driving force in their own lives. For instance they may try to live out their ideals through those who seem to possess the passion and ruthlessness they cannot locate in themselves.

Some women who feel that sex is inevitably associated with submission and self-sacrifice choose to deny their need for erotic pleasure altogether. There has been much focus in contemporary psychoanalytic literature on mothers who become erotically pre-occupied with their children (Welldon 1988). In this chapter I look at the relatively neglected question of how motherhood affects women's adult sexual relationships. Drawing on clinical material I suggest that withdrawal from sex may be an uncon-scious way for some mothers to gain a sense of power in the face of feelings of increased helplessness, social isolation and devaluation.

I begin with clinical examples which illustrate how difficult it is for women to break the cycle of expressing desire through psychic battles for domination and submission in order to move towards a greater sense of equality in sexual and emotional life. For instance an impasse may be reached in psychotherapy if sado-masochistic fantasies or activities, or the avoidance of sexual pleasure, are used as a defence against a deep depression associ-ated with profound early pain or loss. In the final section I describe how it is possible for women in psychotherapy to begin to re-own the powerful aggression and desire which they so often experience only in a split-off way through fears and fantasies about male sexual violence.

Why do so many women feel unentitled to assert, even to recognise, their own needs and desires? From my case-examples, several reasons emerge. First, female sexuality is structured through early experiences of mothering as well as through relationships with paternal figures. If the girl is to tolerate the essential unpredictability of erotic intimacy she must internalise the capacity to negotiate and make sense of a range of passionate and ambivalent experiences, including physical excitement and sensual pleasure, tenderness, hostility and envy. If she is not helped to do this, desire may become associated in her mind with fear of annihilation or enthralment to a tyrannical parental imago. Passion and desire may then become inextricably connected with self-abnegation and living vicariously through the enjoyment of others (Benjamin 1988).

A second fundamental problem for the girl is the often-expressed fear that in fighting for autonomy or expressing Oedipal rivalry she will destroy the mother who is both the mainstay of identity and her primary love-object. Fantasies of domination and submission can express a craving for 'masculine' ruthlessness which would help the woman free herself from a sense of psychic enslavement to her mother. This process may be all the more problematic if the girl has no way of identifying with the father or with qualities seen culturally as masculine, which may also exist in the mother.

The female patients I discuss have great difficulty in conceptualising their own sexual pleasure, tending to imagine themselves always as the object of male desire. Since there are few cultural images of a powerful, active sexual desire, it is very difficult for a girl to develop a sense of herself as active and desiring without repudiating femininity. If she attempts to escape from a disappointing early maternal relationship into closeness with the father she may internalise a debased image of femininity through identification with paternal contempt for women. The fear in our culture of a selfish, uncontrollable female sexual passion may also reflect a universal inability to face very early feelings of helplessness, fear and envy in relation to a mother who was experienced as all-powerful, possessing everything.

Female sexuality seems to be a more internal experience which draws on the sensual capacities of the entire body, in contrast to men's sexual pleasure which is so pervasively symbolised through a thrusting, penetrating penis. If the girl can internalise the maternal capacities of both parents enough to contain and understand the intensity of her own excitement, pleasure and rage, while also gaining a sense of herself as active and autonomous, she may be able to recognise her own desire as emanating from inside her. However, many women, like those I describe in the following section, can only think about their passion and excitement by projecting it outside themselves into fantasies of forceful lovers who would compel them to experience their own pleasure.

THE EROTICISATION OF POWER

Ms S, 35, came to see me in a crisis after her husband had left her. She wanted to understand why she chose men who at first seemed kind and reliable but who later turned out to be cruel, unpredictable, even physically violent. Ms S also felt that, although she had been seen as brilliant academically, she could not find a professional outlet for her talents. For practical reasons I was not able to see her for ongoing psychotherapy so I referred her to a colleague.

Ms S had been brought up to believe that she had had a happy childhood with devoted parents, but she was now convinced that she had absorbed a family myth. She wondered whether her pattern of choosing men who were not what they seemed might have originated in an early relationship with her mother which was presented to the world as idyllic, although it was actually deeply troubled. Perhaps, Ms S speculated, her mother might, beneath a façade of devotion, have actually felt profoundly angry with the baby who consolidated an already disappointing marriage. Ms S might have been forced to comply with her mother's insistence that hatred and resentment were unalloyed love. She now found it very hard to recognise her own negative feelings, and to distinguish people who meant her harm from those who had benign intentions towards her.

Ms S described her father as having been dominated by her mother who had quite openly had special friendships, perhaps even affairs with other men in the neighbourhood. Ms S so dreaded humiliating men as she felt her mother had humiliated her father that she repressed her own aggression absolutely, particularly in her dealings with the male sex. The only way in which she could express this part of herself was through men who behaved towards her in destructive or violent ways. She rapidly terminated relationships with men who would treat her well because of her unconscious fear of acting out her identification with a mother she had experienced as castrating. 'When they asked to see me again, I'd say "No" and leave them wondering what was going on', she said. But this did not help her to achieve more equal partnerships. Having rejected her mother's role she found herself constantly taking up her father's position with men who, beneath their urbane public façade, were contemptuous and cruel. Ms S therefore became the helpless victim of men who she unconsciously experienced as the ambivalent mother. In this way she avoided the imagined dangers of rivalling or identifying with a terrifyingly powerful maternal imago.

Ms S had been active in feminist groups for many years, and felt disturbed by what she described as a 'masochistic' sexual fantasy life. Since her teens she had had sexual fantasies about a repulsive, dirty 'macho' man who would penetrate her forcefully. Only through this image could she have an orgasm, whether on her own or with a partner. The fantasies enabled her simultaneously to express and disown a sexuality she experienced as dangerous, dirty and overwhelming. The man in her fantasy would 'overpower me, so the sex wouldn't be my responsibility. . . . He would carry me right away', she said. He forced her to enjoy her own sexuality which she experienced as dirty, dangerous and debased. As Ms S talked it became clear to both of us that this man possessed the 'masculine' ruthlessness she felt she needed in order to differentiate herself from her dominating internal mother.

Because women have so little power in the external world they often invest more of their desire – for recognition, success or other gratifications – in their children. As a working-class woman with an unhappy marriage Ms S's mother both wished for a better life for her daughter and envied her for having this possibility. In turn Ms S felt desperate envy of the mother who dominated the household with a 'masculine' strength, yet could so easily attract men. In discussing how she had sabotaged her chances of professional success, Ms S said that her mother

> pushed me forward, using me as an object to compete with in the extended family. But, I wasn't a son, and so, ultimately she gave me the message – 'It's O.K. to succeed but not too much.' The relationship was so entwined my success would have felt dangerous to both of us. I couldn't afford to arouse her envy, and she'd have lost me if I'd moved into a different world.

Ms S's father had seemed relatively uninterested in his daughter's academic or professional life, and she may also have unconsciously feared surpassing him professionally.

In contrast Ms S described her son as being very well able to assert himself and to get what he wanted by direct means. She admitted that, in producing the son her mother had always longed for, she felt that she was at last superior to her mother in one significant respect. Ms S was simultaneously preoccupied with her son's future achievements and worried that she might alienate him by trying to live vicariously through him, as her mother had done with her. Ms S may have been using her son to express the 'masculine' drive and aggression which she was as yet unable to acknowledge in herself.

Ironically, although Ms S's mother was quite 'masculine' – forceful and penetrating – this only served to exacerbate her daughter's feeling of psychic enslavement, since her mother could not help her to gain a sense of being her own woman. Ms S described how her mother clung to her, whilst simultaneously undermining her. As a result of her inability to gain psychic independence and her unconscious dread of becoming as terrifyingly destructive as she felt her mother to be, Ms S remained stuck in a rigid identification with stereotypical 'feminine' qualities.

The parents' unconscious communications about each other are crucial in determining how the child perceives them. Ms S's father was benign and gentle in his actions but his wife scorned him as ineffectual. This meant that Ms S could identify with him only as another of her mother's victims. She described how her father had tried to intervene between mother and daughter but 'always got pushed out again'. She was angry now that he had not made a serious effort to draw her mother back into the adult world or to create a father–daughter relationship which might have helped her to differentiate herself from her mother. Ms S described how her father had seemed quite unable to acknowledge her burgeoning sexuality. When she was 15 he still bought her sweets and comics as if she were a little girl. Ms S said,

> I imagine that, in an ideal family, the father and daughter are very close, and she means a lot to him. So when she becomes a teenager and has boyfriends he gets jealous, and for a while there may be explosive arguments. But in my family it would be my mother who would fly into ridiculous possessive rages.

In her relationships with men Ms S therefore constantly acted out her internal battles for autonomy from an internal mother against whom she rebelled but could never break free. Preoccupied as she was with the ambivalent yet possessive mother who had been unable to help her differentiate love from hate, Ms S was actually deeply unavailable for heterosexual commitment.

She was constantly anxious about her inability to form a stable relationship with a man, yet since relationships with women dominated her internal world she could be described as emotionally bisexual.

Ms S's problems in expressing aggression were exacerbated by her dread of acting on an identification with a mother who she experienced as destructive to men. Another difficulty was her fear of incurring maternal envy and retaliation if she succeeded in love or professional life. Neither parent had given her a sense that active female sexuality could be a positive force, and she had come to feel that her own desire was dangerous and debased. She had also had few opportunities to identify with paternal forcefulness or ambition. The only way in which she could express 'masculine' aggression and ruthlessness was vicariously, through her real and fantasied relationships with male figures, including her son.

THE CRUEL FATHER

Another woman, Ms T, 31, was also unable to identify consciously with her father and use this relationship to differentiate herself from her mother, but for very different reasons – because she did not want to identify with paternal cruelty. Ms T sought lovers who would physically hurt her, sometimes actually injuring her during sex. She had once been hospitalised with internal injuries. Mostly her partners were men, but she had had one lesbian relationship which she hoped would be more loving. To her dismay she again found herself initiating sado-masochistic activities. She had also been the one to reject her lesbian lover, whereas she experienced men as cruel, neglectful and abandoning. During both lesbian and heterosexual sex Ms T lost herself in elaborate fantasies about a man who was violent and abusive to his pregnant wife and their children. As in Ms S's fantasies the man was notable mainly for his dirty and unpleasant appearance. Ms T came into psychotherapy because she was feeling depressed and worried about the self-destructiveness inherent in her more dangerous sexual activities.

Ms T described her parents as uninterested in her struggles to get on well at school and unsupportive, even obstructive, of her wish to go to university. Nevertheless she had persevered with her studies despite great odds. When she came to psychotherapy she had recently embarked on a career involving art restoration, having through determined effort won a much-coveted job in preference to other applicants with more experience in the field.

Ms T's childhood had been bleak and frightening, although there were no dramatically bad events that she could remember. As the first child of a depressed mother who had recently lost several close relatives Ms T was often left crying desperately on her own. As a toddler she escaped into what she remembers as an idyllic companionship with her father. She felt entirely abandoned when her father suddenly transferred his interest to the first in a long line of sons whom he often hit.

My patient insisted that her father had never sexually abused her, but his interest in her seems at times to have been quite obviously sexualised. For instance, when she was 4 he took baths with her and put great effort into dressing her up prettily to take her out. In her teens she remembers him flying into rages where he would hurl sexualised verbal abuse at her. She experienced her own often pregnant mother as being unable to protect her children from her husband's verbal violence and bullying. She told me that her father had never hit her mother, but he had allowed her to wear herself out with physical work in the home without offering much help or support.

Ms T had identified with a debased image of the sexual mother, seen as subjugated to the father, and now saw all sexual involvement with men as self-abasement. Unconsciously she saw her father's violence towards her brothers as a kind of love and this may have strengthened her childhood wish to be 'one of the boys'. Although she did not continue to get special attention she was the only child who was never hit. Once her father became preoccupied with her brothers Ms T sought out the company of a gang of risk-taking older boys whose leader alternately favoured and mistreated her physically, an experience which greatly influenced her sexual life.

Ms T had read some psychoanalytic literature in an attempt to understand her own pleasure in pain. One paper by Freud, 'A Child is Being Beaten', resonated with her own experience (Freud 1919). Freud explains in this paper that a girl's fantasies of another child being beaten are a disguised, masochistic way of enjoying the exclusive love of the Oedipal father. Instead of saying 'Father loves me', the fantasy expresses the more acceptable, less incestuous, 'Father defeats or beats only me' or 'Father is copulating with me in this painful, beating way because he loves me' (Meltzer 1978, re-phrasing Freud). Ms T could see that in imagination she was receiving a form of painful, sexualised paternal love.

After two and a half years of three times weekly psychotherapy Ms T had successfully reduced contact with sadistic men and given up her more dangerous sexual practices. But then a new set of problems arose. Previously she had projected her own destructiveness onto lovers who had abused her body. Now she began to turn it against herself, unconsciously beginning to unravel the successful life she had so painstakingly built up for herself. Her work, in which she was utterly absorbed, seemed to have had a reparative effect on her emotional life. In fantasy she constantly damaged her internal family, but through restoring works of art she attempted to make up for her own destructiveness. Her sado-masochistic activities may also have temporarily allayed anxieties about her own destructiveness, since in reality she survived the exquisite tortures enacted on the women and children in her fantasies.

She was devastated then, when she was suddenly made redundant in a work-place re-shuffle. After losing her job she began to spiral downwards, becoming increasingly passive and unable to think realistically about how to find a new job. She was reluctant to apply for lower-grade work, or to take steps that might help her to compete with the more highly qualified people who were applying for jobs like the one she had previously. I was seriously worried about how depressed she was becoming, and how near she was to losing all financial security.

I was also beginning to realise how determined Ms T was never to imagine herself as aggressive or persecuting, for instance through acknowledging the brutal father of her fantasies as a part of her own psyche. This was worrying too, since if she were ever to move out of the victim role, an essential first step would be to recognise her capacity to hurt or abuse others, including myself. Ms T insisted that in her fantasies she always identified with the tortured mother and siblings, but never with the sadistic father. She could not even think about the possibility that through her own fantasies about the cruel father she might be punishing her mother for infantile neglect and Oedipal betrayal in producing the new babies, and also torturing the brothers who she had hated as well as loved. Ms T saw both herself and her mother as entirely innocent and benign. She was adamant that her painful early relationship with her mother had nothing to do with her current difficulties in combining love and sexual desire.

Ms T also found it far more difficult to talk about her lesbian relationship than her experiences with men. At first she said that she now considered it to be wrong and did not want to have sex again with another woman. The vehemence of her view on this surprised me slightly, since she was well aware that the sexual violence she allowed male partners to perpetrate against her would have aroused far more abhorrence amongst her friends and colleagues. I later wondered whether there were other reasons why she might now want to avoid thinking about or experiencing lesbian desire. For instance it appeared that she had been more conscious of her own cruelty in that relationship and that she had not been able to see herself entirely or even mainly as the victim, either sexually or emotionally. Perhaps she wanted to avoid her own sadism towards women (including myself in the transference) so absolutely that she would also rule out the possibility of lesbian desire.

At the beginning of psychotherapy Ms T had experienced me as the perfect nurturing maternal figure. But once she lost her job she began to feel intensely critical of me, so that I felt I could do nothing right. If I tried to help her to explore her imperviousness to danger she would become defensive, and accuse me of being critical and undermining like her father. But when I decided to say less she was equally angry with what she experienced as my passive maternal neglect.

I began to feel that I was being tortured in these sessions as she re-created in me her own victimised state of mind. I said that she was letting me know how it felt to be continually criticised and misinterpreted, as she had described feeling with her father. She told me that the therapeutic impasse we seemed to have reached had nothing to do with her. It was I who had changed and become cruel like her father, she said. Again she could see herself only as the innocent victim of other people's aggression. I suggested that she was afraid of acknowledging any responsibility for her difficulties with me, lest she begin to see in herself the aggression she projected so entirely onto paternal figures, including myself in the transference.

When she did not see me as the cruel father, Ms T likened me to her passive long-suffering mother. All women were sexual masochists she said, just as, in her experience, all men could be lured into sexually sadistic practices. At this point she told me that she needed a male analyst who would speak with confident authority and also wield real power in the world of psychotherapy. Her hope now as in childhood was that she'd be rescued by a powerful idealised male who would magically whisk her from the quagmire of her early relationship with her mother, which was re-emerging through the transference.

Betty Joseph, a Kleinian psychoanalyst, describes a feeling of 'being driven up to the edge of things' which may emerge in the transference with patients like Ms T whose internal worlds are dominated by fantasies of destructive parental intercourse. Both patient and analyst feel tortured, Joseph says, as in Ms T's psychotherapy with me. Joseph speculates that in infancy experiences that might have led to depression were felt instead as terrible pain that turned to torment. To defend themselves against this torment the patient took over the inflicting of mental pain onto themselves and built it into a world of sado-masochistic excitement. As infants these patients withdrew into a 'secret world of violence where part of the self has been turned against another part, and parts of the body being identified with the offending object, and this violence has been highly sexualised, masturbatory in nature, and often physically expressed' (Joseph 1982: 322).

This does make sense of the inner world of Ms T who described this quality of frantic sexualised violence both in her play with older boys, and in her solitary quasi-masturbatory games. Instead of moving forward into real relationships with people Ms T seemed as a child to have retreated into herself and then lived out sexualised relationships in fantasy and sometimes in violent bodily activity. In therapy, as elsewhere, she used her enthralment with self-inflicted pain as a defence against emotional growth or dependency on others. Unconsciously she saw vulnerability as dangerous, so in her sexual relationships she used sado-masochistic activities and patterns as a way of controlling intimacy. Similarly she had begun to experience psychotherapy as sado-masochistic.

How is a psychotherapist to break through the impasse that arises when the patient comes to perceive them as so persecutory? One problem is that such patients may well elicit hostile feelings in the countertransference. Yet, although there were moments when I did feel enraged or frustrated, on the whole I knew that I was not attacking Ms T even though she felt that I was. Kernberg in a 1994 lecture suggests that the psychoanalyst must stand their ground and insist that although the patient sees them as persecutory, this is not true, thus challenging the patient to re-own the persecutory parts of themselves which they have projected onto the therapist.

But Ms T did not seem to have the psychic strength to face any challenges to her very fragile emotional equilibrium. Although she had given up many of her masochistic sexual activities Ms T found it excruciatingly difficult to relinquish her sado-masochistic fantasy life. She had come to rely on these fantasised scenarios more than on everyday relationships with others and believed that she would never enjoy sex without them. Her fantasies were also her final defence against suicidal despair or psychic disintegration.

She could tolerate discussion of her sexual sado-masochism as a defence against experiences of loss, pain and abandonment which have never been listened to or understood. She could also see the way she was using physical violation as a substitute and a protection against the re-emergence of that psychic pain (Khan 1989). But the only aspect of her aggression which Ms T could acknowledge was her envy of the maternal riches that she felt I was withholding from her. She had heard that I worked at The Women's Therapy Centre and told me that my female colleagues must be lavishing me with the nurturing that she herself longed for.

Ms T had absorbed from her father a debased view of female sexuality which reinforced her identification with a mother who she saw as subjugated to him. In psychoanalytic theory there is little mention of the father who denigrates the mother as in Ms T's family. There tends to be more discussion about the mother who devalues the father and gives the child the impression that he or she is the only one she loves. There is a particular risk for the daughter who after a painful infancy turns away from an unresponsive mother, as Ms T did, to a father who is contemptuous of her sex. The girl then has no protection against the father's seductiveness, which may be expressed unconsciously, or his contempt for femininity.

Ms S and Ms T share a common dread of acknowledging or

expressing their own aggression towards others. Unconsciously they are terrified of losing their love-objects, both internal and external, through their own destructiveness. Accordingly they sacrifice themselves in order to protect the other, who is unconsciously experienced as an omnipotent parental figure to whom they are in thrall. They feel that they have no option but to submit, becoming what the other wants them to be. To ward off abandonment they recognise other people's needs without expecting reciprocation, accepting that they can make no real difference to what happens while they remain in the relationship. They are prepared to relinquish their own difference and separateness in order to remain the object of desire. Obviously there is a strong component of aggression, submission and domination in all sexuality. When does a play with domination become real domination? If one partner controls the other, perhaps unconsciously, restricting their ability to have an impact on what happens between them, is it useful to describe the relationship as sado-masochistic?

In my own clinical practice I do not use the term 'masochistic' except to refer to sexual masochism, that is, activities which induce erotic pleasure through extreme pain or violation. Even then, I usually wait and see whether the patient uses the word first. I am extremely cautious and sceptical of the broader use of this concept because discussion of emotional or moral masochism so often leads to the denigration of women – and sometimes of male patients also. In this area, where the psychotherapist's own moral and political biases can rapidly emerge, controversy has always raged.

For instance in 1924 Helene Deutsch referred to the masochistic pleasures of childbirth, and also suggested that the enjoyment of the physical and emotional aspects of motherhood might have served as compensation for female exclusion from culture. Her theory was criticised by Karen Horney, who attributed female 'masochism' to economic and cultural discrimination (Horney 1926). In response Deutsch stressed that she did not believe that women want to be humiliated (Deutsch 1930). On the contrary, Deutsch said, women must preserve themselves against injuries to their self-esteem threatened by the cultural association of masochism with mothering by identifying with an active, forceful image of the mother.

Seventy years later these issues still remain contentious, even though late twentieth-century women are free for the first time to delay pregnancy until they have established themselves in a career, or avoid motherhood entirely, whilst also pursuing an active sexual life. Ironically this new freedom has given at least one male psychoanalyst a new opportunity to level the charge of masochism at women. In a 1994 lecture Otto Kernberg described as masochistic those women who are so frightened of having a child that they wait until they are 'menopausal', thus exposing themselves to dangers including badly chosen marriage partners. In fact those women who expose themselves and their children to different, but not necessarily greater, dangers than younger mothers, may well be trying to find a way of balancing their needs for family life and success in the external world. In our culture it is often women rather than men who feel that they have to make a stark choice between prioritising a career or children in early adulthood.

Even if we do not wish to describe such fundamental female dilemmas as 'masochistic', we must still ask why women find it so difficult to assert their right to equality within personal relationships and the culture at large. This question was crucial for Freud, who argued that the girl becomes submissive, accepting her father's desire as her own at the point where she acknowledges that she can never be male and can only possess masculinity by proxy, through heterosexual sex and producing male penis-babies. Freud went on to argue that women become self-sacrificial, renouncing sexual pleasure, if their erotic desire becomes allied to a cruel super-ego, the internalised representation of the sadistic father. Then sadism, allowed no other outlet, is turned back on the self. Freud saw masochism as an expression of 'feminine' passivity in both sexes since unconsciously it implied a wish to take up a defeated (castrated) stance in relation to the father (Freud 1919, 1924c, 1931).

Chasseguet-Smirgel (1964b), from a more mother-centred Freudian perspective, argues that the daughter accepts male domination, offering herself to the father as a dependent 'part object' or 'thing', because of her particular difficulties in differentiating herself from the much-envied early mother rather than because she wants to be male. Arguing that there is no place in psychoanalytic theory for women's active sadism, their aggressive drives, she describes a particular kind of envious guilt suffered by some girls who denigrate the mother and idealise the father in their desperation to gain autonomy (Chasseguet-Smirgel 1964b). Having identified with a mother who she experiences as castrating towards the father, such a woman may feel that her vagina is dangerous and develop sexual inhibitions. She may also dread competing in traditionally male spheres because of an unconscious fear of damaging the father. Chasseguet-Smirgel's account is particularly relevant to Ms S, who feared identifying with her mother's destructiveness towards men, and so became passive and inhibited in sexual and professional life. ·

I agree that women's inability to cope with envy and hostility towards both parents is crucial in maintaining the vicious circle of female subordination. However, I would place a greater emphasis on the way in which social factors, including real sex discrimination and devaluation, interact with psychic difficulties in separating from the mother. Experiences of powerlessness and exclusion are inevitable in childhood. But it is not inevitable that they should become subsumed into a distorted view of sexual difference as children become aware of their position in the gender hierarchy.

According to the feminist psychoanalyst Jessica Benjamin, the masochist does not seek pleasure in pain, as Freud argued, but an opportunity to submit, to surrender the will under conditions of control and safety. Benjamin describes a special variant of female masochism, 'ideal love', where the woman idealises and yearns for unattainable men – the 'heroic sadist' – who can arouse their passion and desire in a way that no one else can. She quotes Simone de Beauvoir who says, 'When woman gives herself completely to her idol she hopes he will give her at once possession of herself and of the universe he represents' (Benjamin 1988: 116). Benjamin argues that the woman is searching for an experience of excitement and containment that she lacked in childhood. She relates this to the failure of our culture to provide images of powerful female desire. Through the relationship the woman feels that she can escape from an internal mother seen as weak, engulfing and long-suffering, as Ms T felt her mother to be. The lover is so detached that the woman unconsciously feels that he won't be destroyed by the intensity of her anger or need, as she dreaded that her mother would be. Beneath the sensationalisation of power and powerlessness lies a distorted wish for recognition and intimacy with an equal other (Benjamin 1988).

This is a most convincing explanation of the way psyche and society interact in creating female submissiveness. But it contains many generalisations about male–female interaction, and does not offer an account of lesbian experience.

As Benjamin points out this dynamic is often played out between partners who continually move together and then detach emotionally. The following extract, where a lesbian sado-maso-chist parodies the emotional power-plays in relationships between women, could as easily describe a heterosexual interaction.

> Let's start a relationship and hurt each other a lot, OK? You be needy and demanding and fearful and manipulative, and I'll be cool and tough and withdraw further from you while meanwhile becoming totally dependent on you. Then you fall in love with someone else and leave me with no warning. We'll both be broken for months by grief and guilt. Sounds like a good time?
>
> (Samois, quoted by Merck 1993a: 250)

In order to understand whether lesbian and heterosexual power-plays really are similar it would be necessary to look more closely at how each woman unconsciously experienced the interplay between psychic 'masculinity' and 'femininity' in themselves and their partner.

In recent years there has been little feminist or psychoanalytic literature on the practice of heterosexual sado-masochism. In con-trast the issue has been the focus of fierce controversy amongst feminist lesbians who have developed an extensive literature on lesbian sado-masochism. Even here, though, there seems to be little discussion of female sadism. Mandy Merck points out that there is often little detailed description of actual lesbian sado-masochistic activities. This facilitates the illusion that women are not really cruel to each other, and do not unconsciously fantasise about attacking or humiliating the internal mother (Merck 1993a). Obviously some women, including Ms T, the patient described earlier, find it easier to experience themselves as suffering victims than cruel perpetrators, especially in relation to members of their own sex. But I agree with Freud that sadism and masochism always co-exist in the personality, even though the individual may be aware of only one of these characteristics. Furthermore, I believe it is vital for women to face up to their aggression, including their capacity to be sadistic towards others. Only once we acknowledge that aspect of our personalities will we be able to draw on this 'masculine' forcefulness and use it creatively to fight for personal and political equality.

In the following section I return to my earlier discussion about the interaction between psychic and cultural factors in maternal self-sacrifice, an issue which has been central to psychoanalytic discussion of female masochism. I discuss how one woman withdrew from sex after her first child was born in an unconscious attempt to solve internal conflicts about domination and submission.

MATERNITY AND SEXUALITY

Ms D came for twice-weekly psychotherapy for over five years, leaving just before the birth of her first child. When she first sought help she had been in a state of shock because her husband had suddenly left her. In that relationship she had relinquished all her own needs, using the withdrawal of sex as a form of covert revenge. Ms D told me that without her husband she realised that she had little sense of her own identity. During psychotherapy she embarked on a new career and eventually began another relationship. Ms D gained psychic strength through exploring her inner world, but there seemed to be a piece of emotional work that she still could not do. 'There's a corner I can't turn', she told me before she left. Her internal world was still dominated by relationships where one figure was powerful and idealised, the other denigrated and submissive. In psychotherapy she had become fixed in a pattern of seeing me as denigrated, and controlling me in fantasy.

Two years after her daughter's birth Ms D returned to see me four times. She told me then that she had become depressed after the birth of her daughter. She did not feel able to afford regular sessions at that time but we left open the possibility that she might come back for more help in the future. My discussion here is based on her reflections in those sessions about what had remained unresolved when she left psychotherapy the first time.

When she returned after the two-year gap Ms D told me that after her child's birth she had again lost all sexual desire, even though her new relationship had initially been exciting and fulfilling. Ms D described how she had at first felt very emotionally secure with her young lover who 'never ran away or pretended not to be interested'. She went on to say,

> In the beginning I was financially and socially dominant. I paid for everything. I could then. I felt in control and could be sexually relaxed, submissive. I play-acted being a feminine soft thing. But in outdoor life I was confrontational, bold and cruel. But what I really loved was getting into the passenger-seat of his old van, and going out on a date. I was 36 then, but I felt fifteen to twenty years younger. Then a man-friend went away and lent me a sleek new black Porsche. When I got behind the wheel, he looked like a poor weak vulnerable thing in the passenger seat. I'd have liked him to turn the tables on that when I was at my most helpless – after having the baby. I've always had to maintain a controlling role and yet because I can't solve our financial difficulties, I feel passive. I can't breathe or function. The only way I know how to be dominant is to say 'No' sexually. We'd both like there to be more give and take, but I don't seem good at equality.

While in the emotional driving seat Ms D could be sexually open, but she was afraid that she would become subservient if she let herself be emotionally vulnerable. After the birth of their baby she initially felt she'd completely lost all control over her life. This was exacerbated by her sudden feeling of being absolutely on her own most of the time with her baby. She had assumed that she and her partner would share the baby's care but this did not happen. Ms D could not find part-time work in her field and her partner did not want to give up his promising career. She felt cheated, since he had wanted a baby at least as much as she did. But after the birth Ms D could see no option other than giving up work for full-time childcare.

Ms D suddenly felt that she had lost all social value once she was out of the workplace. There was some reality in this since in our society motherhood is simultaneously idealised and devalued. But just as significantly the mothering role, whether undertaken by men or women, puts the parent in touch with infantile experiences of humiliation, helplessness and envy from which activity in the external world can provide an escape. Ms D had previously been able to avoid facing those aspects of herself, through living

vicariously through her successful ex-husband and by later achiev-
ing some professional status of her own.

Ms D told me that despite her depression she had soon come
to love looking after her baby. The freedom that at first she felt
she had lost completely quickly came to appear 'a poor empty
thing' in contrast to the joys of motherhood. Since her daughter's
birth Ms D had identified with her mother, recreating the kind
of exclusive twosome that she imagined she might have had in
infancy. But Ms D's inability to envisage equality in relationships
also caused difficulties with her daughter. She thought that as an
infant she might have felt entirely controlled by a dominating
maternal figure. The only way that she felt able to avoid tyrannis-
ing her daughter now was to relinquish her needs entirely and to
submit herself to the child's desires. 'I see myself as a robot, my
daughter's life-support system', Ms D said. 'I'm a safety-net for
her, not an individual apart from her. But the bad side of this is
that sometimes I get lost in her. I simply react to her, rather than
taking up a strong position and guiding her.'

Ms D was worried that her daughter might also find it difficult
in adulthood to create equal relationships. Indeed if the cycle of
domination and submission is to be broken the mother must find
a way of balancing her own needs with those of the child. But
in order to allow her child to experiment with aggression and
independence while simultaneously setting limits, the mother herself needs a sense that she is an autonomous person, a sense of
her own subjectivity which Ms D was still struggling to develop.

Ms D's difficulties with her daughter reflected those with her
own mother, who had been unable to help her tolerate and give
meaning to her own early pain, envy and hostility. Her father's
lack of involvement had exacerbated Ms D's problems in coming
to terms with being separate and different from her mother, a
dynamic she later re-enacted with me. Reviewing her psychotherapy in retrospect she pointed out that she had always resisted
facing the fact that she was my patient rather than my friend.
She thought that she might have maintained the illusion of being
in an idyllic mother–daughter couple with me in order to avoid
facing early experiences of bleakness in relationship to a mother
who had recently told her that she found babies boring. Ms D
thought that her mother might have coped with this lack of
empathy with her children through imposing fixed ideas about
the 'pretty sweet things' infants should be. Ms D thought her

mother might have idealised her daughter when she appeared to live up to this image and rejected her when she didn't.

Ms D imagined that she had probably felt utterly shocked when, during her fourth year, her mother had suddenly arrived home with a new baby sister. She could not remember having been close to her father, who tended to shut himself away from the children even when he was at home. Ms D now thought that her mother might have excluded him from family life. The only child to whom he had paid special attention was the new little sister. By the time my patient had grown up her father had left the family and now made little effort to maintain contact with his children.

In her new family Ms D was again repeating the pattern of excluding the father, so that there was never a threesome or a close parental couple, but two partnerships that revolved around childcare. When her partner was home he looked after their daughter alone and the rest of the time she did. Ms D felt so envious of his capacity to escape from the family and pursue his career that she wrought an unconscious revenge, depriving him of sexual and emotional intimacy, even though she knew she would feel devastated if he left her.

She went on to tell me that she had begun to treat her partner in the same way as she had treated me. 'Why did I always need to criticise you and keep you at a distance?' she asked. Her answer now was that she denigrated me in order to avoid feeling envious and inadequate. 'When I admire someone I want to be them. When I realise I can't become them envy sets in and I start to tear them to bits', she said.

By projecting disliked parts of herself onto myself and others, and then controlling us in fantasy by constant contemptuous criticism, Ms D kept herself from turning the corner into depression. But this was also a way of avoiding psychic change. I remembered how when she was in regular psychotherapy with me she attempted to avoid feeling inferior and envious by unconsciously trying to stir up those emotions in me. For instance, near the end of one session she had suddenly remarked that everyone would agree, it was a fact, that she was prettier and had more sense of style than I did. She went on to say that she hated all pot-plants and particularly the ones I had in my consulting-room. My decor was dated and the plants belonged to a previous era. I felt shocked by the suddenness of this attack, and was momentarily unable to think clearly. Indeed that day I did feel very tired and drab and I wondered whether it really was true that my pot-plants looked that way too.

During the next session Ms D talked about her own current feelings of inadequacy, telling me, 'I can never grow plants and I desperately envy anyone who can keep them alive.' She then went on to talk about her lack of progress in psychotherapy. She felt lifeless and empty inside and unable to grow emotionally. In contrast she envied the fact that I seemed to have more internal resources. She also talked about her alarm at seeing the visible signs of her body ageing. She felt anxious about losing her good looks and appearing to be a relic of a bygone era, a characteristic she had attributed to my pot-plants.

Contempt for women and their sexuality can be one of the hardest aspects of the maternal transference for a female therapist and patient to tolerate and explore. Often there is no man present in the room but the patient speaks with the internalised voice of the chauvinist men she so often criticises. It is difficult for the therapist fully to analyse this aspect of the transference when the patient's comments resonate too closely with her own feelings of self-devaluation as a woman.

Now that she had a child of her own Ms D felt angry that her father had not helped her find a pathway out of the claustrophobic frustrations of infancy into the external world. She told me that she had got from me the kind of 'objective' attention she had seen her father give her sister and it was this that had previously enabled her to begin her new career. Only Ms D's younger sister, her father's favourite, had received special attention from him, and she was the only daughter who had identified with his personal characteristics. She had been the recipient of what Ms D described as a more unconditional love than their mother could give. Her sister had been able through this to develop a stronger sense of her own needs and interests. At 6 her sister already geared her day around hobbies, something Ms D's father greatly admired, while my patient was looking for her own reflection in other girls, and, increasingly, boys. 'I was a flibbertigibbet, a butterfly. Thank goodness I was pretty they said.' It was assumed (quite rightly) that she'd marry young. Accordingly, as with many middle-class girls of her generation, no one bothered to talk to her about what work she'd do until she'd actually left school. In this way her psychological difficulties were reinforced by stereotyped gender expectations.

It is at the toddler stage, a transitional point where the infant begins to test out fantasy against reality, that the mother's own internalisation of women's second-class cultural status impinges on the girl's external world with renewed force. This can result in the inhibition of the daughter's capacity to play with fantasy and experiment with actualities (Ernst 1987). The boy at this stage denies helplessness through identification with the idealised father while the girl has no alternative but to confront her own helplessness, which may result in her losing much of her exploratory enthusiasm. If there is no actual father in the family the mother's own relationship to her internal father and to the male aspects of her own psyche is crucial.

In most psychoanalytic theories there is still a tendency to assume that the movement from the mother is emancipatory: the girl is saved from an undifferentiated immersion in the infantile world into the sturdy autonomy engendered by heterosexual closeness with the father. His authority is supposed to protect us from irrationality and submission. But this theory reflects and reinforces the devaluation of women and motherhood. It also underestimates the way real mothers devote most of their energy to fostering independence, inculcating the social and moral values that make up the super-ego. It is usually they who set limits to the child's desire for erotic closeness and wish for omnipotent control. But paradoxically the father's distance and mother's closeness conspire to produce a disproportionate idealisation of the symbolic father (Benjamin 1988).

The girl needs to identify with 'phallic' masculinity, with an image of active femininity as well as with receptive, containing functions. We need to recognise both the 'holding' mother and the exciting father as elements which make up desire. The child needs to be able to play in infancy with a range of cross-sex identifications, accepting difference by making it familiar. In this way the girl might be able to sustain her own curiosity about exploring the outside world, as well as her agency and desire.

The problem for the women I have discussed so far in this chapter is that they belong to a generation who expect to be treated with the respect due to an equal in sexual, emotional and professional life. Yet both their unconscious fantasy lives and external realities militate against this. For instance Ms D's experience of being able to surrender to sexual passion when she feels financially dominant suggests a very concrete connection between economic and cultural independence and the free expression of desire.

Women whose internal relationships are dominated by patterns of submission and domination will tend to act these out with children as well as adults. The details of these interactions will vary dramatically between different families but the child's sex will have an impact on the way in which the parents negotiate envy and aggression. For instance Ms S's relationship to her son's 'masculine' assertiveness was markedly different from her own childhood experience.

Each of the female patients I have described so far shares a profound difficulty in symbolising and thinking about their own erotic desire. Although their mothers were not necessarily passive or subservient in reality, each had identified with a debased, subservient image of female sexuality. This was reinforced by their inability to identify with masculinity, which had become idealised as unattainable. Their unresolved envy and internalised contempt for their own sex emerged in quite dramatic ways within the maternal transference, evoking intense countertransference reactions in me.

It is clear then that women need simultaneously to fight for cultural and psychic change. In the following section I discuss how one woman began to break through this cycle, through becoming aware of and questioning her own sense of herself as a helpless victim. In psychotherapy she began to integrate the desire and aggression which she had previously projected outside herself through obsessive fear of male violence.

THE WOMAN WHO STOOD UP FOR HERSELF

Ms X, 27, came for a consultation because her colleagues were concerned that she had completely lost her professional air of calm competence and cried all day. This was her story: She had woken up one night to see a young man standing by her bed. He jumped on to her bed. She was terrified but stayed calm, kept the bedclothes pulled up, and asked him what he wanted. 'Sex', he replied. He then asked her whether she had any cash. She said that she had very little because she hadn't been able to get to the bank. She was used to dealing with young men like him, she said – he reminded her of those who used the project for which she worked. 'Do you believe in God?' he asked. She said she did and he left without harming her or stealing anything. But since then she'd become increasingly disturbed, wondering obsessively what the man had broken into her flat for. Her lover of five years had recently gone abroad to work. She wasn't sure why she hadn't gone with him and now thought of joining him. When she mentioned that to her parents, her mother, who had a history of depression, had taken an overdose and put herself in hospital. She was the only child of working-class parents who were determined that she should have greater opportunities for fulfilment than they had.

Ms X felt unable fully to differentiate herself psychically from her mother and was constantly drawn into the middle of conflicts in a passionate yet fraught parental relationship. She felt that her father had always tended to bully her mother. I offered her the only space available at The Women's Therapy Centre – six months' brief psychotherapy – to focus on psychic separation from her mother. She said, 'I can usually do most things with a bit of help.' Professionally she was highly competent, had stable relationships and up to now had sailed through difficulties with aplomb.

It soon became clear that the police were certain what the man was looking for. They were full of admiration for my patient since they believed that she alone had managed to protect herself from a serial rapist who had assaulted many women in her neighbourhood. But she could not accept the fact that she had managed to avoid becoming a victim of violence, something she had always feared intensely.

Her early sessions were full of very chaotic images of sexual violence and attack which had been lurking in her mind since childhood. This alternated with the re-emergence of her cool composed façade. For instance when she talked about her perfect relationship with her absent boyfriend I felt puzzled – it was just too good to be true. The intensities of vulnerability, passion or anger were denied, associated unconsciously with dangerous destructiveness or loss. This repression of passion was associated with two abandonments. The first was very brief. Her mother developed a fever after her birth, and her father had been unable to look after her and had left her in a different hospital for a week. The second abandonment happened when in her sixteenth year her apparently happy mother had suddenly admitted herself to psychiatric hospital for depression.

Even at 16 my patient had demonstrated a capacity to stand up for herself, telling her father who had left her to do all the washing-up while her mother was in hospital that he must do his share, and could not bully her as he did her mother – she had her homework to do. Through the encounter with the rapist she had been able to use this assertiveness. But she had also been confronted with an aggressive part of herself which had previously been projected onto violent men. An incident at work illustrated her attempts to come to terms with these aspects of herself. She'd been advising a couple who'd been illegally evicted. When it emerged that they were members of a neo-Nazi organisation her colleagues pointed out that their anti-racist charter meant that their organisation could not help such people. She argued that she had good communication with the couple and felt they should be challenged into discussion about their politics rather than banned. In the same way she was wondering whether the aggressive aspects of herself could be negotiated with and integrated, rather than being completely excluded as before.

As she began to acknowledge that she had stood up for herself physically she began to think she might risk more emotional autonomy from myself as a maternal figure. After twelve weeks she decided to join her lover but returned six months later, again distraught, because the relationship had ended. We made a new six-month contract, so that in all she would have seen me for nine months.

She now began to see me as an envious maternal figure clinging to her in psychotherapy, begrudging her happiness. She embarked on a new sexual relationship where she could be more emotionally open. But at first she did not tell me about it because she feared that I might spoil it with envious interpretations. On the other hand she was delighted to discover a book I'd edited with a chapter by me on mother–daughter envy. She was relieved to see that I could get on with something in her absence and that I might understand about envious mothers. A different, more resourceful and independent aspect of her mother's character began to emerge within the transference. She remembered that her mother had been a pillar of the local community, always active and highly competent. Now that she was more able to acknowledge maternal strengths with which she had identified, she could also acknowledge her need to depend on others, for instance on me.

I also represented a caring paternal figure who stood by while she faced up to the reality of her relationship with her mother. Before her last session she dreamed that an old bearded man, associated with me, sat at an easel on a cliff-top painting a picture on a piece of cloud. While this therapist-father looked on, creating evanescent images of her internal world, she walked onto the beach. It was entirely covered with driftwood which she knew that for some reason she had to clear into an orderly pile. She felt daunted by this but knew by the end of the dream (and her therapy) that she had tidied up the driftwood, even though she had no visual image of the neat pile.

She had initially disparaged her father, saying that he was thoughtless and emotionally withdrawn. But I was struck by how sensitive he had been in his behaviour to her after the break-in. He also gave her much practical help. When I mentioned this she said that her colleagues always called him 'your wonderful father'. She was interested in but only partially convinced by the idea that he might have been a better parent than she had previously thought. She observed that she had previously feared her mother's jealousy if she acknowledged closeness to her father. But she also pointed out that he had failed to look after her at crucial times – after all, why had he taken her as a baby to the hospital? And she bitterly resented his bullying of her mother and the way her parents burdened her with their marital difficulties rather than sorting the issues out between them. It also became clear that her mother might also have had 'paternal' strengths, for instance the capacity to help her daughter gain confidence in the external world. Ms X linked her own success in most spheres to the absolute certainty both parents had had that she would be good at everything she undertook.

It was now clear that inside her were two separate worlds. The later very positive and affirmative relationship with both parents was a shallow layer on top of a fracture. The rapist's intrusion had precipitated the eruption of an earlier more persecutory relationship resulting from the early separation, and perhaps from the internalisation of an emotional fragility which her mother 'carried' for both parents. In a follow-up visit after the ending of therapy it emerged that the family obsession with protecting her from male violence stemmed from her parents' experience of violent abandoning fathers. She also knew that her mother had suffered some childhood trauma, perhaps sexual. My patient had internalised a threatening male figure, through her father's identification with and dread of being like his own violent father, and her mother's unconsciously communicated experience of having been victimised.

The combination of involvement and protectiveness from a father who is valued by the mother is unusual in women who seek psychotherapy. This woman was also fortunate in that she felt her parents to be devoted to each other despite their rather tortured relationship. This gave her some basis on which she could begin to build loving sexual attachments herself. Her success in the external world had been due to identification with both her father's personal efficacy and her mother's competence. Perhaps even more important was the fact that she did not suffer the same envy or obstructiveness described by the other female patients. Both parents were united in a strong desire that she should do better than they had. A combination of vulnerability – her heightened expectation of attack – and strength – her ability to stand up for herself – had helped her to avoid being attacked. It was also crucial that her parents had been physically and sexually protective, even though her mother might herself have been an abuse victim.

CONCLUSION

How does a woman come to 'own' her powerful desires, to experience them in her mind and body in a way which allows her to assert her wants both in sexual life and in other spheres of existence? And how can psychotherapy assist her in this? In the clinical setting feelings of internal persecution or psychic enslavement, of being the object rather than the subject of desire, can emerge as intense contempt, envy and denigration of women and 'femininity' within the maternal transference. If this resonates with the psychotherapist's own feelings of self-devaluation as a woman, countertransference difficulties may arise. Women who enter the caring professions often have an intensely critical super-ego, which demands continual perfect attention to the needs of others. Thorough analyses may help to increase women's self-esteem but they cannot alter the fact that in our society women's second-class status is continually reinforced in ways we know too well to notice consciously.

In order to forge a psychic link between freedom and sexual desire girls must find a way of attaining autonomy from the mother and identifying with the father, or psychic 'masculinity' without devaluing womanhood (Benjamin 1988). The parents' wishes and desires towards the daughter, and the way she situates herself in relation to these desires, are crucial determinants of the success of this process. In particular, the daughter, who may have the potential for a much more fulfilling life than her mother, can find herself the object of intense parental envy. The unconscious fear many women feel of losing the mother's love if they become too autonomous and successful is a defence against the daughter's own envy, but it may be compounded by real experiences with an envious mother. This fear of maternal envy combines with actual external sexual discrimination to form a serious impediment to change. It is crucial that parents protect daughters from their own envy and rivalry, instilling in girls their own desire that they succeed both in conventionally 'masculine' and 'feminine' activities. This parental belief in the daughter's capacity for personal fulfilment is a vital antidote to the cultural devaluation of femininity.

Ideally each individual's sexuality should be mediated through a range of experiences and identifications which transcends stereotypical gender formulas. The girl needs to develop a mental space where she can think about and symbolise her own desire through identification with the 'maternal' containing functions of male and female parental figures, as well as the 'exciting' qualities of both sexes. She also needs to identify with psychological masculinity, with the kind of active sexuality seen culturally as 'phallic'. And ideally she should have paternal figures (who might be female), to help her gain a sense of herself as psychically separate, and to help her find a way out into the external world.

However, the girl who internalises a range of cross-gender identifications will still have to struggle to synthesise this sense of independent selfhood with the reality of being a woman, since there are so few images of active and autonomous female sexuality. Female sexuality will not alter through psychological change alone. There also needs to be a re-structuring of social attitudes and institutions – including the institution of psychoanalytic psychotherapy. Psychotherapy is no more immune to issues of gender-based power and status than any other arena of activity – indeed, the nature of the therapeutic enterprise makes it inevitable that such issues will be at the heart of the therapist–client relationship. Male social power and female subordination are among the crucial forces structuring the transference and countertransference, as the following chapter explores.

Chapter 6

Gender in the transference relationship

In a classic psychoanalytic textbook the North American psycho-analyst Ralph Greenson wrote in 1967 that 'all cases of eroticised transference I have heard of have been women patients analysed by men' (Greenson 1967: 339). The image of the female patient who falls passionately in love with her male analyst has also become a popular media stereotype. During the 1980s there was intense debate in the *International Journal of Psycho-Analysis* about why this kind of highly eroticised transference has been reported less often between female analysts and male patients.

In this chapter I begin by discussing the impact of gender on the erotic transference, reviewing classical and contemporary theory in the light of my own clinical experience. I argue that the maternal transference of the male patient to the female psychotherapist is just as likely to be overtly erotic but that for psychic and cultural reasons it may take a distinct form and arouse particular countertransference anxieties in the therapist. In the second part of the chapter I ask whether the female therapist is as likely as her male counterpart to represent paternal figures. In this context the psychotherapist's countertransference – his or her emotional attitude towards the patient, and, especially, the patient's transference – is again crucial. I explore how the therapist's own theoretical biases and unresolved con-flicts about sexual identity may make it difficult to differentiate the male patient's homosexual paternal desires from the hetero-sexual transference, and to distinguish the phallic mother from the intervening father.

THE IMPACT OF GENDER ON THE EROTIC TRANSFERENCE

In his 1915 paper on transference love Freud discussed how the (female) patient would inevitably fall in love with the (male) analyst. This would be due to the workings of transference rather than to the analyst's charms. The patient would be projecting aspects of her own internal world onto the analyst – re-enacting past feelings and fantasies. But, Freud went on, this transference love is just as real as any other love. All adult sexuality is at root incestuous. And all love and hate involves illusion, even delusion. The only difference is the context. Ultimately the patient has to face the narcissistic pain of rejection – transference love can never be satisfied. The therapist's countertransference desire is also real. Again the difference from all other desire is how it is dealt with. Ideally it is not acted upon but thought about, and used in ways that might further the work of analysis.

Freud described a certain kind of woman patient who cannot see the analyst 'as-if' they are the desired parent. Instead they insist that the analyst actually become their lover (Freud 1915). Obviously some patients take a long time to understand that they are not actually going to become the therapist's lover or best friend. But what Freud was describing was the very extreme case of the patient who never does grasp that analysis is a meeting of minds rather than of bodies. Elizabeth Zetzel (Zetzel 1970: 243) gives an amusing example – the woman who comes into her analyst's office and says, 'Before I lie down, I would like to get one thing straight. If I divorce my husband, will you divorce your wife and marry me?' Freud said that this 'outbreak of passionate love' is largely resistance, an attempt to short-circuit the process of emotional change. He also notes the intense hostility and contempt behind such idealised love. The patient is trying to reduce the analyst, to 'bring them down to the level of a lover', he says (Freud 1915: 163).

Interestingly I have had only one patient who actually did come to believe that I was the love of her life in a very literal way and she was a woman. I saw her twice weekly for two years, as one of my first counselling clients, before I went on to further training as a psychotherapist. Ms V was a lesbian, but women who think of themselves as heterosexual can also develop intensely sexualised transferences to female therapists. Her erotic transference was idealised. She described me as a perfect mother, but rejected any links between this and her sexual desire for me. She was in love, she said, and wanted me to be her partner. In fact she had had very similar feelings for another female professional during her long psychiatric history. She found it very hard to tolerate intervals between sessions and would connect these with constant separations from her mother in babyhood. Her idealised love seemed to be partly a defence against the pain and rage that she felt about these abandonments. I constantly worried that her intense erotic feelings towards me might become uncontainable or that I might unwittingly be acting in a provocative way. My situation was all the more difficult because in the organisation where I worked the boundaries between client and counsellor were often blurred and she frequently managed to see me in extra-therapeutic contexts.

When it became clear that the counselling centre for which I worked had lost its funding, her idealisation of me broke down and she began to threaten me with rape, even murder. She had identified with a childhood aggressor, an uncle who'd raped her at 8, and had originally sought help because of fears that she would injure her son. She also told me that she had raped her last lover when the woman ended the relationship. My personal reaction to her threats was one of anger. I was only slightly frightened and wondered whether I did not feel seriously threatened by her because she was a woman.

Fortunately this enforced therapeutic ending helped her to work through some of her feelings of destructiveness towards her love-objects so that she became less terrified of acting them out. I met her by accident some years later and was delighted to discover that she had formed the kind of stable (if stormy) partnership with a woman for which she had longed. She was also getting on much better with her son. Nevertheless she followed up this meeting with a letter telling me that I was still the love of her life, thus suggesting that she might not have entirely resolved her transference love.

Whatever their sex, clinicians sometimes gain narcissistic gratification from a highly sexualised transference and may collude with it rather than looking at the more unpleasant feelings beneath it. It can be flattering to be idealised and exciting to be the object of intense desire. One of my male patients expressed his own confusion about the origins of his sexual feelings towards me by telling me that he could not decide whether his mother really had been seductive or whether he had wished to see her in that light. He went on to say that he had found one of my interpretations, made in the last session, 'charming ... it wasn't that you fancied me but you were behaving in the way that we all do without realising it in order to please people'. He then told me how difficult he himself had found it to tell when he was flirting. His friends had said to him, 'That girl fancies you and you were flirting.' He'd said, 'No I wasn't! I was just being nice.'

On reflection I thought he had a point. My interpretation had been entirely accurate, but I could see that the words I'd used could have been seen by him as seductive or flirtatious. At times this patient was extremely enjoyable, seductive and entertaining. Yet beneath all this was a desolate psychic wasteland and he often had fantasies of killing off a family experienced as neglectful and abandoning. I had momentarily acted out my reluctance to engage with his hatred and cynicism about me as a maternal figure.

I was surprised when in the 1980s I began to read papers by women psychoanalysts who argued that highly sexualised trans-ferences from male patients to female analysts are rare, because they seem to occur frequently in my own practice and those of many colleagues and supervisees. Yet some contributors to a 1982 American Psychoanalytic Panel on the subject concluded that for sociocultural and psychological reasons such transferences did not often happen (Lester 1982). The reasons given included the stronger cultural taboo on mother–son than father–daughter incest and on sex between younger men and older women.

Women psychotherapists often say that the transference changes as they age, but male clinicians do not necessarily make the same observation. Here, as so often in discussion of gender in the transference, it is very difficult to know whether such reports reflect the emotional reality of the patient or the thera-pist's own countertransference reaction. For instance some women therapists have told me that they do not expect younger male (or indeed female) patients to have sexual feelings towards them, and sometimes miss these when they do appear in the transference. Male patients may feel more anxious about express-ing sexual feelings towards a female therapist who is old enough to be their mother but this does not mean that they do not have these feelings.

Female clinicians may have had less to say about the sexualised transference of male patients because their experience of it is different. They might not have been able to identify with the agenda set by their male colleagues. Contemporary male analysts often discuss the erotic countertransference, sometimes stressing the positive ways in which it can be used, arguing for instance that patients need to be able to express their own Oedipal desire in a safe context and see that even when this is reciprocated within the countertransference it will not be acted upon, an experience they may not have had with their opposite-sex parent (Samuels 1993, Mann 1994). Or, on the other hand, male analysts may discuss the temptation for their own sex to collude with or to act out the sexual countertransference (Lasky 1989, Meltzer 1973b). In other words, they seem interested either in dispelling anxiety about the dangers of therapists acting out their own social desires towards patients, or concerned to understand the unconscious fantasies that might underlie such a misuse of the countertransference.

Female therapists do not seem nearly so interested in this issue. This may reflect a particular difficulty in discussing their erotic countertransference feelings and fantasies. But I think that, if this is so, they are more anxious about being seen as provocative or flirtatious than about whether they will commit acts of sexual abuse against patients or be perceived by the public as likely to do so. Certainly this was my anxiety both with the lesbian patient Ms V and with the male patient who thought I was flirting. I also think that women therapists are likely to have their own gender-specific anxieties about containing the aggressive or abusive aspects of their male patients' sexual transferences. In the following section I look in more detail at the way the analyst's sex may affect the heterosexual transference and countertransference.

Freud's women patients presented a veneer of idealised love and flattery, beneath which was hidden enormous hostility, even contempt. This reflects my own experience of the erotic (lesbian) transference with Ms V. In contrast some male patients do exactly the reverse. Their sexuality is extremely overt and their hostility is out on the surface. An aggressive form of sexuality operates as a defence against dependency needs and loving idealisation.

Chasseguet-Smirgel argues that male patients do not usually fall in love with their female analysts in the way Freud describes. Usually, she says, the female patient retreats into the love-transference, using idealised love as a resistance to change. The male patient, on the other hand, retreats from love into sex. If the transference of a male patient to a female therapist is sexualised it is aggressive rather than loving (Chasseguet-Smirgel 1986a). The male patient who idealises the female analyst will, according to her theory, keep sex out of the transference. She describes one man who did idealise her in the sexual transference, something she considers rare enough to designate a 'special case'.

An example of this is the patient, Mr A, already described in Chapter 4, who sexualised the transference, like all his other relationships with women, as a defence against anxieties about childhood loss and separation. He constantly fantasised that I would make him tea, have a chat or stop the session and make love. In this way he tried to eradicate the differences between us – represented by the therapeutic boundaries – in order to return to an illusion of symbiosis with me as a maternal figure. The woman patient who fell in love with me, Ms V, found me perfect physically and mentally. In contrast Mr A accompanied his requests to stop the session and make love with fantasies of 'tearing my body to bits' – a very primitive aggression which emerged initially as a criticism of bits of my body. Before each break he defended himself against overwhelming feelings of loneliness and abandonment through threats of murder and rape, an unconscious attempt to project his own fear and helplessness onto me. The transference was highly sexualised for a long time. Sometimes it was arousing or flatteringly seductive. At other times it was charmingly innocent and childlike. But my greatest anxieties were about the sexualised hostility and contempt with which he masked his infantile vulnerability. At one point I also looked seriously at whether I might be in real physical danger, or whether he was arousing my own partly irrational fears of male violence.

Aggression and contempt in the sexual transference of some male patients with female therapists may reflect the boy's dread of maternal incest. In this context it is interesting that Mr A felt convinced by the end of psychotherapy that his mother had inadvertently eroticised certain aspects of his physical care. Men may mobilise their sadism and cruelty against the mother in the transference because of their dread of losing their masculine identity through incestuous fusion with the mother's body. Chasseguet-Smirgel argues that the same threat of loss of feminine identity is not there for the girl in father–daughter incest since it does not involve a psychic return to the earliest relationship. This could explain why the sexual transference of female patients to male analysts is not so overtly aggressive, since they do not feel the same dread of losing their feminine identity (Chasseguet-Smirgel 1986a, 1988).

Another explanation for the sadism which accompanies the sexual transference of some male patients is the different relationship women and men in our culture have to sexuality and power. Men are more often in positions of authority and financial control and this often tends to make them more sexually desirable. This may also reflect the fact that the father is initially seen by the girl as having a more limited power than the mother's apparent emotional omnipotence. This dynamic may increase the female patient's idealisation of her apparently powerful male analyst. On the other hand if a woman is in an authority position she may well be regarded by men with a combination of fear and attraction. Perhaps unconsciously she is associated with an imago of the dangerously omnipotent early mother.

By contrast male patients, unaccustomed to taking up the passive, vulnerable role in relation to a woman, may feel a strong need to give up the unacceptable position of the passive analysand for the acceptable position of the male suitor. The man I described earlier, Mr A, told me of a sexual dream, saying, 'it was an equalising experience. . . . If we made love, I'd be quite powerful. I'm much bigger than you. You'd be aroused, surrender passionately.' The erotic transference enabled him in fantasy to turn the tables and restore himself to a dominant position.

Describing this dynamic between female therapist and male patient, psychologist Lisa Gornick points out that in three Hollywood films directed by men (*Spellbound, Zelig, The Man Who Loved Women*) the woman analyst restores her male patient to power through having sex with him. Once the analyst falls in love with her patient he then takes up the dominant position in relation to her (Gornick 1986).

If the sexual transference of the male patient towards the female analyst rapidly becomes overtly aggressive rather than idealised, a defence against love and need rather than a retreat into it, the countertransference difficulties will also be different from those described by male analysts. The female psychotherapist may feel frightened, undermined or humiliated by the aggression which accompanies the sexual transference of male patients more often than she feels flattered or aroused.

Statistics seem to back up the public perception that the mental health professional who abuses is far more likely to be male than female. American analyst Richard Lasky links this to anxieties in the male therapist about his own homosexuality or feelings of 'femininity' which may be stirred up through identification with the active heterosexual desires of female patients. Lasky argues that if these anxieties prove unbearable the analyst may actually sexually abuse the patient, in an unconscious attempt to assert that he is indeed masculine and heterosexual (Lasky 1989). These anxieties may also create particular difficulties for male therapists in acknowledging their own homosexual countertransferences. Donald Meltzer also suggests that male analysts are easily drawn into an infantile form of sexual excitement in collusion with perverse patients, while women analysts are more prone to idealising the patient within the maternal transference (Meltzer 1973b). It has also been suggested that therapists who act out sexually towards patients have themselves experienced some abuse from their own therapist, usually in the form of broken boundaries – although not necessarily sexual boundaries.

Some female therapists do seduce their patients or create a tantalisingly seductive atmosphere. But there is far more discussion in contemporary analytic literature about women clinicians' difficulties in recognising or discussing the sexualised transferences of male patients. It is interesting, however, that when it comes to discussing the erotic homosexual transference or countertransference as they arise with patients of their own sex, clinicians of both sexes seem to have little to say (O'Connor and Ryan 1993). Female clinicians' reticence about sexuality in the consulting-room must to some extent reflect a more general cultural silence about all aspects of female desire. Women psychotherapists have lacked the support of a tradition, language and imagery to express their own erotic experience, including their ambivalence about being the object of male desire.

American analysts Goldberger and Evans re-analysed the published clinical material of female analysts who did not often find sexual transferences and concluded that they were avoiding the perverse contempt and sadism of their male patients (Goldberger and Evans 1985). Spanish analyst Torras de Beà also attributes female therapists' avoidance of sexuality to an unconscious dread of perverse contempt and aggression. She describes an analysis which ended in stalemate because the female analyst could not identify with her male patient's debased projections onto her of a fat, smelly, dirty old prostitute, and so did not engage in the erotic transference (Torras de Beà 1987).

The reality that women are at far greater risk of male sexual violence than vice versa will inevitably affect what transpires in the transference and countertransference. It certainly affects referral patterns. The potential for violent or perverse sexual transferences from male patients seems to be borne in mind both by those professionals who do consultations and by female psychotherapists in private practice, some of whom are careful to avoid such referrals. Lucia Tower mentioned this issue in 1956, describing a patient whose transference was so aggressive that she thought he might not be a suitable patient for any woman. His problems might, she said, be better worked through with a male analyst who the patient could perceive as more of an authority figure and 'better able to control him'. So the female therapist has to deal with the reality that she may be at risk from an aggressive male patient as well as her own irrational anxieties about male violence. She also has to contain the male patient's great anxiety about becoming physically violent towards a woman therapist (Tower 1956).

I suggest that there is a tendency with some male patients for aggression and contempt to appear soon after the maternal erotic transference manifests itself. This aggression and contempt is a defence against anxieties about losing male identity through incestuous merger with the mother and Oedipal feelings of desire and humiliation. In our society defences against these early anxieties are institutionalised and emerge in a different relationship between women and men towards sexuality and power. There are many everyday ways in which men can unconsciously triumph over the female sex, reducing them in fantasy to the helpless position they once felt themselves to occupy in relation to a mother who seemed all-powerful.

When confronted with the emotional power of the female analyst some male patients may therefore have particular difficulty in acknowledging aspects of themselves which are often projected onto women and other less powerful social groups. This can result in particularly aggressive power-battles within the transference with a female clinician. The female therapist may collude with the patient in order to avoid the emergence of the patient's sexualised hostility and contempt by creating a seductive idealising maternal transference, or by denying the existence of the patient's sexual feelings towards her.

In the following section I explore another way that external reality may affect the transference – the impact of the therapist's sex on the maternal and paternal transference. I focus on my own experience of the paternal transference with male patients, although equally complex issues arise in other therapeutic dyads.

THE PATERNAL TRANSFERENCE: FEMALE ANALYSTS WITH MALE PATIENTS

In classical psychoanalytic theory maternal and paternal transferences are equally likely to arise whatever the sex of the therapist. But Freud suggested that women therapists might be more effective in eliciting the early maternal transference. He also admitted that his own feeling of being 'so very masculine' made him feel uncomfortable when his patients experienced him as the mother. On the other hand, I have also come across male psychotherapists who miss the paternal transference because they are working with mother-centred theories and have a strong identification with stereotypical 'feminine' or maternal qualities. It is clear then that this is an area where psychotherapists may be quite unaware of how their own unresolved conflicts about sexual identity affect their ability to detect aspects of the transference.

During the 1980s some female psychoanalysts commented on how rarely female analysts discuss their patients' experience of them as representing the father in the transference (Kulish 1986, Lester 1982). This might reflect patients' difficulty in seeing a female therapist as male. But it is far more likely to mean that the female analyst is unable to see beyond the reality of her gender because of unresolved conflicts about her sexual identity or the current theoretical emphasis on the maternal transference. Even though there has been a recent revival of interest in the father his role tends to be seen as complementary to or sometimes even interchangeable with that of the mother amongst object relations theorists and ego psychologists. This orientation does not help the therapist to distinguish when the patient might be seeing her as fulfilling a paternal function, or representing an aspect of the father.

Psychotherapists of both sexes often find it difficult to distinguish different aspects of the transference because of the kaleidoscopic rapidity with which images merge with each other or momentarily separate. Klein points out that although there may be very few people in the infant's life 'he feels them to be a multitude of objects because they appear to him in different aspects. Accordingly the analyst may at a given moment represent a part of the self, or of the super ego, or any one of a range of internalised figures' (Klein 1952: 54). This complexity results in swift changes even within a session between aspects of the father and mother, omnipotently kind objects and dangerous persecutors, and internal and external figures. Sometimes the mother and father are experienced as combined in a hostile alliance against the patient, as in the dream, described in Chapter 2, of a predatory spider which was a bit male, but mostly female.

Some patients have a particular dread of encountering the paternal transference, and sometimes choose a female psychotherapist with the unconscious hope of preserving the illusion that the father is impotent or non-existent. It may for psychic reasons be easier for male patients to see a psychotherapist of their own sex as female than a female therapist as male. This is especially the case with regressed male patients like Mr C, who may, early on in psychotherapy, cling to the reality of the female therapist's gender, in order to reinforce their very tenuous masculine identity. This can reflect a dread of losing a sense of themselves as different to the therapist lest they find themselves merging with her in an indistinct sexual amalgam, where their identity as male becomes completely obliterated.

In order to work in this area as therapist we need to be able to move freely between our own cross-gender identifications with the maternal and paternal functions of each parent. But, nevertheless, the process of assigning gender to aspects of the transference remains fraught with difficulty, since what the psychotherapist perceives as masculine or paternal, or feminine and maternal, may not accord with the patient's experience. In the limited literature that exists in this area it is immediately obvious that psychoanalysts themselves disagree, ostensibly because of differing theoretical perspectives.

For instance, Kleinians and object relations theorists often assume that the provision of a consistent setting, including an unchanging location and time-boundaries, is a mothering function, which helps the patient internalise a secure containing maternal object. Analytic interpretations might well be seen as facilitating identification with the maternal capacity to reflect and give meaning to emotional experience. From a contemporary Freudian perspective, Chasseguet-Smirgel disagrees, making a clear delineation between the maternal capacity to facilitate regression and wait, allowing gestation, and the paternal function of (penetrating) interpretation and boundary-setting. In the Freudian tradition the father is associated with the acquisition of language, and with providing a way out of the illusion of early symbiosis with the mother. Chasseguet-Smirgel argues that the ending of the session provides paternal reassurance that the patient can return to the everyday world of consciousness. 'In its role as boundary, the setting is law, a cut-off point, a representative of the father. There exists a dialectic relationship between the setting as the definition of a space and the regression which it induces and allows' (Chasseguet-Smirgel 1986a: 41). These different perspectives reflect varying views on the father's role in the psyche. But it is also true that the paternal role can be perceived in different ways, according to family and cultural experience.

The American psychoanalyst Nancy Mann Kulish discusses the psychoanalytic concept of the destructive, omnipotent 'phallic' mother – who is seen by the child as possessing everything, including the male (or paternal) penis. She argues that over-reliance on theories which stress the power of the early mother lead to neglect of the paternal transference. Tracing this psychoanalytic preoccupation with maternal omnipotence to a cultural dread of female power, Kulish argues that clinicians may misinterpret authoritarian or aggressive aspects of the father as the castrating 'phallic' mother (Kulish 1986).

I have often found that a feeling of boredom or stasis in the therapeutic relationship alerts me to the emergence of a paternal transference. In the following case-example I represented the prohibitive intervening father of a male patient, Mr H. The boredom I felt might have coincided with his own frustration that he felt, as he described it, psychically 'tethered' to me as an eroticised internal mother or elder sister.

Mr H's father had died in his late teens. This made it difficult for him to consolidate a paternal identification which was already tenuous because of unresolved Oedipal rivalry. Mr H told me that he wanted to become a 'better man', to break the pattern of falling out of love with women once he felt sure that he had won their affections. Men who have not fully identified with the father but have instead idealised a cruel, anal version of masculinity often treat women with indifference or contempt. They have developed a homosexual idealisation of their own sex, and reserve their love and admiration for other men, so that women are treated as sexual objects. Mr H described himself as 'roaring round the country' with a gang of male friends 'drinking and whoring', as he imagined his father had done in his youth.

Discussing an anxiety attack he had had while speaking at a conference Mr H said, 'I'm up there on the platform, and it's like saying "I've got the biggest penis, the biggest member. It's a penis in the mind, about having power, being the centre of attention." ' He went off into an eloquent speech, as if declaiming before an audience, and I began to lose track of what he was saying. 'Are you still listening?' he asked, even though he couldn't actually see me, because he was lying on the couch. I said that he feared losing me, as he worried about losing his audience during presentations. This stopped him in his tracks, and he said in good-humoured amazement: 'Are you saying that I'm boring?' I said that here, at work, and in his childhood he felt he had to entertain but was convinced that he was inadequate and empty inside. He said he'd always felt that his mother delighted in her entertaining, loquacious son. But at a certain point his father might have become irritated and said 'Shut the fuck up', and told his mother to keep him under better control. He was experiencing me as a father who could cut him down to size, setting some limits on his grandiosity.

A few sessions later he showed his immense relief at what he'd experienced as my paternal intervention. He said that psychotherapy had felt a bit stuck and slow-moving for some weeks until the session where I'd 'said he was boring'. Now he could see some changes. He was less 'paranoid', had listened to a female colleague without trying to charm her and had talked as an equal with a new friendly boss (perhaps both representatives of myself). He felt strengthened by internalising an aspect of the father and more equal to his internal mother and other women, less in danger of being swallowed up, rejected or defeated. Furthermore his drinking into which he'd retreated after his father's death, had 'fallen away'. He was becoming more able to think about his own emotional experience and did not need to obliterate it through alcohol.

When male patients begin to see a female therapist as having qualities that they associate with the father and men, they often recognise with relief that they can experiment with expressing more of their own psychic 'femininity'. At this point the homosexual transference towards the father may emerge more clearly. This aspect of the paternal transference may be hard for the psychotherapist to distinguish from the maternal erotic transference. These difficulties are exacerbated when transference projections alter rapidly as in the session with Mr H which I describe next. I was the first to speak in the session, something I very rarely do. The consulting-room seemed cold to me, and I asked him if he was warm enough. He said, 'It's VERY warm in here. AND the hallway smells strongly of fried onions.' There was a silence and then he went on,

> When someone keeps their distance, for instance, a job interviewer, or a woman in a relationship behaves as if they can take you or leave you, you think, this person is worth something. Some people are desperate. They say, this is a wonderful job we're offering here. Or a woman you spend the night with will be all over you the next morning. . . . Yes, I am talking about you, as a matter of fact. You've come over all chatty all of a sudden; you are usually very schoolmarmy, cold and distant.

I was about to interpret this within the maternal transference, but realised this felt stale and boring. A bossy, impatient and contemptuous aspect of himself, associated with his mother, was, however, definitely coming to the fore. 'You're slow today', he said as he rushed to make the interpretations he expected from me. The fact that I refrained from making transference interpretations too soon may have helped him to remember aspects of his relationship with his father which had previously been quite inaccessible to him.

Mr H was soon telling me about his teenage years when his father, a big macho heavy-drinking labourer, would escape to the hot steamy kitchen to cook up vats of sausage-stew, wash up and darn socks while the family watched television. My patient, fascinated, would keep going into the kitchen for big plates of the food which was so much better than his mother's cooking.

He'd asked his father whether he minded doing all the cooking. Work was hard to come by, his father said, and now his mother was the main bread-winner it would be a poor show if he did mind. By this time it was obvious to both of us that the heat and fried onion smells were associated with his father's reign in the kitchen. The sausages in his father's stew reminded him of a dream of childhood sexual rivalry and inadequacy in relation to a greatly admired but sometimes denigrated father who could do women's work yet remain a man's man.

I said that he'd felt today a similar combination of sexual fascination and contempt as with his father in the steamy kitchen. There had been something incestuous and overpowering about the unusual closeness possible with his often unavailable father and he had also felt that with me. 'You mean I had homosexual feelings towards my father?' he asked. 'Do you think I did?'

Then Mr H retreated into safer and more familiar territory, the guiltily desired elder sister. 'I don't fancy my sister. But we're so close she's the obvious person for me to have a relationship with.' He wondered whether acting on incestuous feelings was actually harmful for children, or if it was simply a social law that we all felt we should obey. I said that at this moment he was seeing me as a sister figure, so close I was an obvious person for a sexual partnership. He wondered whether it would be actually harmful for him to act this out in reality or if he would merely be breaking a therapeutic convention. He agreed that he did see me as being like his sister, and that they had recently joked about how they might have to marry each other if their sexual partnerships continued to break up, as in the past. Then he said, 'Well, I've talked more about myself to you than anyone else.'

A few sessions later Mr H linked me with his father, describing us both as 'sweet' when we stepped out of our conventional gender roles. His father cooked; I'd used a word he saw as masculine, vulgar. When I pointed this out he agreed, saying that 'sweet' wasn't a word he used often. Then he said 'something came up last week about sex ... it was something to do with my father cooking ... what do we mean by sexual?' He then went on to describe a dream of anal intercourse with a close man friend: 'I don't feel alarmed by having feelings like that. . . . It was cosy, warm, like you're having chatty sex with a woman you're close to, not a great passion.' In fact, he said this was exactly the way he felt about talking to me.

At this point it seemed that Mr H's homosexual fantasies were an attempt to absorb masculinity, to be like, as much as to be with, the father. In order to explore and integrate his own psychic bisexuality the patient needs to see that his therapist can draw on conventionally 'masculine' or paternal as well as maternal capacities. If a patient can move from the maternal to the paternal transference in the same session, as Mr H could, it indicates that he is firmly anchored in his sexual identity (Chasseguet-Smirgel 1986a). Grappling with questions about what kind of man he was, Mr H was fascinated by how his 'macho' father could have maternal functions and I could appear masculine.

Although I have focused in this chapter on quite well-developed transference images of the Oedipal father, as I illustrated in Chapter 2, the paternal transference will be there from the beginning of psychotherapy, even if it is reflected only in very confused images of an undifferentiated parental amalgam, or is represented only by a silence or a gap in the discourse. If the patient has been through a long period of preoccupation with the early mother, as in Mr H's case, a feeling of stasis or boredom within the therapeutic relationship may indicate the patient's willingness to face Oedipal issues in relation to the father as well as the pain of differentiating from the mother.

CONCLUSION

In this chapter I have focused mainly on my own work with male patients, drawing comparisons with written reports of male analysts' experience with the heterosexual transferences of female patients. I conclude that in certain areas the sex of the therapist and patient does make a difference to the way the transference unfolds, and to the therapist's countertransference anxieties and biases. These differences reflect both the unequal position of the sexes in our society, and the asymmetrical nature of boys' and girls' early experience. The countertransference will also be affected by the therapist's own unconscious conflicts about sexual identity, and his or her theoretical biases. But it is impossible to generalise about exactly how these gender-based differences will emerge since each therapeutic dyad is so unique.

This renewed interest in the impact of gender on the therapeutic dyad reflects changing cultural attitudes towards sexuality, and especially that of women. It may well be significant that since the 1970s psychoanalysts' attention has shifted from female patients' idealised love for their male analysts to the countertransference experience of clinicians of both sexes. This different perspective probably reflects the impact on patients and psychotherapists of changing structures of family life, and shifts in gender power relations.

Nevertheless my brief review of classical and contemporary literature suggests that male and female clinicians continue to report different kinds of experiences of the heterosexual transference with opposite sex patients. For instance it seems that female patients (even with therapists of their own sex) often retreat into the love transference, using it as a resistance to change, while male patients are more likely to retreat from love and dependency into overt expression of erotic desire. Men in psychotherapy may feel a particular need to mobilise their sadism and cruelty in the maternal transference as a defence against losing their male identity through incestuous merger with the mother.

These differences reflect the varying relationship each sex has to authority and sexuality. For instance, the female analyst's emotional influence and professional authority may give rise to stereotypically male defences against envy, helplessness and humiliation in relation to an early mother who was felt to be omnipotent. In these circumstances the erotic transference can be a fantasised way of reasserting gender dominance. This use of aggressive sexual fantasies of dominating the needed object as a defence against pain and humiliation can create particular countertransference anxieties in the female therapist, which reflect her position in the gender hierarchy, as well as her own unresolved conflicts in this area.

It is not surprising that male analysts have traditionally been more able to speak about their experience of the heterosexual transference and countertransference. Women psychotherapists' growing ability to articulate their countertransference concerns in this area might well reflect a new cultural questioning of the idea that women's sexuality is constructed around an enjoyment of being the object of male desire. Certainly, as I have indicated in earlier chapters, women psychotherapists are showing a renewed interest in theorising all aspects of female erotic experience.

The new pressures on women to act as father as well as mother to their children, create particular anxieties for contemporary men who are concerned about the increased marginalisation of their sex within the family. It is not surprising then that since the 1980s there has been a renewed analytic interest in the paternal transference. Theories which revolve around the emotional power of the mother often minimise the importance of the father's role in the reproduction of patriarchy and as an object of erotic desire and identification for children of both sexes. This bias may lead to particular difficulties in distinguishing paternal from maternal authority or the male patient's homosexual desires towards the psychotherapist as a father-figure from those towards the mother. The psychotherapist's ability to draw freely on cross-gender identifications will profoundly influence his or her ability to help patients integrate the maternal and paternal strengths of each parent within the transference.

My emphasis in this chapter has been on my experience of erotic maternal and paternal transferences with male patients. In the next chapter I return to the question of female sexuality, centring mainly on transference issues between women patients and therapists, including the psychotherapist's difficulties in recognising and negotiating the homosexual desires of same-sex patients. Chapter 7 explores another important, and highly controversial, intersection between fantasy and external reality within the therapeutic relationship – the question of whether psychotherapists might deny the reality of actual childhood sexual abuse, or encourage the fabrication of fantasies of such events.

False memories of sexual abuse?

During the 1980s the accusation most commonly made by feminists against psychoanalytic theory and clinical practice was that it denied the reality of sexual abuse, so sentencing 'thousands of patients to confused, guilty silence, while exonerating the abusers' (Scott 1988). But by the early 1990s a fierce public debate was raging on whether psychotherapists might be so keen to discover sexual abuse that they would encourage impressionable patients to fabricate fantasies about childhood incest. Within the world of psychoanalytic psychotherapy there have been dramatic swings between theories that assume that patients' accounts of sexual abuse derive from unresolved Oedipal desire, and those that assume that the patient is describing a real event. These theoretical shifts reflect changing public perceptions of the prevalence of childhood sexual abuse.

Freud initially took a strong public stand in favour of tracing neurosis to repressed memories of actual childhood sexual abuse. Whereas hysteria had once been assumed to be physiological, a wandering womb, he linked it to the wandering hands of nursemaids and parents. As Freud began to understand the complexity of unconscious processes he changed his mind and decided that he was often dealing with fantasies about incest rather than actual events. But in his 'seduction theory' Freud had always specified that it is what the mind does with a scene, not the original experience itself, which determines symptoms. Until he died Freud continued to acknowledge that adult neurosis often originated in real childhood experiences of abuse, cruelty and neglect, but his focus of interest shifted away from the actuality of these real events to an investigation of the patient's unconscious fantasies. Nevertheless, Laplanche and Pontalis argue that Freud could never reconcile himself to treating fantasy as the pure and simple outgrowth of the child's own spontaneous sexual life. Fundamentally, they say, his seduction theory expressed the idea that the child's sexuality is entirely organised by something which comes to it from outside: the parents' relationship and their wishes (Laplanche and Pontalis 1967).

But today Freudianism is no longer so loudly accused of complicity with the patriarchal silencing of women and children. Nowadays the most hotly debated issue in child abuse seminars is whether psychotherapists falsify the memories of suggestible patients, planting erroneous scenarios of sexual assault by adults. Recent discoveries about the prevalence of sexual abuse can be seen as a challenge to patriarchal power since they suggest that the traditional father-dominated family is often a dangerous institution for the child. Elderly parents have organised themselves into groups, claiming that their grown-up children have been incited into making false allegations of sexual abuse against them. Mental health professionals see this debate as a backlash against the recognition of the prevalence of sexual abuse. They express alarm that we might be rapidly returning to a situation where children who are sexually assaulted as well as adult incest survivors can find no one who will believe them.

This debate may also express social ambivalence about the expansion of psychotherapy and counselling within Anglo-American culture. Now that counselling is routinely offered in schools, colleges and hospitals, it is not surprising that the public are intensely concerned about the nature of the therapist's influence. Freud always knew that his theory of childhood sexuality would continue to arouse fierce controversy, so perhaps it was to be expected that questions about the cultural power of the psychotherapist would focus on the erotic status of the child.

In this chapter I look at how these rapid shifts in attitude towards psychotherapeutic work with incest survivors have affected my own clinical practice. I begin by describing how childhood sexual abuse which has either been forgotten or kept secret might emerge in the course of psychotherapy. For many decades up until the 1980s there was profound pessimism about the possibility of helping incest survivors through analysis, which was reflected in the idea that they were not suitable cases for students (MacCarthy 1988). But the new public awareness about the prevalence of childhood sexual abuse was paralleled by increased optimism and interest in work with incest survivors.

This emphasis on the 'real event' is very facilitating for those who are relatively certain that they have been sexually abused. But the recent climate of sympathetic interest may exacerbate the confusion of those who are not sure whether they really are incest victims. In the second part of the chapter I explore the interplay between fantasy and the 'real event' in the psycho-therapy of a woman who suspects that she may have been sex-ually abused, but has no concrete memories. My work with her raises fundamental questions about whether the psychotherapist can distinguish memories from fantasies, and the relative thera-peutic importance of reconstructing 'real' events as opposed to working entirely in the 'here-and-now' transference relationship.

AN ENCOUNTER WITH A SPIRIT

Some patients come into psychotherapy unable to talk about childhood experiences of sexual abuse. Perhaps they have told no one at all up to now, as in the case I discuss next, where through working intensively in the transference and counter-transference, secrets from the past emerged quite spontaneously. Ms Y was a 27-year-old woman whose parents had immigrated to this country before she was born. She sought help from the clinic where I worked because she was having difficulty in study-ing for professional exams. She told me that it was no coincidence that she had begun this training as soon as her mother had left the country on a long visit to relatives abroad, since she felt that she was particularly susceptible to her mother's destructive influence and that she had always undermined her academically. Ms Y told me about how her mother provoked terrible rows and talked about spirits and ghosts in a way which disturbed the entire family.

While her siblings had all done extremely well at school, Ms Y had been labelled a slow learner. She described how, as the only black girl in a secondary school in a small provincial English town, she had been victimised and unfairly picked out as a trouble-maker. At first I found it difficult to believe that this solid, quiet, vulnerable woman could ever have been seen in this way. Ms Y went on to say that after a visit to her home-country her schoolwork dramatically improved, but when she was

14 her mother had visited a spirit-medium, who told her that it was dangerous for her daughter to carry on studying for the exams she was about to take. Ms Y's academic progress again plummeted, and it was only now, in her mid-twenties, that she had begun to train for the professional life she had always wanted.

Ms Y described how, although she worked hard, accidents continually happened on her course. For instance a long essay had got lost in the post and she did not have a copy. In psychotherapy she seemed similarly highly motivated, but sometimes she would not turn up to her sessions or would arrive when I was away. She always seemed terribly distressed by these mistakes and told me that she had left phone-messages or written letters which I had not received. The situation was complicated because I knew that the office in the clinic was going through an organisational crisis and messages did sometimes get lost. But when she told me that a message cancelling the session had been left on her sister's answerphone, apparently by me, I knew something very strange was happening. I tried pointing out the similarity between the mis-communications with me and at college. She agreed, but could offer no explanation, although she made it clear that she felt disturbed and unhappy about what was happening.

Eventually I summoned up the courage to suggest to Ms Y that we might be dealing with a haunted transference. Perhaps, I ventured, a spirit had materialised between us, as in her relationship with her mother, and maybe this could explain the mysterious answerphone messages and the letters that were posted but never arrived? Ms Y looked at me for a moment and then burst out laughing. When she stopped, she said that yes, it did seem that a poltergeist, or some very mischievous destructive spirit was disrupting communication between us. We had now found a way of talking about a part of herself which was identified with a 'possessed' mother, and Ms Y was clearly delighted that I was not dismissing her as a trouble-maker because of it.

Ms Y then told me a secret she had never revealed to anyone before – that she had been sexually abused by a family-lodger when she was 8. Around then she had started to tear things apart – she would pull all the petals off flowers and take clocks and watches to pieces. Soon after this Ms Y came in to her session distraught because her mother, newly returned from her travels, had become possessed by a spirit one weekend. Her mother's belief in spirits was frowned on by their church, Ms Y explained, but the family had called a priest who was skilled at exorcism, who understood all about spirits, and was not at all condemnatory. But unfortunately, although he knew how to calm her mother down, he was available only for short periods of time and then the family were left alone with her again, knowing the spirit might well return.

In discussing this, Ms Y admitted for the first time that she too believed in the literal presence of spirits, although she thought it was only her mother who was possessed, not herself. Ms Y went on to say that she was greatly relieved to be able to talk to me and that the weekly sessions provided a haven from the disturbing family events. I said that she was finding it very difficult that the anti-therapy, anti-learning part of her had become so powerfully disruptive of her studies and her work with me. She felt that I was – like the priest – liberal, able to lessen the power of the parts of her that could sabotage all her efforts to learn and communicate. But the problem was, I went on, that, like the priest, I was only available for a limited period of time. Ms Y agreed with this and talked about how paternal the priest was. She had had no other way of communicating these parts of herself other than by unconsciously acting them out, so creating between us the experience of being possessed, taken over by chaotic disruptive forces. This enabled me to help her put her terrible childhood experiences into words, so beginning the process of exorcism.

Ms Y knew that she had been sexually abused, but had never been in a situation where she felt able to disclose her secret without being blamed for it. Other people enter psychotherapy with no conscious knowledge that they have been sexually abused. This was the case with my next patient, Mrs P.

TAKING A PROFESSIONAL INTEREST

When she first came to see me, Mrs P worked with incest survivors and attributed her interest in this field to the fact that she had seen her father touch her teenage sister in a sexualised way. I asked whether he had done anything similar to her and she was absolutely adamant that neither he nor anyone else had done so. She did tell me, though, that her mother thought it possible that her father had been abused by his own mother. And seeing her father touch her sister had created intensely contradictory feelings for her, including simultaneous relief that he had not done that to her, outrage on her sister's behalf, and jealousy that her sister had so clearly been the preferred object of paternal desire. Mrs P also felt some guilt that, after both sisters told their mother about the sexual abuse, her mother had told the police and then left the house with the children. Eventually her parents had been reunited and the family had lived together again. Mrs P now felt that what her mother had done was in the best interests of everyone concerned, but she could also remember how much pain the entire family had suffered during that period.

After several years of twice-weekly psychotherapy, Mrs P had made significant changes. The witnessing of her sister's abuse had not been the main issue in her psychotherapy by any means, but nevertheless she had talked about it at length and seemed to have resolved many of her feelings about it. I was puzzled, however, by her continuing preoccupation with the whole question of childhood incest. It was beginning to be clear that she felt compelled to continue voluntary work with abused women, even though for practical reasons it no longer suited her to do so. I again asked her whether she was sure that she had not been sexually abused, and again she said she had not. But she did begin to talk more about her confusion about the boundaries between affection and eroticised touching. Like many feminists she was concerned that her daughter should feel proud of her female body and genitals, especially since she herself had always questioned her own sexual desirability. She told me that she was not sure how to engender an atmosphere of sexual openness in the family without over-stimulating the children or being intrusive.

While talking about this she suddenly remembered that when she visited her father's mother, as she often did on her own as a child, her grandmother would lay her down to rest and then stroke her thighs in a way that had made her feel scared and distressed. In retrospect she could see that this had been a very sexualised form of touching, but that, because she had felt lonely and neglected at home, and her grandmother had made her feel so special, she had never been able to face the fact that there had been an abusive element in the relationship.

Mrs P's question about how to talk openly about childhood sexual experience without being intrusive or stirring up an atmosphere of over-eroticised fantasy is equally relevant to the therapeutic transference. When I look back on my work with her I wonder whether I would now ask such direct questions about sexual abuse given the present climate of anxiety over psychotherapists inciting false memories. But if I had been more reticent, I think it is possible that Mrs P might have left psychotherapy without acknowledging her own childhood experience of sexual abuse. Might she then have repeated the cycle by sexualising the relationship with her own children instead?

CAN MEMORIES BE FALSE?

Had Mrs P repressed – turned away, or kept at a distance from consciousness – her grandmother's uncomfortable stroking? Or had she never thought of it as abuse before? And what enabled her eventually to put herself in the position of the abused child rather than continually thinking of her sister, or the women she cared for at work? Mrs P told me later:

> I needed to retain the 'good' grandmother in the absence of other attention and love. When my grandmother abused me something got buried or died. I repressed the memory because I did not want to feel that someone I loved deeply was bad. Therapy helped me make a link between childhood experience and adult feelings. For instance, discussing my father's abuse by his mother led us into talking about my experiences with my nan and that opened up the possibility of her doing that to me.

In his discussion of screen memories in 1899, Freud addressed the way in which we can keep a link with a memory we have repressed by substituting another, less significant memory. Although the memory of her sister's abuse was highly significant, Mrs P's preoccupation with it may have screened out her experience with her grandmother. Freud says that screen memories represent the forgotten years of childhood. 'It is simply a question of knowing how to extract it out of them by analysis' (quoted by Laplanche and Pontalis 1967: 405).

In his paper on screen memories, Freud goes on to ask whether there are memories that emerge from childhood, or merely memories from those years. According to his theory, past events will constantly be re-interpreted in the light of later thoughts, impressions and feelings. We are continually re-writing our own history. As Ann Scott points out, 'real memories' can be of thoughts, as well as of actual observable events, and thoughts may sometimes take the form of fantasy. For many people in analysis, Scott continues, it is the very complexity, indeed inaccessibility, of their own personal store of memories 'with its interweaving of accuracy and distortion which is at the centre of the analytic process' (Scott 1988). The complex issue of disentangling real events from fantasy was central in the psychotherapy of the woman I discuss next.

Ms N

Ms N, a 35-year-old divorcee, came to twice-weekly psychotherapy for help with depression and difficulties in relationships. After her divorce she had a series of short-lived affairs with men and then a more long-term sexual relationship with a close woman friend, which also ended. She had enjoyed sex with this woman more than with men, and now felt unsure whether she wanted to settle down with a man or a woman. To her embarrassment, many everyday experiences were sexualised. At present she was very lonely and any social overture made to her immediately became eroticised in her mind – she did not think anyone could want her except for sex. She would have an orgasm having her back manipulated by the osteopath, or her hair washed at the hairdresser's. She told me that her father had left the family to work abroad when she was 1, and returned when she was 3. As the third of four siblings, she described her mother as being more interested in older children than little ones. She also emphasised that there had been unusually little physical contact between family members. At this point I wondered whether she had eroticised a deprivation, a lack of early parental affection and interest.

The childhood physical contact she could remember was all linked with sex or its prohibition. She described how at 6 she had touched her father's penis curiously while sponging his back in the bath and he had quietly moved her hand away. She also remembered being hit by her mother for playing stimulating back-tickling games with her sister in bed. At 8 she knew that she had shocked girlfriends with sexual jokes. Other memories were of seeking affection from male visitors to the house who praised her prettiness and singled her out from the other children for special attention.

I asked more about these experiences, letting her know that I wondered whether her relationships with adults had actually become sexualised. She was adamant that their behaviour towards her had always been restrained and protective. I accepted this and did not raise the subject again. My reason for wondering about possible sexual abuse was her unusual difficulty in distinguishing physical affection or everyday touching from erotic stimulation.

In most situations Ms N felt great confusion about the boundaries set by others and found it difficult to distinguish between different kinds of relationships. For instance she became infuriated with me because I wouldn't 'chat' to her at the end of sessions. She also became resentful that I would not touch her, even when she was very distressed. Her silent rage and humiliation intensified after we encountered each other in the street. I said hello and agreed that the weather was warm but did not stop to talk. Apart from my usual professional reticence I was late and in a hurry. Nevertheless, she dodged along beside me, asking questions about my flat which I found puzzling and intrusive and to which I gave noncommittal answers. For over two years she returned continually to her feelings about this event, telling me how hurt and angry she felt that I was so distant in the street when she shared so much of herself in the sessions.

Whereas at first she had idealised me as benign and giving she now began to tell me that I was cold, distant and formal, like her mother. What surprised me was that she would often say this straight after a session where I had felt warm and empathic towards her, moved by her pain and loneliness. She began to greet me with an unfailingly resentful stare at the beginning of every session, regardless of how understanding she had found me the last time she saw me.

Ms N had always been well able to function in certain areas of her life and since she had been coming to psychotherapy she had made some radical changes. For instance, she had returned to college to study, overcoming her lifelong inhibitions about learning. But within the sessions she remained frozen in a rigid, persecuted stance. She continued with her angry complaints about my maintenance of the therapeutic boundaries, but would become deeply suspicious that I was trying to manipulate her if she saw any sign that I might be deviating from them. She did not see my interpretations as a point of view that could be explored while retaining her own. Either I was right or she was. Often I would feel that we had negotiated some middle ground, only for her to come back next session having obliterated any memory of this, angrily insisting that I had imposed my view on her.

Although Ms N often compared me to her mother who had died ten years before, I noticed that her view of her father accorded with what she said about me. She always described him as implacably cold and uncaring, but when he discovered that she was seeing a psychotherapist he made what seemed to be a magnificent effort to reach out emotionally to her. I was astounded when she rejected him, responding with absolute cynicism about his motivation. I asked myself whether she was so rigid that she was unable to detect warmth when it was offered.

Around this time she described a vivid image of being a toddler hanging onto the bars of a cot, enraged at the pain and excitement of being forced to watch a copulating couple. She didn't know whether this image was a memory or a fantasy. I suggested that this might have been how she had felt about her parents' sexual relationship, whether or not she had actually witnessed it. This image fitted in with the rest of her sexual fantasies, which were often of watching others having sex. As soon as she entered psychotherapy she began to have fantasies which involved her looking at a male homosexual couple, as well as lesbian and heterosexual intercourse. Her dreams frequently contained images of coercive sex. One, in which a younger, smaller person of uncertain gender was anally penetrated by a large male bully, had been set in a location reminiscent of my consulting-room. She immediately assumed that I must be the sexual bully, forcing my penetrating interpretations on her. She was astonished when I suggested tentatively that this figure might also be a part of her.

Eighteen months into her therapy she engrossed herself in a book about how to remember forgotten childhood sexual abuse. She noted that the victims had similarities with her and wondered whether she had been sexually abused. She mentioned the frequency of sexual coercion in her dreams and also said that she had never come across anyone who confused body zones as much as she did, getting orgasms so easily from casual touch, especially to her back.

I was very surprised by her idea that she might have been sexually abused, since she had at first seemed so convinced that nothing like that had happened to her. I decided to make no judgements but to listen with an open mind. During the next few months she became more convinced that she had been abused, even though she had no concrete memories. Gradually she began to think that the abuse had been by a man, and most likely her father, perhaps after his return to the family when she was 3. She linked this with the number three, which kept recurring in her dreams. She was aware that learning difficulties often result from sexual abuse and connected her frequent dream-images of children who could not speak or learn – with her own childhood academic problems. She speculated that she might have tried hard to tell her mother but not been believed, and then 'gone to great lengths' not to believe in the abuse herself.

We were both well aware that she still had no actual memories of such events. One session Ms N demanded angrily, 'How can I know whether I was sexually abused or not? There's still no concrete proof. Maybe it's all your idea.... After all you raised the issue.' I felt stunned into silence. Eventually I managed to think more clearly and told her that it was true that I had raised the question in her first session, but I had not mentioned it again until she did. I was by now feeling very confused indeed and rather terrorised. She seemed to be re-creating in me an experience of having her sense of reality denied – but what had really happened to her? I determined to say as little as possible when she mentioned the topic of possible sexual abuse. She muttered darkly that she'd become more special to her father during the abuse and now felt that she'd made herself into a more interesting patient.

Soon after this Ms N produced a quite appalling and very precise image of herself as a toddler being held aloft and abused by her father. As with the image of exclusion from parental sex she did not know whether it was a memory or a fantasy. I was simultaneously shocked and puzzled by the image. Physiologically it did not make sense and I could not reproduce it in my own mind. Finally I said that I was having difficulty in picturing it because the two human bodies could not fit together in the way she described.

She came to the next session furious with me, but what she said appeared entirely contradictory. She felt that I had disbelieved her image of abuse. But she also said 'it's only with your support that I've uncovered what I have.... I've never felt you loved or cared for me. My mother was not capable of those feelings ever.' She went on to say that I had been right – if she had been abused it could not have happened in the way she described. She didn't know whether the image represented a real event. It might also be symbolic of her state of mind – an unbearable state of suspension between the certainty that she'd been abused and her lack of actual memories. At this point my experience was that everything I said was likely to be wrong – a feeling she had often had in childhood.

Gradually my patient's certainty of having been sexually abused eroded in the face of a continuing lack of concrete evidence. She felt humiliated and furious with me for letting her explore the topic as long as she had. 'Didn't you know how susceptible I am to attention-seeking?' she demanded. Later she said,

> I was trying to please you, to make myself special. But it was more than that. I was also trying to answer questions about my history that I've wondered about for a long time. I wanted to find a concrete reason, a cause for my problems, someone to blame. I always felt terribly in the wrong as a child. If I was abused it wouldn't be my fault. I wanted drama, an actual event. Now I'm not so concerned about the reason. It doesn't matter.

It was now clear that my patient might have felt herself to be the victim of an assault on her personal sense of reality rather than an actual sexual violation. 'My family say that nothing happened to me, but something did', she said. Again she connected this trauma with her father's return to the family during her third year. She described how she had hated and rebelled against the strict rules her father had imposed on the easy-going, mother-dominated household and her pain at his apparent lack of interest in her.

During this discussion I said that I had never before heard her imply that there might have been anything warm or positive in her early relationship with her mother. To my complete surprise she burst into tears and began to talk about how she had withheld affection from her mother in her final illness, even though she knew that her mother really depended on her children. She went on to wonder whether she had wiped out early experiences of maternal warmth around the time of her father's return to the family, creating an internal image of someone cold and remote. I compared this to the way she had in the past obliterated experiences of feeling understood by me, returning to the next session furious at my coldness. She agreed with this and also speculated that her anger at my therapeutic boundaries might have been connected with that old rage towards the paternal rules that closed off her previous easy access to her mother.

Ms N began to remember feelings of sensual or erotic pleasure in relation to her mother, and described how recently she had begun to lick her fingers and curl her own hair, as she had been told she did with her mother's hair when she was very small. She now linked this with the eroticisation of her scalp. Her confusion of bodily zones might then be connected with an intense eroticisation of the sensual pleasures and humiliations of infancy, such as feeding, holding and nappy-changing rather than in the later Oedipal experiences she had been describing. Ms N wondered whether her mother might have also eroticised the relationship in her mind. She concluded that there was no way of knowing. It was just as likely, she thought, that she herself might have sexualised some early feelings of insecurity, avoiding pain and anger through a sense of being 'exalted', her mother's special companion.

Around this time she dreamed of saving the life of a paternal figure, who she linked with me, and then being selected from a group of women as his sexual partner. Perhaps, she now said, she had avoided facing the pain of feeling unimportant by fantasising that she had been secretly selected for sexual favours. Ms N then described how she felt she had to 'build a wall' psychically between herself and her parents, shutting them out because of their failure to understand her pain at exclusion from their intimacy. She now linked the recurring threesomes in her dreams with a lifelong hatred of triangles.

Some patients do, like Ms N, discover that they have many similarities with sexual abuse victims, and spend time in psychotherapy discussing the issue. I usually assume, as I did with Ms N, that, if I listen carefully, they will eventually reach their own conclusion, or lose interest in the topic. I am aware that the psychotherapist can find it difficult to accept the reality of sexual abuse, to bear the patient's pain and tolerate being seen as the neglectful or molesting parent. Freud's Hungarian colleague,

Sandor Ferenczi, who always believed that incest was an actual cause of much adult disturbance, said that adults were 'often dangerous fools to whom one cannot tell the truth without risk of being punished' (quoted by Stanton 1990: 113).

When she first began psychotherapy Ms N seemed relatively well able to differentiate internal and external reality. But after a while it became clear that she was liable to confuse memory and fantasy. In psychotherapy she retreated into a fantasised past at a point where the transference relationship became particularly difficult. I asked myself whether I might have colluded with this. Certainly I had become frustrated with her fixed hostile transference towards me and worried that she might be so preoccupied with cold, uncaring, internal figures that she might be unable to change psychically through psychotherapy. So I could have unconsciously welcomed a diversion from an exclusive focus on our 'here-and-now' interaction.

I might also have felt anxious about the intensity of Ms N's fantasy of becoming close to, perhaps even part of, me and of penetrating into my habitat and activities. Long after she met me in the street she told me that she had thought I looked nice that day – she liked the dress I was wearing. And her puzzling questions turned out to be an attempt to add to the astonishingly complex picture she had already built up through observation and deduction about my lifestyle and the layout of my flat.

I wondered whether, if I had been able to help her acknowledge the eroticisation of her maternal transference feelings towards me, she might have felt less need to retreat into explorations of actual abuse. At the time of our meeting in the street I had suggested that her need for me to touch her and talk to her outside the sessions might indicate that she had sexual feelings towards me, as she did towards so many others in her life. But Ms N insisted that I was different and that she had no sexual feelings towards me 'because I was cold' towards her. Only after she had eliminated the possibility of paternal abuse could she acknowledge that she had wanted special attention – perhaps in the form of an overt, unsolicited sexual gesture – both from me and from each parent in childhood.

Homosexual transferences to the mother or the father can be particularly hard for heterosexual psychotherapists to detect and work with. The therapist's own unresolved psychic conflicts about such transferences may well be shown by blind spots and defensive displacement of analytic interest rather than by conscious sexual arousal or acting out. O'Connor and Ryan argue that psychotherapists who are anxious about containing the patient's homosexual erotic transference may too easily accept professions of sexual disinterest, as I possibly did. Or they may unconsciously infantilise a patient in order to perpetuate a sense of mother–baby fusion, thereby avoiding conflict and sexual feeling (O'Connor and Ryan 1993).

There were other reasons why I was slow to know whether we were dealing with repressed or dissociated memories, or fantasies of paternal abuse. Ms N was quite right in her observation that her confusion of perception, bodily zones and roles was similar to that of many incest survivors. Ferenczi argued that 'confusion of tongues' is intrinsic to abuse. Child and adult speak different languages, the child wanting maternal solicitude, as my patient clearly did, while the adult responds with guilt-laden desire – the 'language of passion', rather than the 'language of tenderness' (Ferenczi 1932). British analyst Brendan MacCarthy describes how in the first abuse experience the child is swamped by a confusion of tactile, olfactory, zonal and emotional sensations and overwhelmed by the adult's anxiety and need (MacCarthy 1988). Ms N's capacity to change me absolutely from an empathetic to a persecutory figure by distorting her own perception of the previous session has similarities with the abused child's confusion between good and bad, love and abuse. Shengold writes, 'If the very person who abuses and is experienced as bad must be turned to for relief of the distress that the parent has caused, then the child must out of desperate need register the parent delusionally as good' (Shengold 1979: 533–99).

Ms N also knew that learning difficulties and distortions of thinking can be associated with childhood sexual abuse and she linked this with her own childhood inhibitions about studying. Valerie Sinason points out that the really terrible effects of sexual abuse are

> not so much on the sane outraged child who has been assaulted once and has been able to tell and believed, but on children who have been perniciously, secretly and lovingly corrupted over a long period in their own homes; children who in order to keep any image of a good parent have to smile or become stupid or blind to what is happening.

Layers of stupidity and numbing are needed in order to accomod-
ate both the abuse and the precocious sexual awakening. 'To
throw out the knowledge of an abusing trusted adult means
throwing out other learning; to not see terrible corruption
means becoming blind' (Sinason 1988: 104).

I also wondered whether we really were dealing with dissociated memories, or with assaults which had happened at too
young an age for her to integrate emotionally. Although figures
in fantasies represent internal rather than external objects fantasies can also relate to bodily experiences. This may also be true
of memories, which can emerge in bodily sensations and dreams.
The reality of traumatic events is so compelling that knowledge
prevails, although it may not be consciously accessible or complete. In their 1993 paper American psychoanalysts Dori Laub
and Nanette Auerhahn describe a range of different ways of
not knowing about massive psychic trauma. At one extreme are
complete dissociation and fugue states, where events are re-lived
only in an altered state of consciousness. Both amnesia – partial,
temporary or complete forgetting of an event – and hypermnesia
– the inability to escape from memories, which are relived over
and over again, often in a compartmentalised, undigested way,
for instance through flashbacks – are characteristic of post-trau-
matic stress disorder. Valerie Sinason argues that those who have
suffered in well-known and publicly shared disasters are more
likely to suffer from compulsive remembering, while traumas
which are private, secret, unwitnessed by others may well be
repressed (Sinason, private communication).

The tendency to 'forget' entirely when in one state of mind
and to 'remember' in another, becomes vastly exaggerated when
trauma occurs at a very young age and is repeated over and over
again. When the brain cannot process all the information it is
given, memory and emotion become severed. Severe childhood
trauma may permanently alter the neurobiology that integrates
cognitive memory and emotional arousal. This helps to explain
the existence of body memories and flashbacks. The trauma
returns at these moments of very high arousal, but not as words
or memories. Because it has not been integrated into the totality
of emotional experience it will emerge in the form of flashbacks,
nightmares or visual images (Sykes Wylie 1993).

Once Ms N became convinced that her father had not actually
abused her sexually, I began to think more about the implications

of my work with her for the current debate on 'false memories'. Like many of the psychotherapy patients we now read about in the media, Ms N was utterly convinced for a while that I had brought up the subject of sexual abuse a second time, or perhaps, had never really dropped it. This was not true. Fundamentally she and I had a good working alliance. If anything the therapeutic relationship grew stronger through this experience. But what if this had not been so? Might I have been denounced publicly as a psychotherapist who planted false memories?

Another problem is in knowing how to define sexual abuse. Incest is obviously very prevalent. But there are many other ways in which children can be overstimulated or intruded on sexually, and this often leads to a sense of having suffered some kind of abuse. Ms N may indeed have felt traumatised by the sight of some sexual act. She might have been touched in an eroticised way, or exposed to the disturbed sexual fantasy-life of adults round her, although she had no direct evidence that this was so. Very concrete fantasies about incest may also be an unconscious way of drawing attention to some less tangible or visible sexual-isation of parental care. It is then quite possible that someone might feel that they have been sexually abused in childhood while the adult might be equally convinced – consciously – that their conduct had been quite proper.

Patients often need to speculate about the past, and may create hypothetical scenarios which they later discard as false. This pro-cess may be prolonged if there is something about their childhood that continues to puzzle them. It is always difficult to know whether a patient is struggling to acknowledge something they cannot bear to remember. Ms N said that it might have been necessary for her seriously to explore the possibility of a real external trauma in order to dispel her absolute conviction that there must be someone to blame for her problems. Sometimes both patient and analyst may be avoiding difficult aspects of the transference and countertransference. False memories of child-hood sexual abuse may, for example, be the expression of the patient's desire for special love from the parents or psychother-apist, and a way of avoiding the pain of not being the object of parental desire. The psychotherapist might be defending against anxieties about an eroticised transference, or the feelings of aggression or intrusiveness associated with it.

RECONSTRUCTING THE PAST – AN ESCAPE FROM THE PRESENT?

Clinicians have very different views about how important it is for them to help the patient piece together their own history. For Freud a principal aim of analysis was recollection of what had been forgotten, enabling the patient to fill in the gaps in his own story. Writing about the little boy Hans, Freud says that a thing which has not been understood inevitably reappears. Like an unlaid ghost, it cannot rest until the mystery has been solved and the spell broken (Freud 1909).

Many contemporary analysts still see it as crucial to link present experiences in the transference with unresolved past issues. But others disagree. For instance, Betty Joseph, a post-Kleinian, says that discussion of the patient in the past or in other settings is distant and intellectual, like talking about a 'third person'. The main analytic task is, Joseph argues, to elucidate how the patient's deeply engrained mental structures are revealing themselves in the therapeutic 'here-and-now'. The analyst's primary focus should be on understanding the patient's desperate attempts to draw her into collusion with avoiding the pain of psychic change. Joseph argues that once emotional experience has become real in the present, the patient will be able to make historical links which consolidate it (Joseph 1985).

This exclusive reliance on interpreting the transference gives the analyst enormous power to define what is happening in the therapeutic relationship, especially when the patient is as impressionable and anxious to please as Ms N. Yet at the same time the psychotherapist may lack the necessary information to understand what is actually happening in the room. For instance, sometimes children's memories are tampered with by adults, so that distortions of fact are woven into their psyches, as in the case of a patient who said that his memories had been 're-written' by a parent.

During psychotherapy we discovered that he had lived all his life with a false version of events – a story which had been told to him in childhood about an event he had witnessed but could not remember. Once we realised this it became clear that we had not known enough to make accurate interpretations of what happened in the consulting-room. It was not so much that I had been wrong, just that now everything took on a subtly different meaning. But, although work in the transference alone could not help my patient make links with the past, it is highly probable that it did strengthen him enough emotionally to enable him to face the truth. My work with this patient has made me aware that when an adult risks criminal prosecution or losing custody of their children, as may happen in cases of incest or sexual abuse, there may be very strong blocks on the memory of young victims or witnesses.

The approach that suits a particular patient may depend on their history. For instance traumatised patients usually need to go through a period in psychotherapy where they concentrate on elucidating the traumatic past events in all their manifestations. If the analyst does not listen sympathetically to this, but instead relates everything to what is happening with her here and now in the room, the patient might feel she is being subjected to a repetition of the self-centred behaviour of parental figures, who always demanded to be the centre of the patient's attention and concern (Rosenfeld 1972). Alternatively the patient may feel that once again someone influential is concerned to avoid discussion of, perhaps even to distort, her version of reality.

The psychotherapist must be open to exploring that mysterious interface between memory, unconscious fantasy and imagination while absolutely relinquishing any assumptions about what may be discovered. If the analyst relies too strongly on interpreting the 'here-and-now' transference, the patient may become fiercely resistant, fearing that once again her psychic reality is being distorted by a powerful figure on whom she is dependent. The opposite danger is that the therapist may, because of her own countertransference anxieties, collude with the patient's resistance to psychic change through prolonged escape into a fantasised past.

There is a wide spectrum of subtle and invisible ways in which the physical care of children can be eroticised. This can lead to later confusion in adults who feel they may have been abused but have no concrete memories. Alternatively a difficulty in distinguishing between memory, fantasy and desire can reflect a childhood experience of psychic abuse. Patients may feel that their sense of reality was obliterated or ignored, or that there was some more systematic attempt to distort or sabotage their memory-process.

Chapter 8

Female and male perversions?

In 1905 Freud made the observation that girls from some families grow up to become neurotic while their brothers develop aberrations (perversions) of sexual behaviour. This view of gender-differentiated psychopathologies has recently become a focus for the exploration of psychological difference between the sexes. In this chapter I explore why certain psychological problems predominate in one sex rather than the other. I compare a bulimic woman with a man who felt compelled to use hard-core pornography for solitary masturbation. Through this comparison I hope to shed further light on the debates which have emerged around Freud's theory of perversion, and in particular the challenges which have been mounted to his view of perversion as predominantly male. Certainly some types of perversion, such as fetishism and exhibitionism, are still found almost exclusively in men. But some psychotherapists have argued that women too suffer from their own specific types of perversion. These do not focus on the genitals, as in men, but on the woman's entire body or the products of her body – her children. Predominantly female problems such as self-starvation (anorexia) and bulimia (binge-eating and vomiting), which in the past might have been seen as neurotic or hysterical, are now sometimes described as female perversions (Welldon 1988, Kaplan 1991). Is this re-categorisation helpful? How do women's psychological problems differ from men's, and why?

According to Freud sexual perversion is a deviation from genital intercourse with an opposite-sex adult as the main focus of desire and satisfaction. The sexual object may be perverse – for instance a child or an animal. Or the sexual aim may be perverse, so that activities which should lead rapidly towards intercourse

become an end in themselves, as in fetishism, voyeurism or exhibitionism. In perversion the pleasures of infancy and the anal
stage are idealised, and the sexual instinct goes to 'astonishing
lengths in successfully overcoming the resistance to shame, disgust, horror or pain' (Freud 1905a).

Freud stressed that there is no clear dividing line between
perverse or infantile and 'normal' sexuality. For instance, although
there is always a strong element of sado-masochism and rigidity
in perversion, fantasies of mastery and childlike submissiveness
are universal in erotic life. Initially Freud tried to avoid pathologising homosexuality, by defining it as an inversion, but his
developmental theory inevitably implied that emotional maturity
is synonymous with reaching the Oedipal goal of genital heterosexuality.

Freud's theory of perversion revolves around the boy's search
for the penis which he knows his mother does not have. The son
'disavows' maternal 'castration', because he cannot face his own
dread that he too will have his penis cut off, a fate he imagines
his mother to have suffered. The pervert, whose sexuality is rigid
and compulsive, is arrested at the anal stage of the toddler who
battles for control over the mother and his physical functions. He
clings to the illusion that he still exists in narcissistic union with
a phallic, all-powerful mother, so that he does not have to face
loss, pain or humiliation by his paternal rival.

The boy who simultaneously denies and affirms the maternal
penis holds two contradictory beliefs at once, so that his ego or
conscious awareness becomes split. This twisting of reality is
fundamental to perversion, Freud argued (Freud 1940). The fetish
represents the sexualisation of a crisis – the boy's rude awakening
from the dream of being fused with, undifferentiated from the
mother. The fetish may be the last object the boy sees before
the mother's genitals. It is an object or part of the mother's body
(for instance a foot or a corset) which functions as a symbolic
representation of the mother's penis. So for instance the trans-
vestite – who gains sexual arousal through cross-dressing – identifies with the mother and makes the paradoxical statement that
he has no penis but he gets an erection (Stoller 1979). Fetishism
is bound up with the most primitive misogyny, the 'aversion,
which is never absent in any fetishist, to the real female genitalia'
(Freud 1927: 353). Women do not become fetishists because the
Oedipal girl has no reason to cling to the belief that her mother

has a penis. It is her own lack of a penis which the girl may be concerned to deny.

It is clearly vital that children recognise the differences between the sexes and the generations. But within the psychoanalytic literature on perversion it is often assumed that the recognition of Oedipal difference is synonymous with a heterosexual orientation. This assumption, with which I disagree, has led to persistent questioning by clinicians and feminists about the usefulness of the theory of perversion (Cunningham 1991, O'Connor and Ryan 1993).

PORNOGRAPHY AND MALE PERVERSION

It is notoriously difficult to define what pornography actually is, and to distinguish it from erotica, especially given that attitudes towards sexual representations shift constantly between different historical epochs and cultures. Pornographic literature, like perverse sexuality, is not a separate and distinct category. Donald Meltzer refers to the 'knife-edge balance' where the depiction of passion in art tips over into pornographic destructiveness (Meltzer 1973c). Within pornography itself, there is a range of explicitness. The male patient whose case I discuss in this chapter bought videos depicting explicit heterosexual intercourse and lesbian sexuality, material which occupies an intermediate category between soft-core 'girlie' magazines and the most overtly sadistic hard-core pornography.

Contemporary psychoanalysts argue that pornography differs from erotic art in the intensity of its sadistic fantasy and the perverse way it parodies sexual love. According to Stoller, in *Perversion: The Erotic Form of Hatred*, at the heart of pornography is a fantasised act of hostile revenge. 'There is always a victim, no matter how disguised' (Stoller 1975: 65). The favourite fantasy of the pornography user will encapsulate his sexual life history. Stoller argues that this usually includes a passively experienced trauma connected with sexuality or gender. The adult user of pornography, no longer a helpless child, now reverses his childhood trauma, controlling and triumphing in fantasy over those who once humiliated and attacked him. Beneath the hostility of each perverse act is a dread of emotional surrender.

Donald Meltzer describes pornography as an attack on the viewer's inner world, on the capacity for love, creativity and reparation of damage to the self and others. The attack is on the original source of life itself, the mother and her sexual relationship with the father. For this reason there is no procreation, and sex is entirely dislocated from romantic love. As my male patient pointed out, 'No one gets pregnant in pornography.' The infant's pain at exclusion from parental sex proves so intolerable that the adult still needs to debase and ridicule that relationship in a parody of idealised romantic love (Meltzer 1973c).

In *Creativity and Perversion* Chasseguet-Smirgel argues that pornography expresses the perverse desire within all of us to push forward the frontiers of what is possible and to subvert reality. She describes the pornographic obliteration of differences and distinctions, especially those between the sexes and the generations, as an attempt to avoid the reality of human helplessness in the face of psychic pain, loss and death. Pornography, which glorifies a universe of sham and pretence, reflects the little boy's idealisation of his pre-pubertal penis, his fantasy that he does not need to grow up in order to become his mother's perfect sexual partner (Chasseguet-Smirgel 1984).

Mr B

The difficulties of my patient who used pornography, Mr B, originated in infancy and were compounded in his toddler years. He came to psychotherapy at age 27 because of depression about the breakdown of an affair with a woman ten years older. He could have been good looking were it not for an air of isolation, as if he were set apart from others. He was very lonely despite working in a large sociable organisation. His recently ended affair was the third of its kind – his ongoing relationships had usually been with an older woman who selected and then dropped him after six months exactly. Not surprisingly, after what he experienced as a six-month 'honeymoon' with me he began to find the therapeutic relationship excruciatingly difficult. Gradually evidence emerged that he may well have experienced weaning from the breast at six months as the first in a series of humiliating, bitterly resented losses. Mr B referred to a too rapid 'cut-over' point, a sudden shift from breast to bottle which may have coincided with his mother being hospitalised for an operation.

Like his elder brother, Mr B had slept in the parental bedroom until he was 3. It seems likely that he experienced this constant

exposure to his parents' sexual relationship as a traumatic violation which he was forced to tolerate in isolation. The awareness
that his father retained possession of his mother's body continually reinforced his pain and jealousy. He defended himself against
desperate feelings of loneliness and exclusion by turning away
from his parents to his own penis, seeking reassurance that he
could satisfy his own needs. His compulsive masturbation was a
defence against early infantile fears of falling apart or ceasing to
exist as well as against the Oedipal pain of exclusion. Masturbation also represented a rebellion against his mother who habitually tried to stop him from touching his genitals.

Mr B initially abandoned himself to the therapeutic relationship with the passive vulnerability of a very young infant. It was
a long struggle for him to begin to engage with me in a real two-
way exchange. I often felt overwhelmed by his sense of despair
about being genuinely close to another human being.

In psychotherapy Mr B came to link his mother's use of Mills
and Boon novels – mass-market romantic fiction – with his own
obsessive retreat into pornography. He was aware that both were
addictive, escapist ways of avoiding the pain and frustration of
emotional life. Feminists have argued that popular romantic
literature functions as a form of female wish fulfilment and vicarious titillation. These books suggest that 'a woman doing what
women do all day, is in a constant state of potential sexuality'
(Snitow quoted in Segal 1987: 154).

Mr B described how he had been seen as his mother's child,
while his brother was closer to their father. His mother expected
him to be 'more than a son'. He had felt as if he was her life-
companion. His mother was highly eroticised in his mind, an
object of intense desire, but he also identified strongly with her.
It was she who 'wore the trousers' Mr B said, dominating a father
who he initially described as chronically passive and withdrawn.
Within his culture women were expected to be strong-minded,
and often headed the household. However, in dismissing his
father and identifying with a maternal figure who laid down the
law, Mr B could deny the strength of his Oedipal rivalry and
homosexual desire.

Occasionally Mr B would refer to his mother as 'he' and his
father as 'she'. He expressed this confusion of identifications
through a fascination with pornographic images of lesbian sex,
one of the most prevalent images in male heterosexual porno-

graphy. The female couple represented Mr B and his mother. It may also have represented the narcissistic mother who satisfies herself. By banishing his father from the Oedipal scene Mr B protected himself from infantile anxieties about separation from his mother and from unresolved Oedipal conflicts with his father. Lesbian sexuality has an enormous fascination for many heterosexual men because they can bolster themselves against anxieties about heterosexual potency by controlling the two women in fantasy and imagining that only they can truly satisfy them (Spector Person 1986). Such men are psychologically similar to transvestites since, like Mr B, they simultaneously identify with and desire the phallic, all-powerful mother. Women are far less likely to be erotically preoccupied with fantasies of male homosexuality. This may reflect the fact that for the boy the mother is the first object of identification and of desire.

Although Mr B spoke of his father as weak and castrated at the beginning of therapy, this contrasted sharply with the parental relationship as depicted in one of Mr B's childhood dreams. There his father was represented as a powerful, unassailable sexual rival, an evil knight who kidnapped a beautiful princess-mother. After hearing him denigrate his father for several years I was amazed when he suddenly disclosed that this weak pitiable creature was actually physically strong and handsome – 'a fine figure of a man'. He now told me for the first time that his father had been an amateur boxing champion and a teenage war-hero who'd survived gruelling experiences as a prisoner of Hitler's army. Mr B could also now acknowledge that a childhood revulsion against touching or sitting near his father might have masked a powerful homosexual fascination with him.

As the omnipotent voyeur of heterosexual pornographic couplings, Mr B unconsciously engaged in a shifting kaleidoscope of painful and pleasurable identifications with each parent. Through his total power over the celluloid images in whose intercourse he could intervene at will, Mr B reversed his helpless infantile exclusion, and revenged himself on both parents. 'My dad stole mum away . . . she chose him over me. Perhaps when I see women being dominated, I feel I'm getting my own back.' He was, he acknowledged, unsure whether the women he watched were crying out in anguish or delight. Through this confusion Mr B satisfied his conflicting desires simultaneously to protect his princess-mother from the evil knight and to punish her for her unfaithfulness.

Gradually this Oedipal battle moved from the video screen into my consulting-room. Mr B fought to maintain an illusion of being the centre of my emotional life, as he had imagined himself to be the focus of his mother's. After seeing a mechanic in the street mending a car he believed to be mine, Mr B embarked on one of a series of bitter and prolonged battles for control of my presence and the therapeutic environment. It began with him noticing a weakness in one of my chairs. 'Chairs that might break', he pointed out later, 'are like mothers who aren't there when you need them.'

Soon, his attention shifted to the perimeters of my flat. He declared my neighbourhood dangerous and the doorlocks flimsy. Angrily projecting his own aggression outside himself, Mr B pointed out that I might be intruded upon or attacked by violent men. He then stayed away for several sessions. During one of his session times he occupied himself with a pornographic book in which a man violently attacked and seriously injured his girlfriend in a sexualised assault. He came back worried about having for the first time bought such overtly sadistic material. He did not want this to continue.

Mr B realised that he used pornographic fantasy to 'bind', or contain aggressive urges that had arisen originally in relation to his mother. But at the same time he dreaded that constant exposure to debased or cruel sexual imagery would corrupt him, leading him actually to become violent or murderous towards women, including myself within the maternal transference. Unconsciously he had stayed away to protect me from an actual aggressive attack and was mortified to realise how violently he had assaulted me in fantasy.

Interestingly, given my focus on escapist psychological activities, I responded to this alarming incident by immediately forgetting the vicious details of this fantasised attack on my body. This imaginary assault seemed temporarily to suspend my ability to think about the therapeutic material, and I only remembered it when re-reading my notes months later. Presumably Mr B was projecting onto me his intolerable anxieties about acting out his aggressive feelings, and I was reacting with an only partly conscious fear of male violence.

For his part, Mr B gradually admitted how anxious he was with me, as he had been with his mother, that the boundaries between aggressive or sexual fantasy and real events might become blurred. He experienced this with particular acuteness at the beginning and ending of the sessions, 'when the barriers go down and then come up again'. If we really looked at his inner feelings and fantasies, would we, he wondered, be able to maintain the transference as an 'as-if' relationship? Would I be able to ensure that the professional boundaries remained intact, or could we be talking about a real love-affair, or an actual physical attack?

Pornography had provided an addictive means of escape from unresolved infantile anxieties. I was becoming increasingly aware that Mr B might be using the therapeutic relationship in a similarly escapist way. He acknowledged that one part of him wished to remain forever enmeshed in a therapeutic re-enactment of the eroticised relationship with his mother, rather than tackling the hard work involved in genuine emotional growth. 'I was waiting for you to do all the work . . . become my girlfriend, take me out', he said. With me as with her, his façade of passive compliance belied a silent eroticised rebellion.

Mr B's use of pornography was a compulsion rather than an addiction. It was not an organised perversion, since he could enjoy genital sex without the use of pornography and reduced his dependency on it greatly during his short-lived relationships with women. Yet Mr B's fantasies were perverse, and I found much of the literature on perversion helpful in understanding the therapeutic relationship with him. Freud observed in 1914 that people whose sexual lives are deeply committed to perversion do not come to analysis to be cured. Like all those for whom addictions or perversions have become more real than social relationships, Mr B wanted initially to moderate his use of pornography so that he could continue to use it without danger of interference (Meltzer 1973c). Pornography was like a treasured love-object, always there when he needed it, unlike an actual woman whose wishes could not be predicted and who might eventually leave him. It was a great struggle for him to give up such a reliable love-object. He would tell me he had incinerated it all, but later confess that he had kept one pornographic magazine, which would eventually become the basis of a new collection.

The danger for a therapist with a patient like Mr B is that he will 'make a concerted effort at certain stages . . . to dislodge the analyst from his accustomed role and to convert the entire procedure into one which has the structure of their perverse or addictive trend' (Meltzer 1973c: 136). Indeed, falling prey to a common therapeutic hazard, I did not notice this attempt to pervert the transference until the process was well under way. For instance, in one session I was puzzled by jokes he was making about a bawdy passage of Shakespeare and only realised afterwards that he was trying (with some success) to draw me into collusion with a pornographic discourse.

The perverse transference is characterised by extremes of idealisation for the analyst and the psychotherapeutic process, combined with cynical contempt (Meltzer 1973c). Mr B's view of me did shift with extreme rapidity between scorn for me as a deluded fool committed to a useless process and idealisation of me as the source of all wisdom.

Likewise at times I found myself idealising Mr B's progress in therapy. I was like a doting mother, seeing signs of change always around the corner, however slight the evidence. Meltzer argues that the female therapist can easily fall into this countertransference trap, taking up the role of the adoring mother who idealises her son. Male therapists are in Meltzer's view more likely to be drawn into a collusive form of infantile sexual enjoyment with a perverse patient. For instance after one session in which I thought that Mr B was working hard and using all my interpretations creatively I discovered that his main preoccupation had been with the strip-show he planned to visit as soon as he left my house, the prelude to a weekend 'pornographic binge'. This replicated the way he had bided his time helpfully until his unsuspecting mother went shopping so that he could then raid his brother's hidden stock of pornographic magazines.

Mr B wanted to become more capable of intimacy while clinging to his use of pornography, an essentially contradictory wish. The despair at the root of this determination to keep the perverse or addictive habit must, Meltzer argues, be resolved in therapy before the struggle against the underlying problems can be initiated. Mr B was also desperate not simply to 'paper over the cracks' but to achieve radical change.

He decided to end psychotherapy after beginning a new sexual relationship, the first since he had begun seeing me. After four difficult years distinct changes were visible. I suggested to him that he might stay longer to consolidate some of these psychic shifts, but he felt strongly that he was ready to leave. It had been noticeable for a while that he had developed sociable hobbies, a network of real friends and, astonishingly, a reputation as an informal social organiser. His air of being set apart from the world, perhaps the result of an identification with an elderly sick mother, had dissipated and his natural good looks were now visible.

His new girlfriend was different from his previous lovers in being just slightly younger than him and more an equal than a maternal figure. His use of pornography had diminished and then stopped a few months before he met her. Through his transference to me he had developed a capacity to think about his need and destructiveness in a new way. He did not now feel so compelled to 'bind' his aggression through perverse eroticism for fear of actually acting on his impulses. His ambivalent preoccupation with a dominating internal mother had lessened now that his father had emerged as someone worth identifying with.

BULIMIA: HYSTERIA OR PERVERSION?

Mrs K was a depressed 28 year old whose marriage had recently ended. As far as she knew her infancy was relatively contented until, at eighteen months old, her much-loved father died. She might have coped with that loss were it not for another death. Her little brother died during her fourth year. She held herself responsible for this accident, the mysterious circumstances of which were never discussed in her family.

Mrs K remained constantly preoccupied with this second death. Through her bulimia, which began when she was 20, she attempted to vomit up a dead internal object, which her guilt had prevented her mourning. Childhood compulsive-eating and casual sexual 'binges' in adulthood were both attempts to escape from this utterly unassimilable inner reality. In her family, Mrs K said, eating was seen as 'the only legitimate female pleasure'. Yet, like Mr B, Mrs K felt that her mother had unwittingly aroused her sexually, by stroking her legs in a way she found tantalisingly erotic. She experienced her mother as possessive and controlling, yet also absent or preoccupied at crucial moments, as Mr B had done. During and after her marriage Mrs K rebelled absolutely against the strict religious prohibitions against female sexual pleasure which she had internalised as a child. Her adult sexual relationships had always had a sado-masochistic quality. She and her husband had for a brief period looked at pornography during sex, a more characteristic way for women to use it than for lone masturbation.

Mrs K's mother had avoided facing her own reactions to these two tragic family deaths through immersing herself in fundamentalist religion. She expected her daughter to do the same. 'God wanted little James' was all Mrs K's mother would say about the accident. As a result, whatever capacities the little girl had developed to tolerate and digest emotional experience disintegrated. This was clearly evident in her early therapy sessions. She would rush in, flood me with desperate, disorganised emotion, gulp greedily at my interpretations like a starving infant, and rush off again to binge sweet milky food and vomit up the whole experience in secret.

Mrs K's fear of damaging me was intense, since she felt that her childhood rivalry had killed the little sandy-haired brother who was now re-emerging in the transference relationship with me. Initially, her intense need, rage and rivalry were evacuated secretly through bulimia and random, occasionally dangerous, sexual exploits. During one of these encounters, she thinks she may have risked being murdered. As her brother's mysterious death was slowly reconstructed from fragments of memory and dream her actions and feeling-states communicated to me her overwhelmingly powerful sense of guilt. I became worried by the strength of her urge to destroy herself or allow herself to be destroyed.

IS BULIMIA A NEW FORM OF HYSTERIA?

The theory that women tend to express unresolved psychic conflicts through their bodies was crucial to Freud's early writing on hysteria and is also central to contemporary arguments about female perversion. Freud described how his female patients, whose sexuality was more culturally repressed than men's, tended to express infantile sexual desire in a disguised way through hysteria – physical symptoms which are emotional in origin, such as anorexia, nervous 'tics' and partial paralysis (Freud with Breuer, 1893–5).

Contemporary object relations analysts, who have abandoned Freud's central emphasis on erotic life, would relate Mrs K's somatising of emotional pain to the dilemma of the daughter who must differentiate herself psychically from the mother with whose body she identifies. They argue that because of changes in the menstrual cycle and their childbearing role women remain in more constant contact with the rhythms and developmental changes of their bodies than men. The daughter's process of psychic separation is lifelong and unresolved conflicts in relation to the mother re-emerge at crucial points of the physiological life-cycle, such as puberty, pregnancy and the menopause (Pines 1986). As Luce Irigiray says,

> The girl has the mother, in some sense, in her skin, in the humidity of her mucous membranes, in the intimacy of her most intimate parts, in the mystery of her relationship to gestation, birth . . . she does not want to master the mother, but to create herself.
>
> (Irigiray 1989: 133)

Freud's grandson Ernst threw a spool of cotton backwards and forwards in an attempt to come to terms, in a symbolic way, with his mother's coming and going from the room. Irigiray points out that the girl cannot objectify the female body as the boy does, symbolising it as something quite other, a reel. Instead the girl is more likely to react to the mother's absence by becoming so distressed that she can neither eat nor sleep – symptoms which may be precursors of adult eating disorders.

Girls do not, Irigiray says, play with the backwards and forwards, angular, in-out movements made by Ernst with his reel, movements which are reminiscent of the penis in masturbation. In play, girls keep their entire bodies moving, their skipping games, dances and drawings often describing a series of womb-like circles, turning around and inside themselves. The girl is 'split differently in two', and the aim of all her movements is to re-unite, to make whole, while keeping separate, the lips of her vagina, her breasts, her mother and herself (Irigiray 1989: 134).

Mrs K's intense physical identification with her mother's body was crucial to her unconscious choice of bulimia to control unassimilable psychic pain. This maternal preoccupation was exacerbated by the lack of a significant third force – a paternal presence – in her early life. She experienced herself and her mother as identical, both simultaneously beautiful and repulsively fleshy. In Mrs K's therapy sessions it was as if, in fantasy, she wrapped herself around me and became me. When this first happened, I had the sudden alarming feeling that, without understanding how or why, the ground had been cut from under my feet and I had lost all sense of who I was. When I expressed this feeling of intense disorientation, Mrs K. then began to voice her fantasy of having stepped into my skin, sat in my chair and become the therapist rather than the patient. At this point, I began to regain my capacity to think and understand.

During this phase of the therapy Mrs K arrived wearing clothes as similar to mine as possible. For the first time she became visibly enraged with me in a session. Her anger focused on the fact that I wore an unpredictable colour, one she disliked too much to copy. If she could actually experience herself as being me or her mother, rather than a separate individual in her own right, then in fantasy she could control us. Imagining that she possessed all our attributes, she could avoid experiencing her usual envy of us.

Through her bulimia Mrs K expressed her ambivalence about psychic autonomy from her mother. But her symptom also revealed a deep dilemma about her sexual orientation. In her fantasy life, Mrs K exemplified Freud's old category of the hysteric. The prevalence of hysteria in women, Freud had argued, was due to the peculiar difficulties women faced in resolving Oedipal conflicts, and transferring their love from mother to father. Poised between the maternal and paternal object, the hysteric 'wanders' between them, forever rejecting those who love her, always seeking the unattainable (Kohon 1986). She is unable to love when sex is present because of her inability to resolve the incestuous Oedipal conflicts at the root of all human desire.

This was certainly the case with Mrs K, who constantly oscillated emotionally between men and women, as representative of her internal mother and father. She wanted to come between her parents and have exclusive possession of each. She could not, she insisted, face the idea of her mother or myself being part of a sexual couple. 'It makes me feel ill', she said. After arriving an hour early for her session one morning, she acknowledged fantasies of bumping into the man in my life and luring him away. Her feelings about parental sexuality may have remained unresolved because of her father's premature death. They were exacerbated by her own guilt about her brother's death which meant that she could not feel positive about creating new life. But she also felt a desperate need to bring her parents together, accepting them as a couple inside her, so that she could relinquish her obsession with them and build her own adult emotional life. In her therapy, as in her life, Mrs K wanted a woman when she was with a man, and a man when she was with a woman. This was illustrated graphically when, soon after a holiday break and feeling overwhelmed by a combination of rage and devouring need for me, she attempted to vomit up the therapy by visiting a series of male psychiatrists. One of them gave her a strict fatherly lecture when she finally refused his offer of treatment, having decided to remain in therapy with me. Yet in reality her mother had acted as both parents, and was, Mrs K told me, a 'sexually ambiguous figure whose behaviour was sometimes more male than female'. She associated the psychiatrist's emphasis on adjusting surface behaviour with her mother's methods of control. But he also 'gave her licence', as she imagined her father might have done, to risk a period of depression if she gave up her bulimic symptom. Angry at the psychiatrist's confrontational style, she decided 'out of cussedness' that she could now tolerate her feelings enough to give up bingeing and vomiting while remaining in therapy with me, 'rather than doing it with strangers'. In fact, she did give up vomiting, and also more gradually stopped binge-eating. She was becoming more able to contain her emotions and avoid addictive activities especially during breaks in therapy. This was an indication that she had begun to internalise me as someone who could set limits and boundaries, perhaps as a paternal figure.

Mrs K sees herself as very feminine, yet simultaneously rejects conventional definitions of womanhood. For instance she insisted that, although she wanted a permanent love-relationship with one person, psychically she would always be bisexual. She struggles to differentiate herself from a mother who she perceived as possessing everything, including stereotypically male as well as female personality traits. She knew that she needed a stronger identification both with an imaginary father and with the forceful decisiveness and personal authority that she associated with men. Mrs K expresses her desire to absorb masculinity through fantasies of having a penis temporarily attached to her, or making her entire body into one. For instance she told me that, when she stood up tall and erect to give an important paper at an international conference, she had the momentary feeling that her body was like a penis.

This subversive attitude towards gender norms typifies the hysteric, as described by Lacan and some of his feminist followers (Mitchell 1984). From a Lacanian perspective the hysteric does not know whether to identify her body as male or female. This fundamental question reveals the impossibility of reducing identity to gender. The culturally imposed sexual divide is, according to Lacan, the cause of a fundamental psychic split which sets both males and females on a path towards incompletion. Hysterics are not always women. If anyone is pushed beyond the limits of their knowledge and capacity to articulate emotion they can become hysteric, Lacan argues. In the Lacanian culture hysteria is seen as an expression of dissatisfaction with the limits of existing knowledge and convention. Attention to the questions underlying the hysteric symptom can advance cultural, clinical and academic knowledge. Anorexia, bulimia and 'complaint' (lack of direction) are seen as modern manifestations of hysteria and are treated as such in Lacanian clinics (Ragland-Sullivan 1992).

So far I have explored different theories about women's predisposition to somatise psychic pain. But why exactly are they more prone to serious eating problems than men? Clearly the girl's identification with her mother's capacity to produce food from her body before and after birth must be crucial. Unable to 'exhibit' any physiological difference from the mother, the woman – Mrs K – expresses her conflicts about psychic separation through continually incorporating and evacuating sweet, milky food. Mrs K's observation that within her sexually repressive culture eating was women's only legitimate pleasure is vitally important. She described early experiences of pleasurable gorging within her female-dominated family, where, stereotypically, her mother's life revolved around the providing of food.

The cultural ambivalence towards women's bodies and procreative capacities – which are simultaneously idealised and denigrated – is another fundamental reason for female anxiety about weight and size. Physical attractiveness and youthful fertility are two traditional sources of female self-esteem. The desire to maintain a certain image of femininity may serve to exacerbate eating problems which might otherwise remain minor.

Most crucially, the ambivalence so fundamental to eating problems is an expression of a typically female dilemma about sexual orientation and identity. Having been required to transfer her love at the Oedipal phase Mrs K remains poised, as many women are, between her first and second love-object. The girl who accepts her own autonomous womanly body simultaneously acknowledges her unequal position within patriarchy, and this is what the female bulimic – or the hysteric – refuses to do. Instead she clings to an illusion of omnipotence through unconscious attempts to control the maternal body. It is significant that Mrs K both sought and resisted identification with what the father represents in our culture, eventually managing to relinquish her symptom as she took up a more influential position in the wider world.

In contrast men often act out their dilemmas about differentiation from the mother and identification with the father through a preoccupation with the penis, and with eroticisation of early need and aggression. In this way the man tries to strengthen his tenuous grasp on masculinity and 'phallic' potency, agency and mastery. The male propensity towards 'perverse' denial of sexual difference has its origins in the boy's early pain about sacrificing his illusion of physiological fusion with the mother, and accepting that he can neither be like her physiologically nor satisfy her sexually with his tiny penis. Many boys deal with early loss and Oedipal humiliation by making a false separation from the lost maternal object, which is seen as absolutely alien, external and other, although unconsciously all differentiation is denied. For men in our society there are many institutionalised ways of simultaneously denying and clinging to the repudiated 'feminine' aspects of their own psyches, most obviously through a preoccupation with denigrated representations of the female body which can be controlled in fantasy.

In different ways bulimia and the compulsive use of pornography reflect a preoccupation with objectification and sexual looking. 'Where oral fixations occur looking functions similarly to eating, and it is subject to the same intensifications and vicissitudes', Rosen argues (Rosen 1979b: 47). But in our society women are usually the object of the male gaze, while men watch. Mrs K saw her entire body as a pornographic object, which she tried to control. She described herself as feeling from infancy onward like a pretty, passive doll, to be displayed enticingly and played with by others. It had, she said, taken her a long time to realise that she could actively engage in and feel herself a part of her own sexual life. This sense of objectification was reflected in her concern with the physical functions of her body and its fluctuations of weight. It also revealed itself in her anguished fascination with attracting and repelling the advances of voyeuristic men.

Mr B's main preoccupation was in looking at others, who represented his mother or the parental couple. But the voyeur is always an exhibitionist, and he also experienced himself as a passive feminine object awaiting the advances of motherly princesses, an identification which was enacted through pornographic images of lesbian sexuality.

Each of these patients identified with a maternal figure committed to emotional escapism – romance and fundamentalist religion – through whom they could not internalise the capacity to process and learn from their own psychic life. Instead there was a demand that they maintain a veneer of total filial conformity or 'polished perfection'. There was no paternal figure (of either sex) who could set benign limits, so helping them to develop their own psychological boundaries. This contributed to their difficulties in developing an internal regulatory capacity through which they could set limits on their physical and emotional appetites. Instead they each remained preoccupied with psychic struggles against a dominating internalised mother, who laid down the law, against which they secretly rebelled.

SEXUAL PERVERSION – IS IT MALE?

Is perversion a gendered category? Freud, as we have seen, categorised perversion as male, arguing that the boy's pride in the penis induces great castration anxiety, a fear of losing access to paternal potency and privilege. In Freud's theory the perverse male clings to the illusion of undifferentiated symbiosis with the mother by disavowing his knowledge of sexual difference. He avoids Oedipal rivalry and identification with his father by idealising his own infantile sexuality and becoming fixated to a perverse search for the maternal penis.

The boy fantasises that his penis is a magnificent weapon, and can in imagination use it to externalise aggressive conflicts and sexualise psychic pain (Freud 1924a). In contrast, Freud argued, the girl reacts to her genital lack with humiliation and envy. When reinforced by the cultural repression of female sexuality this narcissistic wound leads to a stronger sense of shame, disgust and compassion (Freud 1910b). The female sex is therefore less ruthless and directly sadistic, more tender and sentimental in all areas of life, including the sexual, he claimed.

Janine Chasseguet-Smirgel endorses Freud's view that boys are far more likely to short-circuit development through perversion. She argues that mothers often collude with the son's fantasy that he is already her ideal sexual partner, as Mr B's may have done. Chasseguet-Smirgel says that the daughter cannot compensate for early infantile humiliations in this way since her mother will not desire her sexually as she does the son, unless she herself is perverse. The mother of the neurotic girl does not make her feel special, but excessively devalued (Chasseguet-Smirgel 1988).

Chasseguet-Smirgel goes on to say that the girl who has been loved too seductively by the father becomes neurotic rather than perverse, because she has usually been 'made to wait' until toddlerhood for her father to become interested in her. The daughter, who will have experienced inevitable frustration in her early relationship with her mother, is not so easily seduced into the illusion of being the centre of a parent's life.

The strongest part of this argument is Chasseguet-Smirgel's stress on how the boy is encouraged to overvalue his genitals and his sexuality. But this is not purely because of the mother's seductive attention. It relates to the general cultural fetishisation of the penis, which is regarded with awe and admiration as well as fear. In general, like many contemporary analysts, Chasseguet-Smirgel tends to blame the mother for perversion, thus leaving many questions unanswered. For instance it is obviously true that the father is usually not the primary parent, and so his sexualised attention may not have such a fundamental effect on the child's identity as maternal incest. But Chasseguet-Smirgel weakens her argument by failing to mention the prevalence of actual sexual abuse, which is most often perpetrated by the father against the daughter and inevitably has a fundamental effect on her adult psychosexuality. I also disagree with Chasseguet-Smirgel's assumption that mothers will not desire their daughters unless they are perverse. Many actively heterosexual women have a strong component of bisexuality, and the mother's sensual pleasure in the daughter need not be harmful unless she is unduly seductive. In fact maternal desire is an important component of the girl's sense of herself as beautiful and lovable.

Some analysts agree with Freud that perversion is a mainly male phenomenon, but they give a different explanation for why this is so. Like Horney, Jones and Klein, they argue that each sex has a separate line of sexual development, and that women may not need to resort to sexual perversion because they have other, characteristically feminine ways of defending against psychic pain. For instance Greenacre argues that women do not need fetishes as the sole means of arousal because they can conceal their lack of sexual excitement or pleasure, unlike men, for whom any appreciable interference with potency obviously and drastically affects sexual performance. Female pride is, therefore, usually less invested in erotic performance. Therefore fetishism usually only occurs in women when the idea of being male is strong enough to become a delusion (Greenacre 1979).

Similarly, Freud argued that since women experience their lack of a penis as a narcissistic injury, exhibiting the genitals outside the sexual act as a way of gaining sexual satisfaction does not reinforce female pride. In contrast the male exhibitionist who 'flashes' his genitals protects himself from extreme castration anxiety and gains a gratifying sense of potency through the fear and shock of his female victim (Rosen 1979a). Men may well be more proud of their erect penis than women of their genitals. But what is even more significant is that both sexes associate the male genitalia with rape. Behind many male perversions is an implicit threat of sexual aggression. In contrast, where the female genitals are displayed, as in pornography, the expectation is that the onlooker will be aroused. The woman who shows her genitals offers herself as an object, inviting rather than threatening the viewer.

In some ways Freud's theorising about men and women's different psychopathology seems dated. For instance cultural expectations of female sexuality have changed greatly since Freud's day. Indeed there is no evidence that women have less sexual desire than men although it is often mobilised in different ways. Mrs K, although similar in some ways to Freud's 'hysteric' patients, was actually far more sexually active and adventurous than Mr B whose symptom was more directly eroticised. For instance she acted out her bisexual desire towards women, while Mr B only gradually became able to mention his attraction towards men. There is much current media interest in the idea of a new, sexually assertive and perhaps predatory female who might be interested in soft-core pornography and male strip-shows. Some feminists argue that the 'conventions of gender and sexuality are . . . being actively tampered with. . . . Maybe it isn't a sexuality which wholly breaks free from the oppressive codes of women as sexual commodities but neither does it straightforwardly reproduce them' (Winship quoted in Segal 1987: 154). Yet despite these cultural changes, as Mrs K pointed out, most women are still brought up to think about attracting and pleasing others rather than satisfying themselves sexually.

It is obviously true that some organised perversions are mainly found in men. This seems to be related to men's overvaluation of the penis and their capacity to use it symbolically to sexualise pain and aggression, as well as to a different early relationship with the parents. In contrast women, whose sexuality is more diffuse, tend to remain preoccupied with somatising psychic pain and aggression through their own bodies, unconsciously identified with that of the mother. But perverse fantasies, where aggression is more dominant than loving concern, are just as common in women, who also engage in some of the activities Freud saw as perversions.

THE CASE FOR FEMALE PERVERSIONS

The idea that there is a special category of female perversion has recently become influential. Eating disorders, self-cutting, female prostitution and maternal incest have all been included in this category (Welldon 1988, Kaplan 1991). It is argued that women do not direct sexualised aggression towards an objectified other, as in male perversion. Instead women form a perverse relationship with their own or their children's bodies.

Writers who make this argument draw on a range of contemporary mother-centred theories to show that the entire female body is eroticised, rather than just the genitals. Women's erotic experience is therefore more subtle, complex and diffuse, with pleasure zones located all over the body (Irigiray 1977, 1989). The boy can check that his penis is still intact but the girl's fears about damage to her reproductive and genital organs cannot be so easily allayed by reality-testing (Klein 1928). This means that women may be more prone to an internal sense of rottenness, persecution or emptiness because they cannot so easily escape anxieties about envious maternal attacks on their body. These anxieties may be reinforced by the onset of menstruation which the neurotic girl may unconsciously associate with harm to the interior of the body. Women who constantly feel very concerned about their appearance, as bulimics do, may unconsciously be attempting to compensate for this imagined internal damage and decay.

Those who argue that there are specifically female forms of perversion often define perversion in a different way from Freud, who used the word perversion in an exclusively sexual context. Like many object relations or Kleinian analysts they may focus on whether sexual fantasy life reflects a capacity for loving concern or a sado-masochistic dehumanisation of the other.

From the Kleinian perspective perverse character structures are seen as being equally pervasive in women and men. Meltzer argues that a destructive part of the self which cannot tolerate the mother's closeness to another person gains dominance over more trusting parts of the personality using the slogan 'Evil be Thou My Good'. What is valuable and enviable – originally parental sexual creativity – is twisted and spoiled in the mind, while destructiveness and harm is admired and glorified (Meltzer 1973c). The personality becomes rooted in a fixed position where madness is avoided but the personality cannot develop. Guilt and depression cannot be tolerated, and so reparation cannot be made. As a result the capacity for loving concern within sexual relationships is impaired. Perverse sexual activities do not necessarily exist, but the distortion and twisting of truth (originally Oedipal) leads to a perverse 'borderline' relationship to reality. In analysis the perverse patient 'turns a blind eye' to insight, seeking help but failing to use it. At times there may be the appearance of emotional growth but a 'pathological organisation' of this kind is profoundly resistant to change, which might involve the risk of breakdown (Steiner 1987).

The problem with much of the contemporary literature on female perversion is that the definition has become so broad that it ceases to be meaningful. It often seems to include most typically female ways of mobilising psychic pain. It is easy to see how bulimia can be described as a perversion of the eating process, since it subverts the digestive process and breaks the link between eating and nourishment. But are all eating problems perverse? Similarly Estela Welldon argues that prostitution is a female perversion because it affords the opportunity to practise perverse activities while disowning the desire to do so. Again, questions immediately spring to mind about how to categorise prostitution that does not involve perverse activities (Welldon 1988).

While bulimia can be compared to perversion, there are also considerable differences. Bulimia was likened to masturbation by a female patient who described how her initial overwhelming excitement came to a climax when she vomited, to be followed by a sense of post-prandial depression. For the bulimic the digestive process has become eroticised, but binge-eating and vomiting differs from perversion in that it does not provide direct sexual gratification or orgasmic release. This is very significant in clinical practice. There is less secondary gain in serious eating problems than perverse sexuality, and so, when a patient is highly motivated as Mrs K was, it is much easier to renounce the symptom and begin working on the underlying conflicts.

Mr B's use of pornography was not his sole source of sexual satisfaction, and he could almost give it up when he had a girl-friend, so it was not exactly an organised perversion. But pornography had been since adolescence his most consistent love-object, and when he first came for psychotherapy it was more real to Mr B than social relationships. Although he wanted to moderate his habitual use of pornography, he was extremely sexually and emotionally dependent on it. This led to a particu-larly twisted transference relationship where I sometimes found myself colluding with his attempts to delude me and lead the psychotherapy into a cul-de-sac. When Mr B stayed away from his sessions and consumed pornography, or concealed the fact that he was going straight on to a strip-pub, he was using the sessions as a form of pornography. He was intensely dependent on me, but it had become a quasi-analytic relationship, a pretend psychotherapy, and I was temporarily deluded into idealising a sham.

In contrast Mrs K's transference relationship with me was buli-mic so that she binged and vomited analytic nourishment in a self-destructive way. But, because she did not idealise her bulimia and her erotic life did not revolve so strongly around it, she did not need to involve me in such an insidiously twisted collusion.

In my view the term 'female perversion' is limited in its useful-ness. The really positive aspect of this debate is that it gives women's sexuality a central place in analytic theory. But the focus is still on women's reproductive role and their identification with the mother. There is a lack of discussion of women's actual sexual activity even when this fits in with classical definitions of perversion.

Feminist and gay writers have fundamentally questioned the use of the term perversion because of its deeply rooted biologistic and moralistic assumptions. They have asked whether it can be subverted, and used to include aspects of female sexuality, or to develop a more positive analysis of homosexuality. Alternatively they suggest that the psychoanalytic theory of perversion should simply be discarded.

Some writers draw on the psychoanalytic literature on perversion to develop a radical understanding of how gay and lesbian eroticism transgresses the patriarchal social order (Dollimore 1991). Others suggest that relationships conventionally seen as perverse, such as lesbian sado-masochism, are actually much healthier than 'normal' heterosexuality. From an academic perspective, Parveen Adams argues that lesbian sado-masochism does not display the compulsiveness, rigidity and castration anxiety characteristic of male heterosexual masochism. Instead, desire is freed from a focus around the penis into a myriad more flexible representations. She argues that lesbian sado-masochism subverts patriarchal codes of gender and power and allows the women who practise it to escape the pathology that besets the rest of their sex (Adams 1989).

We each have to make an individual decision about the point where real or fantasised sexual play with power and submissiveness slips into actual cruelty or emotional suffering. Parveen Adams avoids this by leaving out any concrete discussion of physical pain or humiliation in the sado-masochistic encounter. The female sadist seems to have escaped from the feminist frame. Mandy Merck also points out that conventional pornography, which often includes lesbian as well as heterosexual sado-masochism, reflects a profound hatred of life and a vicious attack on the womb that bore it. However, the possibility that hatred of the mother might fuel lesbian sado-masochism is not often discussed in this feminist literature. It is particularly dangerous for women to ignore their own sadistic impulses and see themselves purely as masochists, since in doing so we also avoid recognising the ways in which our aggression can be used creatively in our own interests (Merck 1993b).

I do not think it is possible to reclaim the term 'perverse' for sexually subversive ends unless we entirely alter its meaning.

Intrinsic to the psychoanalytic definition of perversion is the idea of a deep commitment to cruelty, dehumanisation and twisting of individual emotional truth. As a psychotherapist I do find this understanding of perversion clinically useful. Yet at the same time I disagree with the assumption that truth and reality are inevitably bound up with heterosexual reproductive sex. Rather than describing some orientations or activities as perverse – whether these be homosexual or heterosexual – I would define perversion in a more general way, focusing, for instance, on the degree of love and concern in unconscious sexual fantasy life.

CONCLUSION

Both 'perversion' and 'hysteria' have become pejorative terms and are used in ways which are normative and biologistic. The only justification for using them is that a clinical literature exists which is illuminating in working with some patients. I do not see perversion as a gendered category, although there are some organised perversions which are mainly male.

I am dubious about defining stereotypical ways of mobilising psychic pain as female perversions. Often they can more easily be understood as neurosis or even hysteria. For instance, Mrs K's bulimia was a compulsion, but it did not stand in place of a sexual love-object and was therefore easier to relinquish. Her constant oscillation of identity and desire is closer to hysteria as described by Freud and Lacan than to perversion. She also fitted into this category by virtue of her subversive attitude towards conventional norms of gender and identity.

Both Mrs K and Mr B had retreated into their bodies in order to control unbearable emotional pain through quasi-addictive physical rituals. But in stereotypically female fashion, Mrs K enviously attacked and devalued her entire body through an indirectly libidinised relationship to food. A combination of psychic, cultural and physiological factors cause women to experience themselves as the object rather than the subject of desire. The cultural denial of the power of female sexuality reflects unconscious envy and anxiety in relation to the early mother.

In contrast Mr B sexualised his pain and rage, focusing on his genitals – which are overvalued in our culture – and attacked an objectified female body in fantasy. In this way he also denied his early envy since in fantasy he possessed himself of the femininity of the object he mastered. Through refusing fully to face the reality of genital difference he expressed his ambivalent desire to re-enter the maternal womb, with its accompanying dread of losing what distinguishes him from the mother – his identity as male.

A lack of paternal involvement and of possibilities to identify with psychological masculinity has different consequences for the girl and boy. The boy who is unable fully to identify with the privileges and prerogatives of his sex may become fixated, continually needing to reassure himself in very literal sexualised ways that he has a grasp on virility and potency. The girl who has been offered no pathway out into the external world and who cannot find a way of identifying with the psychic 'masculinity' of either parent may act out her sense of being trapped in a destructive symbiosis. Clearly there is a relationship between gender-linked symptoms, early development and male–female power relations. Much more work needs to be done on these areas, and particularly on the interconnection between physiological experience, unconscious fantasy and social forces.

In the final chapter I continue this discussion of recent debates which have emerged around Freud's theory of perversion. It has been pointed out by lesbians and gay men that, while women have continually been able to challenge psychoanalytic theorising about femininity, including raising questions about female perversion, the exclusion of homosexuals from many professional trainings has prevented them from having a similar input into analytic thinking about sexual orientation. Nevertheless the question I explore next – whether homosexuality is pathological – has become a source of profound and painful controversy within the world of psychoanalytic psychotherapy.

Chapter 9

Is homosexuality pathological?

Homosexuality created an irresolvable theoretical dilemma for Freud who argued against those who wanted to 'abolish' it. Writing to James Jackson Putnam, an American colleague who wanted analysts to take a strong moral line with patients, Freud said, 'Sexual morality as society – and indeed American society – defines it, seems very despicable to me. I stand for a much freer sexual life' (Dollimore 1991: 172). Freud and his early followers tended to have a liberal cosmopolitan stance towards homosexuality, placing great emphasis on the cultural and artistic achievements of homosexual scholars and thinkers throughout the centuries. Sandor Ferenczi campaigned for the legalisation of homosexuality (Stanton 1990) and in 1935 Freud wrote a 'Letter to an American Mother' in which he said, 'Homosexuality is . . . no vice, no degradation; it cannot be classified as an illness; we consider it to be a variation of the sexual function. . . . It is a great injustice to persecute homosexuality as a crime – and a cruelty too' (Freud 1935b).

Freud stressed the continuity between heterosexual and homosexual love, saying that he had never conducted a single psychoanalysis without 'having to take into account a very considerable current of homosexuality' (Freud 1905b: 95). Freud also emphasised that inhibitions in the capacity to love may stem as much from difficulties with the same-sex parent, as with the parent of the opposite sex.

It is ironic then that in 1993 the writers of a book on lesbianism and psychoanalysis should conclude that homosexuality has been 'the site of some of the worst excesses of psychoanalysis – gross and inaccurate generalisations, explicitly manipulative goals of therapy and a striking failure to consider vital countertransference issues' (O'Connor and Ryan 1993). In fact Freud never finally decided whether homosexuality was a valid sexual orientation or evidence of pathology. Initially he described homosexuality as an 'inversion', differentiating it from other deviations which he called perversions (Freud 1905a). Later Freud wavered, sometimes placing it more clearly amongst the perversions. Despite his liberal convictions, he explicitly associated homosexuality with arrested development, describing it as a narcissistic object-choice – seeking the self in the guise of another.

In this chapter I highlight these theoretical contradictions and question the applicability of some psychoanalytic assumptions about homosexuality to cultures where attitudes towards sexual life are rapidly altering. My emphasis is on the precariousness of all sexual orientation and the subtle oscillations there are in all of us between heterosexual and homosexual desire.

DIFFERENT CULTURAL ATTITUDES TOWARDS HOMOSEXUALITY

Freud's theories, which shifted the emphasis of erotic life away from genital and procreative sex, developed at the point when in parts of Western Europe and the United States, sexuality was for the first time becoming divorced from reproduction. The idea of a homosexual identity, as referred to by Freud, is a phenomenon of late-nineteenth- or early-twentieth-century western society. In ancient Greek there were no nouns corresponding to the English words for 'homosexual' or 'heterosexual'. It was assumed that at different times everyone would experience love and desire towards males and females (Liebert 1986). Freud's *Three Essays* were written at the point when medical and psychiatric theories were being elaborated which described homosexuality as a condition, a part of someone's nature, perhaps even biologically determined. Freud's theories reflected awareness of a new way of thinking about and organising sexual life (Freud 1905a).

The American psychoanalyst Robert Liebert in a historical survey of male homosexuality (Liebert 1986) points out that most societies have found ways of simultaneously permitting and suppressing overt homosexuality while giving some outlet for bisexuality in order to preserve an enduring social fabric. This might be by rigidly codifying homosexual behaviour as in ancient Greek society, so that it could co-exist with, but not threaten, the family.

Homosexuality has often been permitted as long as it does not infringe culturally sanctioned male and female behaviour. Liebert argues that a prohibition against deviation from whatever gender roles are culturally prevalent is almost universal. For instance, although certain male homosexual acts were permitted in Ancient Greece, sexual passivity, in the form of oral and anal receptivity, was permitted only among men of the lower social orders (non-citizens). In post-renaissance Europe and America, 'special friendships', and sometimes even sex between women, were tolerated, as long as these relationships could clearly be seen as an adjunct to heterosexuality. It was when women demanded masculine social privileges, or made open declarations of a sexual preference for their own sex, that they were condemned or punished (Faderman 1992).

For a number of social reasons, including the need for an educated, mobile workforce involving large numbers of women, it has during this century for the first time become possible for increasing numbers of people to live outside the nuclear family in the USA and some parts of Europe. As a result there has been a marked increase in self-esteem among lesbians and gay men, and a growing cohesiveness of their emergent sub-cultures. Simultaneously there has been a rapid erosion of the nuclear family.

Despite this increased visibility and toleration of homosexuality, persecution has continued throughout this century. Homosexuality became legal in Britain for males over 21 only in 1967, and it remained classified as a mental illness by the American Psychiatric Association and the American Psychological Association until 1973. Twentieth-century culture has expressed simultaneously the urge to displace rejected aspects of social and emotional life onto homosexuals, and the liberal desire to integrate different sexual orientations. In its theoretical contradictions, psychoanalysis reflects both of these cultural tendencies.

MALE HOMOSEXUALITY

Freud always believed that sexual orientation might be determined by a combination of constitutional and environmental factors. He offered a number of quite distinct explanations for different forms of male homosexuality, all of which signalled an unresolved Oedipus complex. One type of exclusive male homosexuality arose when the boy defended himself against extreme castration anxiety through 'over-valuation' of the male genitals. Where such intense horror of the female genitals exists it precludes heterosexual relationships. Freud described another form of exclusive homosexuality as a defence against excessive incestuous desire for the mother. The son who identifies with an over-intense seductive mother (Freud 1905a) may later shun sexual contact with women not out of hatred and fear, as in the first explanation, but as an unconscious attempt to remain faithful to the mother. In adulthood the son may seek to re-enact that first relationship in a narcissistic way with a man he can love as his mother loved him.

Two other forms of homosexuality described by Freud could easily co-exist with heterosexual behaviour, since they did not involve such an exclusive preoccupation with the mother, or such an intense dread of her genitals. One example was that of the boy whose profound love for his mother led to exaggerated jealousy towards his siblings (Freud 1922). Through a reaction formation, this murderous rivalry was transformed into homosexual love. Since there was no hatred or dread of the woman's genitals the outcome of this constellation might be a bisexual or even a heterosexual adult orientation. This unusually early sublimation of rivalry towards other men, Freud argued, explained the frequency with which homosexual men devote themselves to enriching the lives of others in community and cultural activities.

Freud described another form of homosexuality which is in fact very common in both sexes. Instead of retaining his mother as the object of desire and identifying with his father, the boy takes both parents as erotic love-objects, while identifying with each (Freud 1918). Freud pointed out that the resulting passive homosexual longings are often repressed but lead to inhibitions within heterosexual relationships. Here Freud made a distinction which has become crucial to later psychoanalytic theories of homosexuality. You cannot be what you desire or want to possess, and you cannot have what you wish to be, or to identify with (Freud 1921). This difference between identification and desire is consolidated at the Oedipal phase, where the child takes one parent as a love-object and identifies with the other. If the two are the same it leads to disappointment or inhibition in love, as in his example above (O'Connor and Ryan 1993).

Yet even as he elaborated this theory, Freud cautioned against over-simplification in this area. He suggested that it may not be so easy to make an absolute distinction between desire and identification (Freud 1921). Sometimes we might want to possess those who are like us. Freud had already pointed out that male homosexuals are often very 'masculine' in appearance and personality, while men who take up a conventionally 'feminine' role in love-relationships may well be heterosexual (Freud 1905a).

While Freud recognised that there are many different kinds of homosexuality his followers often threw caution to the winds in their search for global explanations for the existence of 'the homosexual'. For instance it has often been argued that male homosexuals have an over-possessive, seductive or castrating mother, and an absent, ineffectual or rejecting father, with whom the son cannot easily identify. (See Friedman 1988 for a review of the literature.) But this is the most common family-pattern in our society and is described by the majority of men who come for psychotherapy, whatever their sexual orientation.

The shift since the 1920s towards theories about the mother's pre-eminence in psychic development has led to an increasing emphasis on the oral and anal origins of homosexuality. Homosexual desire is typically seen as emerging from an infantile identification with opposite-sex characteristics, rather than from a mature, Oedipal recognition of sexual difference. For instance the gay man might be seen as enmeshed in an early identification with the mother, and to be seeking in his male partners a sense of masculinity which he feels himself to lack (Freud 1949).

FEMALE HOMOSEXUALITY

If male homosexuality is seen as a perversion, lesbianism is hardly viewed as sexuality at all. In his 1920 *Psychogenesis of a Case of Female Homosexuality* Freud set out a number of themes which were to emerge consistently in the sparse later literature on lesbianism. His 20-year-old patient had had a disappointing early maternal relationship and envied her more favoured brothers. This girl had taken her father as the primary love-object at the Oedipal phase, but partially reversed this in her teens when her beloved father gave her mother another baby. Incensed at her father's 'betrayal' in making her mother pregnant again, Freud's patient 'changed into a man and took her mother instead of her father as love-object' (Freud 1920: 384). Freud, who argued that a predominance of psychic 'masculinity' was found more often in lesbians than femininity in gay men, saw his patient as a feminist who could not accept conventional notions of female passivity. She fell in love with a prostitute and courted her 'cocotte' actively, taking up what Freud described as the conventional role of the male lover.

Yet at the same time Freud's concept of bisexuality enabled him to explore the intricate oscillations of homosexual and heterosexual desire which influence the choice of love-object. He pointed out that his patient fell in love with a woman who fitted in with both her masculine and feminine ideals, since she was a mother-figure who also looked like the patient's favourite brother. Freud observes that male homosexuals also choose objects who fit masculine and feminine ideals (Freud 1920).

Freud's case history is also typical of later writings on lesbianism in that it reveals an extremely unresolved countertransference which he attributed to the patient's resistance. When we studied this text during psychotherapy training our entire seminar-group was stunned by Freud's dismissal of his patient's dream of passionate love for a man and the wish for a husband. We could see no evidence for his interpretation of this dream as a lie, a transference wish to deceive him as she had her father. Nor could we understand why, after that dream, he suddenly ended her analysis, recommending that if she started again it should be with a woman. Freud observes that it was her parents who found the young woman's sexual orientation problematic, and that her lack of personal motivation for psychoanalysis made his task difficult, if not impossible. But he may have added to his own difficulties by exaggerating his patient's hostility towards men, and identifying too strongly with her father. He seems to have been unable to accept that she might have been telling the truth when she described the heterosexual desire that still co-existed with her rage towards her father.

In later psychoanalytic literature lesbian desire is usually associated with a very early ambivalent attachment to the mother, as in the case above. There has also been a tendency to see all sexual desire as revolving around the penis, which women either desire or wish to identify with in fantasy. The idea that lesbians are likely to be male-identified has been very common amongst analysts. Freud also raises questions in this paper about whether sexual orientation can be changed through psychoanalytic treatment.

Despite his criticism of Freud's 'phallocentrism', Ernest Jones set a trend for analysing lesbianism almost entirely in terms of women's attitude towards the penis, the father and men, without any investigation of the positive reasons why women might become lesbian. In his influential 1927 paper, Jones described two types of 'masculine' woman. One type was the heterosexual woman who would like to be acknowledged as one of the men. The second was the lesbian who identifies with the idealised father. This latter type projects her own femininity onto her partner and relates to her with a male (internalised father) aspect of herself (Jones 1927a).

Five years later Helene Deutsch disagreed, arguing that psychic masculinity was not a motive for lesbianism. She warned that a mannish façade might well conceal more infantile wishes. One patient's relationship is described by her as 'a perfectly conscious mother-and-child situation, in which sometimes the one and sometimes the other played the part of the mother.... One received the impression that what made the situation so happy was precisely the possibility of playing both parts' (Deutsch 1933: 40). She stressed the flexibility of women's sexual orientation and the great variety of forms lesbian attachments could take, even amongst women who consider themselves to be heterosexual.

Joyce McDougall, whose papers have been profoundly influential, returned to the theme of lesbians' 'masculinity' (McDougall 1964, 1979). In the 1960s and 1970s she argued that lesbians defend against serious psychic disturbance through identifying with a father who they describe initially as destructive, brutal and repulsive. The mother's qualities are idealised and sought in sexual partners. This idealisation of the mother is actually a defence against the threat of succumbing entirely to a destructive state of symbiotic merger desired by the mother. Since the daughter can neither define herself as separate, nor identify with the mother's heterosexuality, taking on the father's characteristics is seen as the only solution other than utter submission to the mother. Some of my lesbian patients have similar histories to that described by McDougall, but many more have had quite different experiences.

McDougall agreed with Freud that homosexuality must fit in with the ego-ideal, the sense of personal values. In the histories of lesbians she has treated there has always been a relative or other influential figure who has either approved of, or tolerated, her sexual choice, as did the mother of Freud's patient (Freud 1920). This latter idea is for me the most interesting aspect of McDougall's work, since it could offer some explanation of why some bisexual women act out their lesbian desires directly, while others do not.

McDougall is typical of many contemporary analytic writers in adopting a liberal façade which belies her assumption that lesbianism is profoundly pathological. She consistently denies the possibility of 'real' desire between individuals of the same sex, asking, 'How is it possible for a woman to maintain the illusion of being the sexual partner to another woman?' (quoted in O'Connor and Ryan 1993: 106). Lesbian desire is 'false' in her view because it emerges from the fictitious position of identification with the father. She also seems to be arguing that the woman who thinks she is experiencing fulfilment in a lesbian relationship is actually defending herself against a very persecutory early maternal relationship by idealising her lover.

McDougall assumes that the lesbian is denying sexual difference, and therefore has a twisted and distorted relationship to psychic reality. But what does she mean by 'psychic reality' and how does she know more about what is emotionally true for her patients than they do? She does not question the objectivity of theories derived from clinical work, which is, after all, an intense engagement between two individuals with their own values and prejudices. Nor does she consider the social biases which might lead some forms of fantasy and desire to be seen as less good, healthy or true than others in any given culture.

In this view of homosexuality as a psychic denial of the sexual relationship between the parents and a defence against severe depression or paranoia, McDougall is drawing on the theories of Klein and her followers. From the Kleinian viewpoint homosexuality, like certain perversions and psychosomatic illnesses, is a 'third position' between paranoid-schizoid chaos and the depressive position. In all perverse sexuality, Kleinians argue, parental intercourse is enviously attacked through the idealisation of the diffused, pre-genital sexual play of children. Homosexuality is equated with (infantile) foreplay (Meltzer 1973a: 121).

According to Klein, heterosexuality is phylogenetically inscribed, presumably for reproduction of the race. In the unconscious of the infant an awareness of the sexual organs of its own sex is waiting to be complemented by those of the opposite sex, because of an innate knowledge of parental intercourse. Within the Kleinian tradition Meltzer argues that since loving sexual intimacy can only be based on the internal fantasy of a creative parental couple, it does necessitate the choice of a partner with different genital organs and the 'sexual qualities of mind' that accompany these biological differences (Meltzer 1973a: 121).

At the root of many classical and contemporary psychoanalytic theories is a similar assumption that homosexuality is unnatural, a transgression of biological and psychic reality. The poet H.D., describing her analysis with Freud, writes, 'When I told the Professor [Freud] that I had been infatuated with Frances Josepha and might have been happy with her, he said, "No – biologically, no" ' (H.D. 1956: 152). The American psychoanalyst Socarides wants his patients to know that homosexuality is not what culture requires, that it is meaningless and extra-territorial to the biological realities of life (Socarides 1979).

The conservatism of many contemporary psychoanalytic writings on sexuality contrasts sharply with recent developments in philosophy and in social and political theory. Rachel Cunningham (1991) points out that Kleinian psychoanalysts still accept on trust the theory of innate ideas and 'Ideal Forms' which philosophers have long challenged (Cunningham 1991).

Through her abandonment of Freud's theory of bisexuality Klein reinforced the equation of homosexuality with pathology. But her emphasis on the underlying state of mind, rather than specific sexual acts, can be used to argue that 'perversity can be equally present or absent in heterosexual and homosexual relationships alike' (Waddell and Williams 1991: 206). According to Klein the resolution of rivalry for the opposite-sex parent and feelings of depressive concern for the parental couple are vital for loving sexuality. But, as Cunningham points out, homosexuality does not necessarily involve hatred towards the parental couple. If homosexuality resulted from real love for the same-sex parent, or admiration, love and identification with the opposite-sex parent, then it would not be perverse (Cunningham 1991).

Today lesbianism is often discussed entirely in terms of the early mother–infant relationship. But why are contemporary analysts so ready to take gender at face value? In fact lesbians often experience their partners as representing significant male figures, including fathers and brothers. Similarly, when the analyst (or, by extension, the lesbian lover) is experienced as an eroticised maternal figure, we need not necessarily assume that the sexuality is infantile or 'archaic', a precursor of Oedipal genital eroticism rather than actual desire. The American psychoanalysts Welles and Wrye point out that the mother–daughter relationship can be erotic in its own right. Sexual wishes and fantasies may be directed towards an Oedipal mother, who is separate from the self, a source of pleasure as well as identification (Welles and Wrye 1991).

It is not just the sex of the partners which determines whether a relationship is heterosexual or homosexual, but the nature of the unconscious fantasies of both participants. For instance, a female patient told me of a 'revelation' in a dream, that she was actually a lesbian and her male lover was gay, although neither had ever had homosexual sex. 'It works because he is attracted to me with his homosexual part and I'm attracted to him with my lesbian part', she said. Similarly a child may be born into a heterosexual relationship where the underlying parental fantasies are homosexual – when for instance one partner is unconsciously preoccupied erotically with their own sex. Chasseguet-Smirgel describes a heterosexual marriage which is unconsciously lesbian since the woman has married the 'bad mother' (Chasseguet-Smirgel 1964b). This is clearly a pathological marriage. But what if the woman had married a man who unconsciously represented a beloved female relative? Presumably this would also be an unconsciously lesbian match, but it might afford more fulfilment than if the woman had married a hated father-figure. It is also possible that a homosexual partnership might actually be unconsciously heterosexual.

CAN SEXUAL ORIENTATION CHANGE?

If homosexuality is a defence against profound internal disturbance, a perversion or a blockage of the heterosexual impulse, then deep psychic change is impossible unless there is a 'cure' in sexual orientation. But is this possible, even if the patient wants it? Freud was pessimistic about the chances of altering a fixed sexual orientation. 'In general, to undertake to convert a fully developed homosexual into a heterosexual does not offer much more prospect of success than the reverse, except that for good practical reasons the latter is never attempted' (Freud 1920: 376). Freud argued that a confirmed homosexual would never become fully heterosexual, but might, if strongly motivated, become bisexual and decide because of social pressures to live a heterosexual lifestyle (Freud 1920).

In the USA after the 1950s some analysts became evangelical about converting homosexuals into heterosexuals, claiming a high success rate (e.g. Socarides 1979). It is often unclear whether the patient shares the analyst's zeal.

One of the major resistances continues to be the patient's misconception that his disorder may be in some strange way of hereditary or biological origin, or, in modern parlance, a matter of sexual 'preference' or 'orientation', that is, a normal form of sexuality. These views must be dealt with from the very beginning.

(Socarides 1979: 264)

Discussion of 'curing' homosexuality is now less fashionable.

A comparison of the writings of two contemporary psychoanalysts illustrates the profound effect of the analyst's personal values upon contemporary theory and clinical practice with homosexuals. Adam Limentani and Richard Isay write in a very similar way about different types of homosexuality, but, whereas Limentani pathologises homosexuality, Isay does not. Each describes one kind of homosexuality as a defence against heterosexual, Oedipal anxieties including fears of the internalised mother (and therefore women) as engulfing or castrating, or of the father (and men) as brutal or abandoning. Homosexuality for this group creates guilt and personal conflict since it doesn't fit in with the ego-ideal, with fundamental personal values. Theoretically, if the patient wished to become heterosexual he or she could do so. Each analyst then describes another category of 'true' or fixed homosexuals who do not feel intense personal conflict about their sexual orientation (Limentani 1989, Isay 1986).

Although their observations about types of homosexuality are almost identical, Limentani and Isay have entirely different views about the clinical outcome of work with gay men and lesbians. Limentani, like Joyce McDougall, argues that homosexuality is a defence against serious psychic disturbance. Isay argues, on the other hand, that psychoanalysts pathologise homosexuality because they have internalised cultural homophobia. The role of the analyst working with a gay patient of fixed orientation is to help resolve the neurotic conflicts that prevent the establishment of the stable, gratifying and loving relationships that are possible for homosexuals, Isay argues. He points out that research (other than that done by psychoanalysts, see Friedman 1988) does not support the view that there is significantly more psychological disturbance amongst the homosexual community, especially when it is borne in mind that cultural persecution may well intensify any existing personal tendencies towards depression, paranoia, and low self-esteem.

Freud argued in 1905 that many more people would live as homosexuals were it not for forceful social prohibitions. Today bisexual women and men may choose to be gay or lesbian. This was the case with the patient I describe next, a gay man who had left his own country at a point where AIDS was decimating the homosexual community. Ostensibly he came to Britain to develop his extremely successful business. However, one of his unconscious motivations had been to explore the possibility of relationships with women, a course followed by several of his gay friends. He was miserable and lonely in London and quickly decided to return home. Although he described an incident where he had been surprised into a sudden burst of heterosexual attraction he was reluctant to re-experience some of the intensely claustrophobic feelings he had felt in childhood in relation to a mother who had often been left on her own with him and his sister by her workaholic husband.

Because this man did rapidly begin to feel an uncomfortable flicker of heterosexual desire for me as a maternal figure, I think that he might have been right in thinking that relationships with both sexes were a theoretical possibility. But he chose again not to pursue whatever heterosexual desires he might have had. His decision to return home was certainly reinforced by his enjoyment of life within a vibrant and flourishing gay community there, which contrasted greatly with the life he would have led during Freud's lifetime, when homosexuality was still illegal in many western countries.

Freud suggested that actual experiences of sexual satisfaction with one's own sex may be crucial in 'sealing' a lesbian or gay orientation (Freud 1920). This may have been true with my patient who had, from his teens to his late thirties, been exclusively gay. Ethel Spector Person argues, on the other hand, that in some male patients entering treatment in order to change orientation, the greatest obstacle is not the inability to have intercourse with women, nor a preference for sex with men, but an unwillingness to give up a homosexual identity. She suggests that in cultures where there are no other stabilising features (e.g. rigid class distinctions or geographical rootedness) a sense of identity focused around sexual orientation may play an essential role in anchoring the personality, especially when that orientation differs from the norm (Ovesey and Spector Person 1973).

I have rarely come across committed lesbians or gay men who do want to become heterosexual. This may reflect a greater social acceptance of homosexuality. But some patients are uncertain about their sexual orientation, or are actively bisexual and feel the need to choose a partner of one sex with whom to make a permanent relationship. Patients who are in conflict about their sexual orientation usually make it clear, however, that they need an atmosphere of absolute analytic neutrality rather than a therapist who is predisposed to steer them in one direction or the other.

THE DIFFERENCES BETWEEN LESBIAN AND GAY SEXUALITY

In psychoanalytic theory it is often assumed that homosexuality is a psychological entity with shared characteristics. For instance lesbians and gay men are often described as having strongly identified with the opposite sex and as seeking the characteristics of their own sex in partners. But the idea of a separate homosexual identity is historically very recent, and many gay men and lesbians do not see themselves as being set apart from their own sex in this way. Instead, they suggest that lesbians have more similarities with heterosexual women, and gay men with their own sex as a whole. Obviously this raises another set of questions. Many individuals are able to identify with some of the psychological characteristics culturally attributed to their sex but there are as many differences within each sex as between them.

One very clear difference that I have found between male and female patients is that, whatever their sexual orientation, adult women seem to experiment more with bisexuality than men. Many of my lesbian patients have had sex with men at some time in their adult lives. I have also had a number of actively bisexual female patients, and many heterosexual women who have had lovers of their own sex in adulthood. In contrast, none of the gay men I have seen in psychotherapy have had sexual experiences with women, an observation which is backed up by the research of Bell and Weinberg (1978). And although many heterosexual male patients have had homosexual experiences in their youth and remain unconsciously ambivalent about sexual choice, they seem by their mid-twenties to be less able to envisage the idea that they might take a lover of their own sex than their female peers (Bell and Weinberg 1978).

The greater prevalence of heterosexual experience amongst lesbians may reflect social and cultural pressures on young girls to have heterosexual experiences. There is also a physical reality that women can passively experience sex, whereas men find it physiologically harder to conceal a lack of desire. But I think that psychic factors are deeply significant here. The strength of the early attachment to the mother may, paradoxically, lead to bisexuality in women and to exclusive homosexuality or hetero-sexuality in men. Anxieties about engulfment by a very early, primitive and terrifying imago of the mother may lead the man with an insecure sense of his male identity to cling to his adopted orientation for fear that experimentation might threaten his frag-ile psychic equilibrium. Women may not feel the same anxiety about losing their female identity through sexual experiences with their own sex. Indeed, if early issues in relation to the mother remain unresolved the woman's heterosexual orientation may be more tenuous than her 'feminine' identification.

It is extremely hard to generalise about the problems that each sex brings to psychotherapy. Yet it is possible to discern slight differences in the issues that gay men and lesbians find problem-atic in intimate relationships. For instance lesbians frequently discuss a tendency for their relationships to develop a symbiotic 'merged' quality, a lack of psychic separation and distance. Gay male patients more often describe their wish to give up a pattern of casual promiscuity which they have come to see as a defence against sexual intimacy with one loved partner. Ryan and O'Con-nor point out that the intensity and depth of bodily closeness gives lesbianism a special appeal for women, who can rapidly experience themselves as re-enacting primary experiences of inti-macy with the mother (O'Connor and Ryan 1993). But this can also lead to subsequent difficulties, such as a premature breakdown of sexual intimacy. American feminist Diane Elise argues that this tendency to 'merge' is women's issue rather than a gay issue since gender differences become exaggerated in relationships between two individuals of the same sex. In heterosexual relationships, she argues, a stable tension is created between the woman, who 'clings' through fear of abandonment, and the man, who 'distances' through unconscious fear of being trapped (Elise 1986). This is clearly a recognisable stereotype, although many heterosexual couples do not fit it.

Maintaining love and sexual passion in long-term marital relationships is a problem for everyone, whatever their sex or orientation. Martin Dannecker, a German gay academic, argues that the promiscuity which is a feature of male homosexual behaviour is a flight from intimacy, but an escape also chosen by some heterosexual men. Gay promiscuity may, he says, be an attempt to compensate for narcissistic wounds inflicted by a culture which still holds homosexuals to be inferior men. At the same time Dannecker argues that through structures that valorise promiscuity rather than passionate long-term love and commitment, the gay community also strengthens defences against homosexual intimacy (Dannecker 1978).

The tendency towards promiscuity and anal obsessiveness often associated with male homosexuality may be generally more common in the fantasy-life and personalities of men than women. The boy who has not fully resolved his Oedipal rivalry with the father may idealise a caricature of masculinity, which is cruel and unfeeling, while feeling intense contempt for 'femininity' in himself and in others. Anal obsessiveness is also associated with a strong unconscious need to control a maternal figure who may be both an object of desire and identification. Whatever his sexual orientation, the man who is unconsciously preoccupied with anal power-battles may be unable to bring together love and desire. This may lead a gay man to have a long-term partner who he loves but no longer desires, while he has transient objectified sex with others. Or a heterosexual man may value his male friends more than women in whom he may lose interest after brief affairs.

Some men may be more aware of a desire to withdraw from intimacy, while some women are only in touch with their vulnerability and 'clinginess'. But in psychotherapy it is not possible to maintain such splitting, and the patient may rapidly be confronted with the aspect of himself which he so often projects onto others.

This was the case with a gay man in his twenties, who came to see me for a consultation. I had said that I did have some spaces but it was unclear whether he would be able to fit in with my times. For the first session, he arrived forty-five minutes late. He was determined to see himself only as a victim of traffic hold-ups, but I was struck by the fact that he seemed to have lengthened his journey by changing his mode of transport mid-stream. I was immediately aware that he was erecting a fence around himself, lest I pursue the issue.

He then began talking very openly, about how, for the first time, he was desperately in love with a man who made him feel like a 'lady-in-waiting'. I felt as if I was listening to a well-rehearsed soap-opera, but knew at the same time that he was in great emotional pain. Indeed he acknowledged that he would tell anyone about himself in this way, to an extent which his friends considered inappropriate. He continually longed for devotion from his majestic lover, who randomly alternated between affection, withdrawal, and sudden scathing, humiliating comments. In his previous relationships, he told me, he had been the less involved partner, and had experienced his lovers as possessive, controlling and manipulative. He hoped for insight – but mainly about how to win his beloved's constant affection. A lesbian friend had given him a book entitled *Women Who Love Too Much* (Norwood 1986), he told me ruefully.

He described a childhood dominated by a mother who had tried to rule every detail of her children's lives. Always rebellious, he had eventually evolved ways of resisting her domination. He now realised that she had sexually abused him through ritualistic punishments carried out in front of his sisters, where he had felt extremely humiliated, his male body mocked. His father, although benign in his own actions, had done nothing to prevent his wife's cruelty and humiliation of the children.

Since the session was cut short by his late arrival we agreed that he would return for another consultation the following week. As he was leaving he told me that there was little flexibility about the fees he could pay or the times he could attend sessions and that he would have to find a psychotherapist who would accept that. The following week he did not arrive at all at the agreed time. Instead he came on the dot a day later having got the times confused. I could not see him then, so we arranged a third time the following week. He arrived exactly on time and immediately began telling me about how his mother had fascinated him with her majestic unpredictability and obsessiveness. He marvelled at the way she managed to encompass every emotion in its most extreme form. This time, I persisted in discussing his previous mistakes with time. I said, as delicately as I could, that he was telling me how he himself had grown up to be as majestically unpredictable as his mother. He was showing me exactly what it had been like to have had his childhood structured entirely around her rules. We had agreed on the session times, but, as with his mother, he had felt that I had simply told him when he was going to come. He had then made his own arrangements about times and dates, ignoring what he experienced as my attempts to control and manipulate him. In this way he ensured that I, rather than he, was the 'lady-in waiting', a role he had taken up both with his mother and his lover.

He was astounded by this idea, and at first almost shouted me down. Then, as we continued to discuss it, it became clear that he was as fascinated by my interpretations as he had been with his mother's pronouncements. I later said that he was letting me know that he would want a therapist who could be very flexible and take his needs into consideration in a way that he had not remembered his mother doing.

This man had a fixed view of himself as his mother's quasi-female sacrificial victim. As a result both myself and his current lover could only be cast as controlling, manipulative maternal figures. Nevertheless he could operate successfully in a competitive conventionally male profession, having identified both with the gentle distant father and his mother's 'masculine' strengths.

Many psychoanalytic case histories reflect the experience of cultures where homosexuality was illegal. For instance, in 1949 Rosenfeld argued that his paranoid male homosexual patient actually chose his orientation because homosexuality was then illegal and it gave him a concrete reason for his feelings of persecution. Cultural changes as the twentieth century progressed have facilitated the open choice of a lesbian or gay lifestyle by women and men who might previously have lived a restricted sexual life or sought to hide their orientation (Rosenfeld 1949).

SEXUAL ORIENTATION AND CULTURAL CHANGE

The following account of short-term focal psychotherapy with a lesbian highlights similar questions about the impact of culture on the psyche. The patient I describe shares some important similarities with the lesbian patient Freud saw in 1920.

Sharon, 29, came to The Women's Therapy Centre in a state of extreme anxiety, fearing the loss of all financial and emotional security. She had fallen far behind on the mortgage repayments on a house she shared with her partner Carol and Carol's small son. During their two-year relationship, Sharon had agreed to support Carol financially so that she could go to college. Sharon had also paid the bills on the house she had shared with her previous female partner, with whom she had lived for eight years. Sex with Carol had long-since ceased, and now that she could no longer support her financially, Sharon felt constantly criticised and belittled by Carol. Embittered, Sharon had begun having affairs with other women.

She was the younger of two sisters. The elder had been very much her mother's favourite, with Sharon feeling constantly excluded from their intimacy. She had compensated for this by closeness to her father who clearly preferred her to her sister. Her father had also been constantly devalued by her mother. Like Sharon he was seen as emotionally inarticulate, his role being solely to support the family financially. I pointed out that Sharon was re-enacting with her lovers the role her father had played in the family. Sharon agreed with this, with a mixture of interest and reluctance, corroborating my observation by saying that she also thought he had had affairs, as she did when her relationships deteriorated.

In two further ways, re-enactments of family patterns were contributing to Sharon's current difficulties. She feared losing her job because she had come into serious conflict with a woman, only slightly senior, who, it transpired, resembled her sister in crucial ways. Furthermore, she had managed to make an enemy not only of Carol, but also of Carol's younger sister, Lucy, through a highly complex triangular relationship. She had earlier had a brief affair with Lucy who had left her. It was after this abandonment that Sharon had quickly become sexually involved with Carol, despite continuing to feel far more attracted to the fickle younger sister, Lucy. Thus she had managed to recreate and reverse the infantile triangle. Now she was the powerful older maternal figure over whom both sisters competed, and it was the younger one (herself) for whom she felt more passion. Sharon declared herself utterly bemused by the aggression both sisters now felt both for her and for each other.

The only space available to offer her at the centre was for thirty sessions of focal psychotherapy. We agreed to concentrate on resolving some of the past issues which were being re-enacted in the current acute crisis, with particular emphasis on her recreation of the dynamics of her parents' relationship with her lovers. However, it was clear to both of us that issues about sexuality might well emerge. Sharon did not enjoy sex, she told me. In fact, the only time she had had any glimmer of pleasure was in the weeks she had been with Lucy, the younger sister, who had curtailed the relationship all too rapidly. She had never had sex with a man, and told me that she had no desire to. I said that we would not be able to discuss her sexuality in any depth during these thirty sessions, but that if Sharon did want to explore this area, I would make a referral for private psychotherapy which she might be better able to afford once her present crisis was resolved.

Painfully, in those early sessions, Sharon recalled more of the traumas that had left her feeling so bitter and despairing about being with, or like, her mother. At around 9, her mother had 'terrified' her by beating Sharon so violently that she broke the stick she was using. This attack was rendered even more unforgiveable in Sharon's eyes because her sister was never hit by her mother. Her father was always gentle, 'good at playing', although often out of the house. He was proud of Sharon's athletic ability. 'Did he want me to be a boy?' she wondered. She had been called after the mother he had lost in childhood. When she was 13 her mother had become acutely ill. Sharon was staying with her relatives in Cyprus, and was left there, separated from her mother. Sharon felt desperately abandoned, terrified that her mother would die and she would be to blame. Soon after this, her periods started, but her relationship with her mother was now so difficult that Sharon could not tell her. Sharon reacted with defiance to this abandonment, denying that she needed her mother. She had asked her parents whether she could stay in Cyprus, where she felt accepted by her aunt, and enjoyed playing with her cousins, 'the other boys', as she unwittingly referred to them.

As a result of her mother's violence, a part of her, associated with her sexuality and sense of herself as a girl, had died. She had lost touch with an inner world of feeling and imagination that she began to re-discover in the sessions. She described how, before her mother's violence, she had happily played on her own for hours, but had afterwards become totally outer-directed. Now in therapy she was beginning, with delight, to keep a journal, to read novels, and to enjoy exploring her fantasy-life. She told me about a new woman friend she had made outside therapy, with whom she discussed her feelings in a way she had never done before.

Sharon sold the house, and moved in temporarily with an older lesbian couple she had known since her teens. They had, she told me, once questioned why she had become a lesbian, wondering whether it might reflect a rebellion against her mother, an inability to bear being like someone towards whom she felt such intense hostility. At 16 she had got engaged briefly, but there had been little physical contact because 'you know how girls dread sex'. Then, through a friendship with a gay male couple, she had come across the idea of being a lesbian. When her mother discovered she was going out with girls, at 18, she had thrown her out, and for almost ten years they had hardly talked. Her father, however, had gone out of his way to keep contact with Sharon, and to give her money, reassuring her that 'whoever her friends were', she was always his daughter. As Sharon extricated herself from playing her father's familial role with Carol, her parents' marriage immediately went into crisis and they temporarily separated for the first time in thirty years.

Sharon associated sex with madness, danger, and the apparently irreparable emotional 'rift' between her parents. She described how her first long-term girlfriend would complain that they weren't having sex. Sharon would then make love to her, without much enjoyment or understanding of how her partner might be feeling. The attitude of Lucy, the younger of the two sisters, that sex was 'about exploring' had been a revelation and a release from the feeling of responsibility for a burdensome duty. She could not see herself giving up being a lesbian and still felt no attraction for men. Yet she found herself pondering the fact that she had always had easier relationships with men than women.

'It's generally said that you should taste a drink before saying you don't like it', she ventured thoughtfully.

At this point, three months into the therapy, I missed a session through illness. Sharon was devastated by my absence of which she received very little warning, and took to her bed with acute asthma until the next session. On her return, she talked about a dog she had already mentioned who had died after being taken for treatment with a tooth-ulcer. She had been desperately upset by its death. 'Everyone liked the dog. It was good looking, tall, with a proud walk.' This description also fitted her handsome athletic father, and herself 'a bit'. Like a dog, she felt capable of absolute loyalty or devotion to those who looked after her. But dogs, like children, could turn on people suddenly. Then I, like her mother, might get angry or irritated with her. She might make me ill, as she had felt she made her mother ill. Or one of us might have a breakdown. 'How can I stop feeling like this? Rationally I know you can't make someone get ill – can you?' She was re-experiencing the traumatic teenage months when she'd feared her mother's death. Whereas then she'd started menstruating, now she was asking fundamental questions about her sexual orientation, even considering the possibility of sex with men. And again, she'd been abandoned. She felt alarmed that having, like the dog, come for treatment in a crisis, she would also die – of neglect.

She alternated between experiencing me as the idealised, accepting Cypriot aunt, and the mother into whose rigid notion of how girls should be she could not and would not fit. At these moments I felt the need to consider carefully my own countertransference reactions to her. I asked myself whether, for instance, I was pushing her towards heterosexuality. Could I leave her free to make her own sexual choices?

Sharon's charming, witty and considerate treatment of me was a way of protecting us both from the hostility that she feared might erupt in all her relationships with women. Conflict with men was tolerable, but with women it was, as always, 'terrifying'. Yet it was impossible for her to deny that she was becoming increasingly hurt, angry and frightened about my abandonment of her between the sessions, during holidays, and most of all, at the impending termination. She needed to express the full extent of this rage in order to hold onto the good things she'd got from the sessions, but this continued to be very difficult for her.

'Couldn't we make it come out so I feel good about the ending?' she begged, tearfully.

Apart from ending her relationship with Carol, and moving to live outside a couple for the first time in adult life, Sharon made a number of other significant changes in her life during psychotherapy. For instance, she worked hard, with some success, to communicate again with her mother. She gained confidence that her disagreement at work hinged on genuine professional differences rather than simply on a personality conflict, and expressed her own views forcefully enough to resolve the situation. She began to apply for new senior jobs. She told me that she felt tired of teenagers and in particular of the communication difficulties and narrow-mindedness of 'teenage lesbians'. She'd come to psychotherapy as a 'teenage lesbian', she was telling me, but wanted to move on now and become like me, a woman who worked with adults. And she was becoming more open-minded about what kind of women she herself might be. If she remained a lesbian she saw the possibility of developing more genuinely intimate relationships with women, where loving concern could co-exist more fully with sexual passion. And there was also the possibility that she might sip the untasted heterosexual drink.

Sharon no longer needed to re-enact her experience of her parents' relationship. Taking up the position she imagined her father to occupy in relation to her mother had enabled her to deny any likeness between herself and her hated mother, while winning an illusion of intimacy with her by proxy. In this way she had also avoided rivalry with her mother for her father. This re-enactment had kept her parents apart in her mind – she possessed her father through identification, and her mother in fantasy as a love-object. But this rigid identification with her father restricted her emotional possibilities in relation to both sexes. Her father was generous, charming and witty, but he had profound problems with adult intimacy. Through her very brief experience of the transference relationship she had come to understand more about her mother and to feel less rejected by her. Sharon had access to new aspects of her own personality now that she could tolerate the idea of being like her mother in some ways.

Sharon's psychotherapy enabled her to resolve her present crisis and gave her insight into its origins. She was more able to tolerate and think about her own internal life, to observe herself, and to make choices. She could continue to grow through nourishing the inner world of fantasy and imagination to which she had regained access through the transference relationship. She asked for a referral for ongoing therapy but after a few weeks found an opportunity to bump into me and let me know that she had felt unable to continue with her new psychotherapist. Perhaps she needed longer to resolve all her feelings about the work we had done together. Or maybe she had gone as far as she wanted to.

A woman who appears to have made the Oedipal shift from mother to father as love-object, as Sharon and Freud's lesbian patient had done, may choose later to become lesbian rather than heterosexual. In 1920 Freud's patient, 'a beautiful and clever girl of eighteen', was still so dependent on her parents' goodwill and financial support that she had to enter psychoanalysis to 'cure' desires which she did not want to relinquish, thereby giving Freud a task he could only acknowledge as hopeless. Sharon, although from a far poorer background, had very different possibilities sixty years later. Thanks to women's vastly altered educational opportunities and the creation of a flourishing lesbian and gay community, she could forge an independent life and identity for herself, despite her mother's disapproval. Sharon and the two gay men I described earlier in the chapter might all in another era have tried harder to live or appear to live a heterosexual life. This change in cultural attitudes makes it less easy than ever to predict which kinds of family history or psychic constellation will produce a particular sexual orientation.

This social change raises interesting questions about the interrelationship between identification and desire. Psychoanalytic theory offers little insight into why those who identify with their own sex also desire them, except to imply that they may not be as exclusively homosexual as they think they are (Limentani 1989). Sharon's dress and manner were relentlessly boyish and as a 'butch' she usually took the sexual initiative. Yet in psychotherapy, as in all close relationships, whenever the topic of sex arose she would rapidly flounder into a miserable confused silence, exuding an air of helpless fragility. This fits in with the suggestion made by some analysts (e.g. Deutsch 1933) that the apparent masculinity of some lesbians does not reflect a strong identification with male figures. It may be a defence against a desire to submit, or be looked after, by a maternal figure.

Ardill and O'Sullivan describe the terror some 'butch' lesbians experience about genital contact (Ardill and O'Sullivan 1986). Freud observed that many lesbians dressed and acted like men, splitting off their femininity. But today's feminists argue that early analysts exaggerated the masculinity of their lesbian patients (certainly to a contemporary eye these assertive early-twentieth-century women do not appear lacking in femininity) and they also note how a significant majority of lesbians in our western post-industrialised society consider themselves to be 'femme' rather than 'butch'. The change probably reflects the fact that it is more possible now for women to live outside marriage without the financial support of men. The existence of lesbian communities also obviates the need for women to signal their orientation so clearly (Ardill and O'Sullivan 1986, Merck 1993c, O'Connor and Ryan 1993).

There has been a similar emergence of visible masculinity, even of 'machismo', amongst gay men. Martin Humphries argues that the conventional look alike 'clones' and the 'leather men', with their images of strength and masculinity, are both the result and a contribution to a new sense of pride within the gay community. The existence of such visible maleness means that masculine desirability need no longer be located outside the self, in 'straight' men. Yet apparently 'macho' men are not necessarily dominant sexually – they may take up a more passive role in sexual relationships (Humphries 1985).

In fact identifications are formed through such an intricate process of layering and fusion of fragments of memory, fantasy and desire, that it is extremely difficult to say with certainty which real figure a patient is identified with. Freud himself acknowledged this in 1931, when he pointed out that the little girl who plays with dolls is not necessarily expressing early heterosexual femininity. She may be showing that she is too exclusively pre-occupied with re-enacting her early relationship with her mother to view her father as a significant love-object (Freud 1931).

It is important to separate identification and sexual orientation as far as possible theoretically. Then it may become clear whether homosexuals, like heterosexuals, suffer because they have identified with parental figures towards whom they feel profound ambivalence, rather than because of their sexual orientation. Mandy Merck, a British feminist, argues that this was the case with Freud's lesbian patient. Merck claims that the seriousness of the young woman's suicide attempt and the ferocity of her anger towards men are both evidence of serious psychological conflict, but she links the woman's self-destructiveness to her identification with a father who is simultaneously hated and desired (Merck 1993c). A similar argument could be made about Sharon, who changed significantly in brief psychotherapy through strengthening positive identifications with maternal figures through the transference and loosening the power of negative paternal internalisations, rather than by altering her sexual orientation.

What can psychoanalytic psychotherapy offer to lesbians and gay men who do not wish to, or cannot change their orientation? First of all it is very difficult to work with theories that pathologise homosexuality. These must inevitably exacerbate the psychotherapist's anxieties about their own unresolved conflicts in this area. Many gay men and lesbians may drop out of analytic treatment, not, as is often suggested, simply because they are resistant to change, but because of the countertransference difficulties of their heterosexual analysts.

We need to look more closely at the operation of power within the psychoanalytic world, especially as it relates to knowledge and theory. Women analysts have continually challenged and reformulated psychoanalytic ideas about femininity, but since homosexuals have so often been excluded from training, they have not been able to influence the profession from within in the same way (Lewes 1989). In 1921 Freud and Rank wrote in a circular letter that homosexuality should be no bar to training as a psychoanalyst, but many contemporary training organisations for analysts and psychotherapists do not accept confirmed homosexuals as students (referred to by Lewes 1989). The existence within psychoanalytic theory of unattainable sexual ideals leads to a persecutory attitude towards homosexuals who are seen as embodying all the sexual pathology that heterosexual practitioners are unable to face in themselves.

There is a need for more positive theorising about lesbian and gay identity. For instance, what is required to build a viable homosexual identity? Embedded in psychoanalytic theory is a notion of two sexes which are biologically and psychologically complementary. Is this still appropriate, given the increasing cultural trend towards psychic androgyny? Powerful cultural taboos against homosexual acts may reflect the great need in some previous historical eras and cultures to preserve the species, but our social needs may now be different.

From time to time psychoanalysts have suggested that homosexuals may gain psychological advantages from their sexual orientation and may be able to make a special contribution to society. They may also benefit from being particularly well able to integrate opposite-sex personality traits in themselves. Freud attributed gay men's particular contribution to art, culture and community life to their early resolution of sexual rivalry with the father. Joan Riviere suggested in 1929 that lesbians may have less conflict about professional achievement because they feel less anxiety about surpassing the father. Diane Hamer argues from a feminist academic perspective that lesbianism may be a healthy response to the contradictory position of women who in our culture are educated to expect more equality than they are actually offered. The resulting requirement that women repress some of their active strivings may result in an increased incidence of neurotic 'symptoms' such as anxiety states and depression. Hamer argues that lesbianism is not a repudiation of femininity but a redefinition of the possibilities open to women. Rather than develop neurotic inhibitions lesbians continue to stake a claim to male 'activity'. But there may be a particular price to pay for the challenge lesbian identity offers to patriarchal authority, and individual women may suffer anxiety as a result (Hamer 1990).

Both sexes would benefit from the integration of a wide range of cross-sex identifications, so that conventional notions of gender become more detached from biological sex. Rather than pathologising women who have conflicts about 'masculine' identifications, we need to recognise how girls are disadvantaged by the lack of opportunity to identify with the psychological qualities associated with men which are more highly valued in our society. Similar questions need to be asked about how men can accept and integrate their early identifications with maternal functions and qualities seen as 'feminine' rather than defensively disowning them, and projecting them onto women and gay men who they then devalue.

CONCLUSION

In reading for this chapter, I have been moved by the writings of lesbians and gay men about their experience of loving their own sex within a homophobic society, and their willingness to ask themselves challenging questions. I have been dismayed, on the other hand, by the speed with which some analysts dismiss the possibility of loving intimacy within homosexual relationships. Perhaps the tendency to make categorical statements and to abandon analytic neutrality reflects the high degree of anxiety that the topic arouses in clinicians.

It is difficult to sustain many of the theoretical generalisations often made by psychoanalysts about homosexuality when faced with contemporary clinical material. For instance it may not be useful to describe a category of 'homosexuality' or to assume common characteristics between those who desire their own sex. Lesbians and gay men may have more in common with their own sex than with each other. For example the homosexual preoccupation with anality so emphasised by psychoanalysts may well reflect aspects of the fantasy-life and personality construction of all men, without being particuarly relevant to the majority of women, whatever their orientation. The assumption that homosexuality is a narcissistic search for sameness may be belied by the unconscious fantasies underlying the relationship. Unconscious homosexual fantasies may also dominate the psychic life of those who consider themselves heterosexual.

Since there is now economic and cultural support for women and men who want to have relationships with their own sex, many people, some of whom may well be bisexual, are choosing to adopt a homosexual lifestyle for all or part of their lives. There may also be more scope for the expression of psychic bisexuality within heterosexual relationships, as notions of sexual identity become slightly less rigid.

Perhaps it is time, then, for the psychotherapeutic profession to abandon some of our more facile assumptions about what constitutes a 'normal' sexuality, and acknowledge that such changes may well offer new possibilities for genuine sexual happiness, a more open way of being for heterosexuals and homosexuals alike.

Conclusion

Feminism and psychotherapy: an agenda for the future

The encounter between psychoanalysis and feminism is now almost a century old. What has been gained through this intense off and on engagement? How have feminists dealt with the challenge which psychoanalysis poses to conventional notions of sexual identity? To what extent have psychoanalytic theorists and clinicians been willing to address the political issues which feminists see as central to any dynamic psychology? And finally, at a point when power relations between the sexes are beginning to shift significantly, how can future collaboration between psychoanalysis and feminism promote an agenda for sexual equality?

Both movements have always had much in common, apart from a central concern with sexuality and gender. Psychoanalysis highlights aspects of mental life and behaviour which are usually experienced as unacceptable or at least profoundly uncomfortable. Similarly, feminism has illuminated the disparities between what our society wants women to be and what we, as women, actually want: again, an uneasy insight. As a result, both movements arouse highly ambivalent feelings.

Today psychotherapy seems almost to be viewed as a new religion, a contemporary bastion of truth and morality. As a result, its practitioners are subject to the same type of idealisation/denigration associated with much religious belief (and infantile emotional states). This has been reflected recently in the fierce controversies surrounding childhood sexual abuse, in which therapists are either viewed as perfect parents coming to the rescue of abused children or as evil interlopers into the family scenario. Incest is an issue which invariably blurs boundaries between fantasy and reality in this way. But today the erosion of older patterns of gender relations has made the discussion of incest even more emotive. As traditional family structures give way to new, those who point to the vulnerability of children within the family arouse very primitive anxieties. Both feminists and psychotherapists find themselves sharing this dangerous ground, as they challenge conventional attitudes towards parenting and the place of children within erotic life.

Despite this shared field of concerns, however, the feminist attitude towards psychoanalysis has often been very suspicious. Why is this? Psychoanalytic psychotherapy provides access to a more embodied way of thinking, which opens up the possibility of integrating political ideals with emotional and sexual experience, and exploring how cultural expectations might be imprinted on the body, as well as the mind. There is now an increasing understanding that male and female psychology cannot be considered in isolation from each other. But some of those aspects of feminity which psychoanalysis highlights are difficult to confront, particularly female envy and aggression. Women, who place such a premium on being 'nice', find it hard to think about all those less nice aspects of the human psyche. We would often rather foist these onto men. But in doing so we lose the capacity to mobilise our aggression in creative ways. We also lessen our capacity to understand the forces which lie behind women's apparent collusion in certain forms of personal and cultural subordination. We need to know more about why women tolerate cruelty, frustration or even violence within personal relationships and what makes it so difficult to claim an equal share of cultural power. What is it about femininity that continues to constrain us, and how can psychoanalysis help us to understand or even change this?

The degree to which psychoanalytic perspectives have proved useful to the feminist political project has undoubtedly been limited by the hesitancy and prejudice with which the analytic world has approached gender issues. There is still a clear male bias in all mainstream psychoanalytic theories. Women do not exist as subjects in their own right with their own will and desire. Instead, they are seen through the eyes of men or children. Men, on the other hand, tend to be idealised in most analytic writings (unless they are homosexual) and as fathers they are almost invariably viewed in a positive light.

These biases are strengthened by the tendency of psychoanalytic theorists to present their views as universal and timeless.

Whereas contemporary feminist literature places an increasing stress on the historical and cultural factors behind the formation of sexual identity, psychoanalytic writers have been disappointingly slow to acknowledge the cultural specificity of their theories. Feminist emphasis on the multiplicity of forms which sexual subjectivity and orientation can take has been matched by no corresponding attempt on the part of analytic theorists to understand how different cultural belief-systems and values might be reflected in personality development. Ideas of normal/abnormal development are still offered as universal truths, despite all evidence that such norms are culturally weighted. This is particularly true of theories of sexual orientation, where homosexuality continues to be pathologised despite the greater respect accorded to lesbians and gay men in the culture at large.

But the most significant difficulty in the encounter between feminism and psychoanalysis remains the refusal of the analytic world to recognise the role of power in male–female relations. Although gender and sexual identity are currently highly fashionable topics in psychoanalytic circles, I am often astonished to hear these discussed with barely any mention of the power difference between the sexes. From listening to clinical discussions one might think that the sexes were equal, or even that women really did have the overwhelming power with which the infant invests the mother in fantasy.

Why this refusal to acknowledge the psychic consequences of male power? In this book I have shown how, since its inception, psychoanalytic theory has tended to emphasise one side of the parental couple as more powerful than the other. The first psychoanalytic debate on female sexuality in the 1920s highlighted the issue of which parent appeared more powerful and enviable in the mind of the child. After Freud was accused of male bias, there was a reaction against his father-dominated theory, in which the role of the mother was marginal, and women were viewed as envious and deficient. Klein and Winnicott then focused almost exclusively on the power and significance of the mother, barely mentioning the father. And, although mother-centred psychoanalysts are beginning again to explore the psychic significance of the father, and of Oedipal issues, theoretically the father remains a shadowy figure. But if we are to understand how maternal and paternal power interact in the psyche we must first integrate the parental couple in the theoretical mind. We still do not have a mainstream psychoanalytic theory that brings the two sexes together, while giving due weight to the different kinds of power and control with which each is invested through culture or nature. Perhaps this is because holding in mind different notions of envy and power would necessitate the recognition that the sexual equality our society purports to offer does not exist in reality.

This theoretical limitation in turn limits the way psychotherapy has grappled with gender-mediated problems. For example, object relations theories explain women's propensity to eating disorders in terms of unresolved psychic separation from the mother, resulting in unconscious conflicts which are acted out in fantasy through the daughter's own body. Bulimia and anorexia are sometimes seen as forms of female perversion – indirectly eroticised abuse of the woman's own body, or that of her children. But these mother-centred theories often neglect the more Oedipal aspects of sexuality and the crucial role of the female body as a site both for the reproduction of and resistance to patriarchal power relations. In contrast, Freud's theory of hysteria emphasises how women use their bodies to express in a very concrete way their discontent with their devalued status and restricted opportunities. Drawing on both of these perspectives, I would argue that the bulimic or anorexic woman does not fully accept her womanly body, the concrete evidence that she cannot possess male potency, but instead clings to an illusion of possessing everything, including the maternal body, which she simultaneously reduced to an asexual status. She also refuses to make the socially required Oedipal choice between mother and father. Instead she oscillates unconsciously between men and women, unable to love where sex is present, forever keeping the parents separate in her mind.

Turning to the male side of the gender equation, we need to see how maternal and paternal power interact in the male psyche if we are to understand why men sexualise psychic conflict. The man who focuses in a perverse way on his own genitals is expressing his dread of losing what the penis symbolises – male cultural dominance, potency and privilege. Simultaneously he is expressing his own conflicts about the lost world of early 'feminine' intimacy, through reassuring himself that he has not succumbed to the lure of an imagined symbiosis with the maternal body.

It is also essential that psychoanalysis integrates its insights into maternal psychological influence and paternal power in order that we may understand how the transference is formed. Gender power differentials, as I have stressed throughout this book, are reflected in the transference and countertransference. For instance, a theoretical bias towards maternal power may combine with unconscious conflicts about psychic 'masculinity', causing a female psychotherapist to mistake a male patient's homosexual desires towards the father for a maternal (heterosexual) transference. Or the woman therapist might use a theoretical focus on maternal nurturing to avoid the contempt and hostility which often emerge rapidly in the heterosexual transferences of male patients.

Male psychotherapists who remain unconsciously profoundly ambivalent towards the early mother may collude with a female patient's idealised love-transference towards the father rather than exploring the hostility towards both parents which might lie beneath it. In similar fashion, unconscious conflicts about his own disowned psychic femininity may prevent a male clinician from recognising his homosexual countertransference feelings towards a patient who shares his sex.

Many of the issues raised in the 1920s about the limits and possibilities of change in male and female sexuality remain just as topical and unresolved today, despite vast changes in the daily lives and expectations of both sexes in our society. We still do not know how cultural change impacts on the psyche. There is still no definitive theory of how culture, physiology and unconscious processes interact. I have argued that sexual identity is formed mainly through culture although the experience of erotic life and the physiological life-cycle will inevitably be different for women and men. Language patterns, symbols and values systems determine how bodily sensation is interpreted in each culture, so if we want to eradicate sexual inequality we must understand and radically alter the way we symbolise and interpret the embodied experience of women and men.

There is a tendency in psychoanalytic theory to pathologise those who have intense conflicts about opposite-sex identifications: so-called 'masculine' women and 'feminine' men. But these normative notions of gender identity obscure the way both sexes are impoverished through the inability to integrate cross-gender identifications. Men who project their own 'feminine' vulnerability outside themselves, and transform their own need to depend into real or fantasised domination of an objectified other, will close off the possibility of equal intimacy. The man who cannot resolve early conflicts in relation to the mother, will also be unable to work through Oedipal humiliation and rivalry towards the father. Psychically he may become arrested during the early phase of identification with the father, reacting against a fear of losing a very tenuous male identity by idealising a caricature of masculinity. Even if he consciously believes in sexual equality he may unconsciously treat women in aggressive, domineering and contemptuous ways.

In contemporary society male envy and fear of female strength is becoming increasingly visible. This could be because there are fewer institutionalised ways of inducing feelings of envy and exclusion in women, who are now somewhat less likely to 'carry' that aspect of emotional life for the entire human race. This often leaves contemporary male patients feeling profoundly anxious about their ability to adapt to a less masterful role in relation to sexual partners and children. For instance they ask whether they should be exploring different ways of fathering, or developing maternal capacities, and express anxieties about whether, if they begin to face up to their own psychic 'femininity', they will become devalued as women and 'effeminate' men have always been.

Female patients are often preoccupied with questions about whether they really can be successful in traditional male as well as female spheres of activity, especially given that men have traditionally relied on the support of a wife in order to do so. They ask whether it is possible to combine the focused instrumentality, single-mindedness and ambition necessary for success in the external world with the capacity for empathy and selfless giving demanded within the home and family. And would this mean becoming more stereotypically masculine, or finding a different way of winning and using power? It is particularly difficult for women to acknowledge the strength of their own will, and to recognise that desire emanates from inside themselves rather than belonging to the other. Often this is because the girl fears that in using her aggression to separate psychically, she will damage or destroy the internal mother, with whom she still feels unconsciously merged. This dilemma is often exacerbated by a lack of opportunities to identify with qualities seen culturally as masculine. The girl may not have paternal figures who can help her gain confidence in the external world, and she may be unable to identify with the 'masculine' strengths of a mother with whom she still feels psychically enmeshed.

Although the woman who succeeds in traditionally male as well as female spheres may now be the greatest object of envy for both sexes, patriarchal structures of cultural and sexual life still give men a myriad of opportunities to place women in the position they once felt themselves to be in relation to the mother: envious, humiliated and excluded. But women also suffer because of the ways they defend against their own envy. Some girls cope with the difficulties of psychic separation from a much-envied mother by idealising the father and men, but the resulting envious guilt and self-contempt can create inhibitions about sexual intimacy and professional competition in conventionally male arenas. Other women are crippled by unconscious fears about losing their mother's love if they arouse her envy through personal fulfilment and achievement, a defence which may be exacerbated by real external sex discrimination and an awareness of actual maternal envy.

Since desire is structured through our earliest childhood experiences it is inevitable that the image of a helpless being acted upon by a powerful other will at times feature within the erotic imagination. But if we are to break the cycle whereby gender inequalities are structured into psychic and sexual life, men and women need to be able to find different ways of expressing and resolving the narcissistic wish to deny pain, helplessness and psychic separateness, other than through denigrating the mother and subordinating the female sex.

The most crucial and difficult task for all of us is to face the fact that the sexes are equal in potential yet anatomically different. To accomplish this, the envy, fear and inadequacy engendered by sexual difference must be resolved through identification with the psychological qualities associated with both sexes. For women this means finding a way of differentiating from the mother and identifying psychological masculinity without devaluing their own sex. Male identity can be strengthened through a greater integration of the boy's early identifications with maternal nurturing functions, and with psychic femininity. The male patient who recognised within the maternal transference the ways in which he is like the mother psychologically, even though he lacks her reproductive and sexual capacities, will become more secure in his own masculine difference from her. He will then feel more equal to women, and less driven to denigrate them enviously.

If men must come to terms with the loss of some of their

traditional patriarchal privileges, the question for women is how to build on what we have gained. To step outside the victim role and see themselves as the subject of their own desire, women need to face their own sadism and will to dominate others, which we so often project onto men. This will also give them access to creative ways of using this 'masculine' aggression, such as the capacity to insist, demand and take what they need in relationships with others, as in the external world. If girls are allowed to explore their own passion, excitement and destructiveness within safe limits, they will be able to see that strong emotion will not damage themselves or their love-objects. They will then feel more free to exert their own wishes and desires and make a real impact on the world around them.

It has often been difficult for women and men with feminist views to integrate these with psychoanalytic theory and practice, especially within some of the more socially conservative training institutions. They may either become isolated critics, ignored by the psychoanalytic establishment, or give up their radical stance altogether. Is there a need for some institutionalised support for the maintenance and development of a feminist-psychoanalytic perspective, for instance through women-only networks and organisations? Certainly we need to recognise how slow theoretical progress has been on some issues.

In some areas, such as education, female disadvantage is fast diminishing. However, men often respond to this increase in sexual equality with an institutional backlash or personal forms of retaliation, as has happened in the past. There is an urgent need for psychotherapists to give up their preoccupation with maternal omnipotence and to focus equal attention on helping men understand their current dilemmas so that they can develop the psychic resilience to act as equal partners in sexual and family life.

Change at the psychological level will be limited unless it is accompanied by a transformation of attitudes, cultural imagery and social institutions. Men need to find a place for themselves in the realm of 'feminine' emotionality and childcare if women are to move out of their conventional roles. But women themselves must find new ways of speaking for and about their sex, a new language and imagery to express the previously hidden aspects of their experience, and different ways of symbolising power other than through the phallus.

All of us, women and men alike, need to feel that we can take risks, while having our emotional vulnerability accepted, if we are to embrace the challenges life offers. We must be able to look to each other for support and love without feeling that such dependency overthrows our sense of independent selfhood, or deprives us of inner worth. Inextricably entwined with all our 'others', as we inevitably are, we need nevertheless to feel in possession of ourselves – travellers on our own paths, the subjects of our own destinies.

Bibliography

Abraham, K. (1920), 'Manifestations of the female castration complex', in *Selected Papers of Karl Abraham*, London: The Hogarth Press and Institute of Psycho-Analysis 1927.

Adams, P. (1989), 'Of female bondage', in T. Brennan (ed.), *Between Feminism and Psychoanalysis*, London: Routledge.

Ardill, S. and O'Sullivan, S. (1986), 'Upsetting an applecart: difference, desire and lesbian sadomasochism', *Feminist Review*, 23.

Balint, E. (1973), 'Technical problems found in the analysis of women by a woman analyst: a contribution to the question: "What does a woman want?" ', in G. Kohon (ed.), *The British School of Psychoanalysis*, London: Free Association Books 1986.

Bell, A.P. and Weinberg, M.S. (1978), *Homosexualities: A Study of Diversity Among Men and Women*, New York: Simon and Schuster.

Benjamin, J. (1988), *The Bonds of Love: Psychoanalysis, Feminism and the Problem of Domination*, New York: Random House.

Benvenuto, B. and Kennedy, R. (1986), *The Works of Jacques Lacan, An Introduction*, London: Free Association Books.

Bick, E. (1968), 'The experience of the skin in early object-relations', in E. Bott Spillius (ed.), *Melanie Klein Today*, vol. 1, London: Routledge 1988.

Britton, R. (1989), *The Oedipus Complex Today*, London: Karnac.

Brunswick, R.M. (1940), 'The pre-Oedipal phase of the libido development', in C. Zanardi (ed.), *Essential Papers on the Psychology of Women*, New York: New York University Press 1990.

Cavell, M. (1985), 'Since 1924: toward a new psychology of women', in J. Strouse (ed.), *Women and Analysis*, Boston: G.K. Hall and Sons.

Chasseguet-Smirgel, J. (1964a), *Female Sexuality*, London: Maresfield 1985.

—— (1964b), 'Feminine guilt and the Oedipus complex', in *Female Sexuality*, London: Maresfield 1985.

—— (1984), *Creativity and Perversion*, London: Free Association Books 1985.

—— (1985), *The Ego Ideal*, London: Free Association Books.

—— (1986a), *Sexuality and Mind*, New York: New York University Press.

—— (1986b), 'The femininity of the analyst in professional practice', in *Sexuality and Mind*, New York: New York University Press.

—— (1988), 'A woman's attempt at a perverse solution and its failure', *International Journal of Psycho-Analysis*, 69, 2: 149–62.

Chodorow, N. (1978), *The Reproduction of Mothering: Psychoanalysis and the Sociology of Gender*, Berkeley: University of California Press.

—— (1989), *Feminism and Psychoanalytic Theory*, London: Polity Press.

—— (1994), *Femininities, Masculinities, Sexualities*, London: Free Association Books.

Cixous, H. (1976), 'The laugh of the Medusa', in E. Marks and I. de Courtivon (eds), *New French Feminisms*, Sussex: Harvester Press.

Cunningham, R. (1991), 'When is a pervert not a pervert?', *British Journal of Psychotherapy*, 8: 48–70.

Dannecker, M. (1978), *Theories of Homosexuality*, London: Gay Men's Press 1981.

Davis, M. and Wallbridge, D. (1981), *Boundary and Space, An Introduction to the Work of D.W. Winnicott*, London: Karnac.

Deutsch, H. (1924), 'The psychology of women in relation to the function of reproduction', in J. Strouse (ed.), *Women and Analysis*, Boston: G.K. Hall and Sons 1985.

—— (1930), 'The significance of masochism in the mental life of women', *International Journal of Psycho-Analysis*, 11: 48–61.

—— (1933), 'Homosexuality in women', *International Journal of Psycho-Analysis*, 14: 34–56.

—— (1946), *The Psychology of Women*, London: Research Press.

Dinnerstein, D. (1978), *The Rocking of the Cradle and the Ruling of the World*, London: Souvenir Press.

Dollimore, J. (1991), *Sexual Dissidence*, Oxford: Oxford University Press.

Eichenbaum, L. and Orbach, S. (1982), *Understanding Women: a Feminist Psychoanalytic Approach*, New York: Basic Books.

—— (1987), 'Separation and intimacy: crucial practice issues in working with women in therapy', in S. Ernst and M. Maguire (eds), *Living With the Sphinx*, London: The Women's Press.

Elise, D. (1986), 'Lesbian couples: the implications of sex-differences in separation-individuation', *Psychotherapy*, 23: 303–10.

Ernst, S. (1987), 'Can a daughter be a woman?, in S. Ernst and M. Maguire (eds), *Living With the Sphinx*, London: The Women's Press.

Faderman, L. (1992), *Odd Girls and Twilight Lovers: A History of Lesbian Life in Twentieth Century America*, London: Penguin.

Ferenczi, S. (1932), 'Confusion of tongues between adults and the child', *Zeitschrift*, 18: 239.

Flax, J. (1990), *Thinking Fragments: Psychoanalysis, Feminism and Postmodernism in the Contemporary West*, Berkeley: University of California Press.

Fogel, G. (1986), 'Introduction: being a man', in G. Fogel, F. Lane and R. Liebert (eds), *The Psychology of Men*, New York: Basic Books.

Freud, A. (1949), 'Certain types and stages of social maladjustments',

Indications for Child Analysis and Other Papers, London: Hogarth Press 1969.

Freud, S. with Breuer, J. (1893–5), *Studies on Hysteria*, Pelican Freud Library (PFL), 3, Harmondsworth: Penguin 1974.

Freud, S. (1899), 'Screen memories', *The Standard Edition of the Complete Psychological Works of Sigmund Freud* (*SE*), London: Hogarth.

—— (1905a), *Three Essays on the Theory of Sexuality*, PFL 7, Harmondsworth: Penguin 1977.

—— (1905b), *Fragment of an Analysis of a Case of Hysteria ('Dora')*, PFL 8, Harmondsworth: Penguin 1977.

—— (1909), *Analysis of a Phobia in a Five-Year-Old Boy ('Little Hans')*, PFL 8, Harmondsworth: Penguin 1977.

—— (1910a), 'Leonardo da Vinci and a memory of his childhood', *SE* 11, London: Hogarth 1953–74.

—— (1910b), *A Special Choice of Object Made by Men*, PFL 7, Harmondsworth: Penguin 1977.

—— (1914a), *On Narcissism: An Introduction*, PFL 11, Harmondsworth: Penguin 1984.

—— (1914b), 'Remembering, repeating and working-through', *SE* 12, London: Hogarth.

—— (1915), 'Observations on Transference-Love', *SE* 12, London: Hogarth Press 1953–74.

—— (1918), *From the History of an Infantile Neurosis ('The Wolfman')*, PFL 9, Harmondsworth: Penguin 1979.

—— (1919), *A Child is Being Beaten*, PFL 10, Harmondsworth: Penguin 1979.

—— (1920), *Psychogenesis of a Case of Female Homosexuality*, PFL 9, Harmondsworth: Penguin 1979.

—— (1921), *Group Psychology and the Analysis of the Ego*, PFL 10, Harmondsworth: Penguin 1979.

—— (1922), *Some Neurotic Mechanisms in Jealousy, Paranoia and Homosexuality*, PFL 10, Harmondsworth: Penguin 1979.

—— (1924a), *The Dissolution of the Oedipus Complex*, PFL 7, Harmondsworth: Penguin 1977.

—— (1924b), 'The loss of reality in neurosis and psychosis', *SE* 19, London: Hogarth 1954–74.

—— (1924c), *The Economic Problem of Masochism*, PFL 11, Harmondsworth: Penguin 1984.

—— (1925), *Some Psychical Consequences of the Anatomical Distinction Between the Sexes*, PFL 7, Harmondsworth: Penguin 1977.

—— (1927), *Fetishism*, PFL 7, Harmondsworth: Penguin 1977.

—— (1928), Letter from Freud to Ernest Jones, 22 February 1928, quoted in P. Gay, *Freud: A Life for Our Times*, London: Papermac 1988.

—— (1931), *Female Sexuality*, PFL 7, Harmondsworth: Penguin 1977.

—— (1933), 'Femininity', in *New Introductory Lectures*, PFL 2, Harmondsworth: Penguin 1973.

—— (1935a), Letter from Freud to Carl Muller-Braunschweig, published as 'Freud and female sexuality: a previously unpublished letter', *Psychiatry*, 1971.

—— (1935b), Letter from Freud, in *American Journal of Psychiatry*, 1951, 107: 786.

—— (1937), 'Analysis terminable and interminable', *SE* 23, London: Hogarth.

—— (1940), *Splitting of the Ego in the Process of Defence*, PFL 11, Harmondsworth: Penguin 1984.

Friedman, R.C. (1988), *Male Homosexuality: A Contemporary Psychoanalytic Perspective*, New Haven, CT: Yale University Press.

Frosh, S. (1989), *Psychoanalysis and Psychology*, London: Macmillan.

—— (1991), *Identity Crisis, Modernity, Psychoanalysis and the Self*, London: Macmillan.

Gallop, J. (1982), *Feminism and Psychoanalysis: The Daughter's Seduction*, London: Macmillan.

Gay, P. (1988), *Freud: A Life for Our Times*, London: Papermac.

Glasser, M. (1984), ' "The weak spot": some observations on male sexuality', in D. Breen (ed.), *The Gender Conundrum*, London: Routledge 1993.

Goldberger, H. and Evans, D. (1985), 'On transference manifestations in male patients with female analysts', *International Journal of Psycho-Analysis*, 66: 295–309.

Goodison, L. (1990), *Moving Heaven and Earth*, London: The Women's Press.

Gornick, L. (1986), 'Developing a new narrative: the woman therapist and the male patient', in J. Alpert (ed.), *Psychoanalysis and Women: Contemporary Reappraisals*, New Jersey: The Analytic Press.

Greenacre, P. (1979), 'Fetishism', in I. Rosen (ed.), *Sexual Deviation*, Oxford University Press.

Greenson, R. (1967), *The Technique and Practice of Psycho-Analysis*, London: Hogarth Press.

Grossman, W. and Stewart, W. (1976), 'Penis envy: from childhood wish to developmental metaphor', in C. Zanardi (ed.), *Essential Papers on the Psychology of Women*, New York: New York University Press 1990.

Grosz, E. (1990), *Jacques Lacan: A Feminist Introduction*, London: Routledge.

Grunberger, B. (1989), *New Essays on Narcissism*, London: Free Association Books.

Hamer, D. (1990), 'Significant others: lesbians and psychoanalytic theory', *Feminist Review*, 31: 134–51.

H.D. (1956), *Tribute to Freud*, Manchester: Carcanet Press 1985.

Horney, K. (1924), 'On the genesis of the castration complex in women', *International Journal of Psycho-Analysis*, 5: 50–65.

—— (1926), 'The flight from womanhood: the masculinity complex in women as viewed by men and by women', in J. Baker Miller (ed.), *Psychoanalysis and Women*, London: Penguin 1984.

Hughes, A. (ed.) (1991), *The Inner World and Joan Riviere*, London: Karnac.

Humphries, M. (1985), 'Gay machismo', in A. Metcalf and M. Humphries (eds), *The Sexuality of Men*, London: Pluto Press.

Irigiray, L. (1977), 'This sex which is not one', in C. Zanardi (ed.), *Essential Papers on the Psychology of Women*, New York: New York University Press 1990.

—— (1984), *Ethique de la différence sexuelle*, Paris: Minuit.

—— (1989), 'The gesture in psychoanalysis', in T. Brennan (ed.), *Between Feminism and Psychoanalysis*, London: Routledge.

Isay, R. (1986), 'Homosexuality in homosexual and heterosexual men: some distinctions and implications for treatment', in G. Fogel, F. Lane and R. Liebert (eds), *The Psychology of Men*, New York: Basic Books.

Janeway, E. (1982), *Cross Sections: From a Decade of Change*, New York: Wm. Morrow and Co.

Jones, E. (1927a), 'The early development of female sexuality', *International Journal of Psycho-Analysis*, 8: 457–72.

—— (1927b), 'The early development of female sexuality', in *E. Jones, Papers on Psycho-Analysis*, London: Maresfield Reprints 1948.

—— (1935), 'Early female sexuality', in *E. Jones, Papers on Psycho-Analysis*, London: Maresfield Reprints 1948.

Joseph, B. (1982), 'Addiction to near-death', in E. Bott Spillius and M. Feldman (eds), *Psychic Equilibrium and Psychic Change. Selected Papers of Betty Joseph*, London: Routledge 1989.

—— (1985), 'Transference: the total situation', in E. Bott Spillius (ed.), *Melanie Klein Today*, vol. 2, London: Routledge 1988.

Jukes, A. (1993), *Why Men Hate Women*, London: Free Association Books.

Kakar, S. (1989), 'The maternal-feminine in Indian psychoanalysis', *International Review of Psycho-Analysis*, 16, 3: 355–62.

Kaplan, L.J. (1991), *Female Perversions*, London: Pandora Press.

Kernberg, O. (1994), *Lecture: Sado-Masochistic Love Relations*, London: Institute of Marital Studies, Tavistock Centre.

Khan, M. (1989), *Alienation in Perversions*, London: Maresfield Library.

Klein, M. (1928), 'Early stages of the Oedipus complex', in *Love, Guilt and Reparation and Other Works 1921–45*, London: Hogarth Press 1975.

—— (1952), 'The origins of transference', in *Envy and Gratitude and Other Works 1946–1963*, New York: Delta 1977.

—— (1957), 'Envy and gratitude', in *Envy and Gratitude and Other Works 1946–1963*, New York: Delta 1977.

Kohon, G. (1986), 'Reflections on Dora: the case of hysteria', in G. Kohon (ed.), *The British School of Psychoanalysis*, London: Free Association Books.

—— (1987), 'Fetishism revisited', *International Journal of Psycho-Analysis*, 68: 213–29.

Kulish, N.M. (1986), 'Gender and transference: the screen of the phallic mother', *International Review of Psycho-Analysis*, 13: 393–404.

Lacan, J. (1964), *The Four Fundamental Concepts of Psycho-Analysis*, translated by A. Sheridan, Harmondsworth: Penguin 1977.

—— (1977), *Ecrits. A Selection*, London: Tavistock.

—— (1985), 'Intervention on transference', in C. Bernheimer and C. Kahane (eds), *In Dora's Case*, London: Virago.

Laplanche, J. and Pontalis, J.B. (1967), *The Language of Psychoanalysis*, London: Karnac 1988.

Lasch, C. (1979), *The Culture of Narcissism*, London: Abacus Books 1980.

Lasky, R. (1989), 'Some determinants of the male analyst's capacity to identify with female patients', *International Journal of Psycho-Analysis*, 70, 3: 405–18.

Laub, D. and Auerhahn, N.C. (1993), 'Knowing and not knowing massive psychic trauma: forms of traumatic memory', *International Journal of Psycho-Analysis*, 74: 287–302.

Lester, E. (1982), 'The female analyst and the eroticized transference', *International Journal of Psycho-Analysis*, 66: 283–94.

Lewes, K. (1989), *The Psychoanalytic Theory of Male Homosexuality*, London: Quartet.

Liebert, R.S. (1986), 'The history of male homosexuality from ancient Greece through the Renaissance: implications for psychoanalytic theory', in G. Fogel, F. Lane and R. Liebert (eds), *The Psychology of Men*, New York: Basic Books.

Limentani, A.(1979), 'The significance of transsexualism in relation to some basic psychoanalytic concepts', in *Between Freud and Klein*, London: Free Association Books 1989.

—— (1989), 'Clinical types of homosexuality', in *Between Freud and Klein*, London: Free Association Books.

—— (1991), 'Neglected fathers in the aetiology and treatment of sexual deviations', *International Journal of Psycho-Analysis*, 72, 4: 573–84.

Littlewood, R. (1992), 'Towards an intercultural therapy', in J. Kareem and R. Littlewood (eds), *Intercultural Therapy*, London: Blackwell.

Lloyd Mayer, E. (1985), 'Everybody must be just like me: observations on female castration anxiety', *International Journal of Psycho-Analysis*, 66: 331.

MacCarthy, B. (1988), 'Are incest victims hated?', *Psychoanalytic Psychotherapy*, 3, 2: 113–20.

McDougall, J. (1964), 'Homosexuality in women', in J. Chasseguet-Smirgel (ed.), *Female Sexuality*, London: Maresfield 1985.

—— (1979), 'The homosexual dilemma: a clinical theoretical study of female homosexuality', in I. Rosen (ed.), *Sexual Deviation*, Oxford: Oxford University Press.

—— (1980), *Plea for a Measure of Abnormality*, New York: International Universities Press.

Maguire, M. (1987), 'Casting the evil eye – women and envy', in S. Ernst and M. Maguire (eds), *Living with the Sphinx*, London: The Women's Press.

Malcolm, J. (1982), *Psychoanalysis: The Impossible Profession*, London: Pan Books.

Mann, D. (1994), 'The psychotherapist's erotic subjectivity', *British Journal of Psychotherapy*, 10, 3: 344–55.

Mannoni, O. (1968), *Freud: The Theory of the Unconscious*, London: Pantheon Books 1971.

Meltzer, D. (1973a), *Sexual States of Mind*, Scotland: Clunie Press.

—— (1973b), 'Perversion of the transference', *Sexual States of Mind*, Scotland: Clunie Press.

—— (1973c), 'The architectonics of pornography', in *Sexual States of Mind*, Scotland: Clunie Press.

—— (1978), *The Kleinian Development*, Scotland: Clunie Press.

Merck, M. (1993a), *Perversions, Deviant Readings*, London: Virago Press.

—— (1993b), 'The feminist ethics of lesbian s/m', in *Perversions, Deviant Readings*, London: Virago Press.

—— (1993c), 'The train of thought in Freud's "Case of Homosexuality in a Woman" ', in *Perversions, Deviant Readings*, London: Virago Press.

Miles, R. (1991), *The Rites of Man, Love, Sex and Death in the Making of the Male*, London: Grafton.

Mitchell, J. (1974), *Psychoanalysis and Feminism*, London: Allen Lane.

—— (1984), *Women: the Longest Revolution*, London: Virago Press.

Munder Ross, J. (1986), 'Beyond the phallic illusion: notes on men's heterosexuality', in G. Fogel, F. Lane and R. Liebert (eds), *The Psychology of Men*, New York: Basic Books.

Norwood, R. (1986), *Women Who Love Too Much*, London: Arrow Books.

O'Connor, N. and Ryan, J. (1993), *Wild Desires and Mistaken Identities*, London: Virago Press.

Odes Fliegel, Z. (1986), 'Women's development in analytic theory: six decades of controversy', in J. Alpert (ed.), *Psychoanalysis and Women, Contemporary Reappraisals*, New Jersey: The Analytic Press.

Ovesey, L. and Spector Person, E. (1973), 'Gender identity and sexual psychotherapy in men: a psychodynamic analysis of homosexual transsexuality, transvestitism', *Journal of the American Academy of Psychoanalysis*, 1: 53–72.

Pines, D. (1986), 'A woman's unconscious use of her body: a psychoanalytic perspective', Carl Dilling Memorial Lecture, New York.

Ragland-Sullivan, E. (1992), 'Hysteria', in E. Wright (ed.), *Feminism and Psychoanalysis: A Critical Dictionary*, Oxford: Blackwell.

Rayner, E. (1991), *The Independent Mind in British Psychoanalysis*, London: Free Association Books.

Richards, B. (1989), *Images of Freud: Cultural Responses to Psychoanalysis*, London: J.M. Dent and Sons.

Riley, D. (1983), *War in the Nursery*, London: Virago Press.

Riviere, J. (1929), 'Womanliness as a masquerade', in A. Hughes (ed.), *The Inner World and Joan Riviere*, London: Karnac 1991.

Rosen, I. (ed.) (1979a), *Sexual Deviation*, Oxford: Oxford University Press.

—— (1979b), 'The general psychoanalytical theory of perversion: a critical and clinical study', in *Sexual Deviation*, Oxford: Oxford University Press.

Rosenfeld, H. (1949), 'Remarks on the relation of male homosexuality to paranoia, paranoid anxiety and narcissism', *Psychotic States*, London: Maresfield.

—— (1972), 'A critical appreciation of James Strachey's paper on the nature of the therapeutic action of psychoanalysis', *International Journal of Psycho-Analysis*, 53: 455–61.

Samuels, A. (1985), *The Father, Contemporary Jungian Perspectives*, London: Free Association Books.

—— (1993), *Politics and the Psyche*, London: Routledge.

Sayers, J. (1991), *Mothering Psychoanalysis*, London: Penguin.

Scott, A. (1988), 'Feminism and the seductiveness of the "real event" ', *Feminist Review*, 28.

Segal, L. (1987), *Is the Future Female?: Troubled Thoughts on Contemporary Feminism*, London: Virago Press.

—— (1990), *Slow Motion, Changing Masculinities, Changing Men*, London: Virago Press.

Shengold, L. (1979), 'Child abuse and deprivation: soul murder', *Journal of the American Psychoanalytic Association*, 27: 533–99.

Sinason, V. (1988), 'Smiling, swallowing, sickening and stupefying: the effect of sexual abuse on the child', *Psychoanalytic Psychotherapy*, 3, 2: 97–111.

Socarides, C. W. (1979), 'The psychoanalytic theory of homosexuality: with special reference to therapy', in I. Rosen (ed.), *Sexual Deviation*, Oxford: Oxford University Press.

Spector Person, E. (1986), 'The omni-available woman and lesbian sex: two fantasy themes and their relationship to the male developmental experience', in G. Fogel, F. Lane and R. Liebert (eds), *The Psychology of Men*, New York: Basic Books.

Stanton, M. (1990), *Sandor Ferenczi: Reconsidering Active Intervention*, London: Free Association Books.

Steiner, J. (1981), 'Interplay between pathological organizations and the paranoid-schizoid and depressive positions', in E. Bott Spillius (ed.), *Melanie Klein Today*, vol. 1, London: Routledge 1988.

—— (1985), 'Turning a blind eye; the cover-up for Oedipus', *International Review of Psychoanalysis*, 12: 161–72.

—— (1987), 'The interplay between pathological organizations and the paranoid-schizoid and depressive positions', *International Journal of Psycho-Analysis*, 68: 69–80.

Stoller, R. (1968), *Sex and Gender*, London: Hogarth Press.

—— (1975), *Perversion: The Erotic Form of Hatred*, London: Maresfield.

—— (1979), 'The gender disorders', in I. Rosen (ed.), *Sexual Deviation*, Oxford University Press.

Strouse, J. (ed.) (1985), *Women and Analysis*, Boston: G.K. Hall and Sons.

Sykes Wylie, M. (1993), 'Trauma and memory', *Family Networker*, Sept/Oct: 42–3.

Symington, N. (1986), *The Analytic Experience*, London: Free Association Books.

Temperley, J. (1984), 'Our own worst enemies: unconscious factors in female disadvantage', in *Free Associations Journal*, London: Pilot edition.

Torras de Beà, E. (1987), 'A contribution to the papers on transference by Eva Lester and Marianne Goldberger and Dorothy Evans', *International Journal of Psycho-Analysis*, 68, 1: 63–9.

Tower, L. (1956), 'Countertransference', *Journal of the American Psychoanalytic Association*, 4: 224–55.

Waddell, M. (1989), 'Gender identity – fifty years on from Freud', *British Journal of Psychotherapy*, 5, 3: 381–90.

—— (1993), 'From resemblance to identity: a psychoanalytic perspective on gender identity', unpublished paper.

Waddell, M. and Williams, G. (1991), 'Reflections on perverse states of mind', *Free Associations*, 2, Part 2, no. 22.

Welldon, E. (1988), *Mother, Madonna, Whore*, London: Free Association Books.

Welles, J.K. and Wrye, H.K. (1991), 'The maternal erotic countertransference', *International Journal of Psycho-Analysis*, 72: 93–106.

White, J. (1989), 'Racism and psychosis: whose madness is it anyway?', unpublished paper.

Whitford, M. (1989), 'Rereading Irigiray', in T. Brennan (ed.), *Between Feminism and Psychoanalysis*, London: Routledge.

Winnicott, D.W. (1957), 'The mother's contribution to society', in *The Child and the Family: First Relationships*, London: Tavistock.

—— (1964), 'This feminism', in *Home is Where We Start From, Essays by a Psychoanalyst*, London: Penguin 1986.

—— (1971), 'Creativity and its origins', in *Playing and Reality*, Harmondsworth: Pelican.

Zetzel, E. (1970), *The Capacity for Emotional Growth*, London: Maresfield Library 1987.

Index

Abraham, K. 21
Adams, P. 194
aggression 31, 35, 68, 169; male 66,
  86–9, 94–9, 102–3, 140–4, 151,
  178; and perversion 190, 191;
  women and 18, 78, 107, 109,
  112, 117, 118, 128, 130, 225, 231;
  see also sadism; sado-masochism
amnesia 168
anal stage, obsessiveness 173, 211,
  223
androgyny, psychic 16, 221
anger 78; see also aggression
anorexia 172, 182, 186, 227
anxiety 5, 24, 25–6, 37, 66, 143, 229;
  see also castration anxiety;
  Oedipal anxiety
Ardill, S. 220
Auerhahn, N. 168
autonomy 39, 100, 105, 111, 124,
  127, 133, 232

Balint, E. 69
Battersea Action and Counselling
  Centre 4
Beauvoir, S. de 120
Bell, A. P. 210
Benjamin, J. 7, 8, 61, 67, 82, 98,
  108, 120, 121, 127, 133
Benvenuto, B. 42, 64
Bick, E. 88
biology, and sexuality 1–2, 5–6, 20,

21, 27–8, 29, 30, 51, 62, 98,
  204–5; see also heredity; women,
  bodies
bisexuality 5, 16, 76–7, 189, 190,
  198, 200, 202, 204, 205, 207, 208,
  209–10, 223; psychic 36, 49, 58,
  104, 112, 150, 185, 223
Bose, G. 25–6
boundaries 2, 42, 72, 142, 146, 161,
  165, 179, 185, 188
Bowlby, J. 33, 53
Britton, R. 35, 40, 45, 47, 48
Brunswick, R. M. 19–20
bulimia 9, 172, 181–8, 192, 193,
  195, 227

castration, castration anxiety 6, 16,
  17, 26, 188, 190, 200
Chasseguet-Smirgel, J. 7, 42, 45,
  46, 59–60, 69, 95–6, 119–20,
  139–41, 146, 150, 175, 189, 206
Chodorow, N. 34, 54, 55, 56
Cixous, H. 76
class 4, 99; changes in 84, 85
clitoris 17, 18, 21
complaint 186
core gender identity 5, 37, 56
counselling 154
countertransference 8, 116–17,
  128, 132, 169, 171, 180, 197–8,
  202, 217, 221, 228; gender and 3,